The Path

of the

Spiritual Warrior

The New Earth Council

and

Raphael Weisman

All photographs by the author except book cover photographs used with permission.

Portrait of the author by Anne Staveley Photography.

Cover painting by Herman Rednick, property of the author, photograph by author.

A portion of sales will be tithed to Soul Support Systems, Inc.

Published by:
All Worlds Publishing
Putney, VT

ISBN: 978-1-880914-11-3

Contents

Contents   III

Dedication   V

Preface by Flo Aeveia Magdalena   VI

Foreword by The Ones with No Names   VIII

Introduction   IX

The Invitation   XIII

The New - Earth Council   *1*

Voice One - Seshat   *5*

Voice Two - Thoth   *22*

Voice Three - Apollo   *41*

Voice Four - Pan   *59*

Voice Five - John Henry   *79*

Voice Six - Ashtara   *97*

Voice Seven - Old Chinese   *117*

Voice Eight - The Druid   *135*

Voice Nine - Joan of Arc   *155*

Voice Ten - Ganesha   *171*

Voice Eleven - Guru Rinpoche   *189*

Voice Twelve - Joy   *209*

Voice Thirteen - The Christ   *225*

Epilogue   **244**

Notes and glossary   **247**

Bibliography and Recommended Reading   **260**

About the Author   **264**

Reviews   **265**

Dedication

This book is dedicated to my grandchildren Elias, Ajah and Lilliana, and my children Elisha, Grace and husband Sage, and to all the children who will inherit and create The New Earth. It is also dedicated to my daughter Joy, whom you will meet shortly.

I also dedicate this book to Mary Magdalene, who has entered my life in such a profound manner. She represents an embodiment of the Beloved, as the emerging sacred feminine essence that is ready now to be the most important energy on the planet, the energy that stands for life.

This book is also dedicated to our friend, Donna Sessler (Donnareyna) who transitioned in October 2021 and is sorely missed.

Preface by Flo Aeveia Magdalena

We are at a time in our human evolution where the voices of many create a decisive and divisive divide in our life experience. As this divide strengthens, fission and friction are created in every corner of the world and in every home and environment. The underlying fears elicited from this divide are quite real in their impact for many. There is war, famine, pestilence, judgement, recrimination and oppression. We are at the time of reckoning. A time when all that we have held sacred is being challenged.

Each of us must choose how we will now face each moment, each day, each encounter. Are there seeds of Union within us that we can bring forth when the seeds of distress are so loud and pervasive? Can we each contribute in some way to transform what appears to be a huge worldwide overturning of the heart? What more can we do as Bringers of the New Dawn? How do we find the courage, vision, strength, and wisdom to hold the Truth of Light? How do we stand in the knowing of this Light and choose to live with honor and dignity while facing huge opposition to the honoring of life and the sacredness of being?

The Path of the Spiritual Warrior brings us these answers through the 12 voices of the Standard Bearers of Spirituality, an amazingly varied cast of ascended masters, avatars and infinitely wise souls representing the unified voices of the New Earth Council.

Their voices join in deeply evocative ways to weave a world where there is no longer an ounce of disparity between these spiritual epistemologies, once thought of as distinct. Each of their messages are given with unifying precepts, concepts, aspects and visions that gently provide One voice. Christ, Old Chinese, Ganesha and others provide deeply relevant guidance that reveals simple, effective and cogent formulas of truth that are applicable and possible for us all, no matter what our spiritual or religious experience or method has been to date.

At a time when our communal beliefs, stories and conditioning have stood in the way of our forward movement as a species, these beings support us in understanding how to remap that difference. The information and specific ways they outline our challenges, answer our questions and give guidance with love and understanding is reassuring and enlightening. They remind us that through both our evolution and our spiritual origins, our very beings and therefore our lives, and thereafter our worlds, will listen and respond to our ancient roots of wisdom — the very wisdom that inspired us to return here to stand for and fight for the ways of the heart.

To receive the encouragement, support and vision of each of these voices and to see how the sum of their messages provide a deep and lasting impression of, 'Yes, I can do this; we can do this; we are doing this,' brings forgiveness, absolution, and sighs of relief and deep joy.

There is a way forward personally and collectively, and this highly diverse group is compelled to bring this to Earth now. Their 'standards of care' are impeccable and life-changing; their voices blend in a harmony that truly provides a model of how we can join our voices together as One.

It is time to fully embody and bring the promise of our life and the Promise of a Million Years of Dreaming into Divine Union. As we go forward then, the knowing that we are ready as warriors of the heart permeates our bodies, minds, hearts and spirits and we bring this Union from above into our lives and into the Earth. We share ourselves fully and openly as we carry the vision of Oneness.

Through the guidance provided here we know how to do this. We recognize the parameters and capacity of our spiritual and etheric 'helpers' to walk with us, as they show us our true essence as spiritual warriors in the human framework.

With the Union that they have shown and related, we now infuse their wisdom with every breath to create a sphere of peace and wellbeing that transcends imposed limitations and opens each of our doors to our spiritual destiny.

Flo Aeveia Magdalena

Foreword by The Ones with No Names

In the beginning-less beginning, we find one voice. That voice is the heart of life and the moment of creation. Wordless, soundless and bottomless, the voice is not held in the hearts of the people, because the people had not yet come forth.

Since then, that one voice has amplified and diversified many times through all voices and through the intent for each voice to increasingly manifest as more and more unique and authentic. Each voice has its own timbre and cadence, message and original way of responding.

However, those differences, in the beginning only a difference in timbre and cadence, became diverse in beliefs, traditions, lineages, genetics, encampments, regions, countries and borders. Now, of course, every human is seen, felt and touched as being outside of the one voice because they have their own voice. This is a way to stand in self-authority and live authentically.

The compendium of voices in The New Earth Council begins the journey "back" to the one voice. The timbre and cadence of each contributor, although aligned in some way with the tradition or epistemology of its derivation, endeavors to provide a road back, a way home, a lessening of the angst caused by difference (defined as separation). They teach us that this somewhat literal re-union of voices, concepts, and traditions is a way to begin again. These learned ones recognize that by unifying, we add our voice as a strand of the infinite in the finite, remembering its call and its destiny without need to call attention to its difference.

The timbre and cadence then, are unique, and yet, as instruments in an orchestra playing a symphony, they provide richness of context, contrast, expanded awareness, deep emotional yearning and gracious acknowledgement.

Each voice in The New Earth Council responds to this call uniquely, as is their wont. And yet, the overall theme is that to embody the promise of the heart requests the presence of the community (common unity), and the intention for co-creating a new way (in a new way). Their invitation calls forth the memory of Oneness - instilled as the yearning to move us forward. This memory rides on the waves of the words shared by these avatars. Each voice carries a wave, which together forms an ocean. And, of course, the ocean brings us home.

The Ones with No Names

Introduction

I was invited to receive and share these messages and the wisdom, love and guidance of a group of Beings of Light, The New Earth Council. Every morning I sit with a cup of coffee and meditate. I place my right hand on my heart and my left upon my right. I create around me a column of light, connecting with Mother Earth below, and Father Sky above me, my heart in the center. I feel a downpouring from above of a golden light and sense of stillness that fills my heart. I am holding a large nugget of Shungite and begin to open my chakras, from the root, moving upwards.

I say a mantra as I connect with the root in a counterclockwise motion. "The love of the Christ fills my heart and soul, body and mind". I move up the chakras, spinning alternately clockwise and counterclockwise. As I reach my heart chakra, the mantra changes; "Your will be done God, not mine, in me and through me. Show me what I must do this day, and let me be a blessing to all." At my heart chakra I open a sphere filled with golden light surrounding and protecting me. At my throat chakra I ask that I may always speak with the voice of God. At my third eye, I ask that I may always see through the eyes of God. When I reach my crown chakra, I radiate light into the world to touch the hearts of my family and friends, the children, all who suffer, then each one on my healing list.

I fill my mug with a second pour and settle again with my journal in hand and wait. Almost immediately words begin to come. I write them down. For many years, John Henry was my companion. He would feed me words, sentences, quotations. He was my buddy. There was/is a great love between us.

Then, in January 2021 I "met" The Magdalen. It started by seeing a painting, a portrait by a master artist on a crumpled sheet of paper at my friend Isis. It had, at the bottom, in beautiful lettering "Beloved Mary Magdalen." I have not been able to find the artist to request permission to reproduce it. My friend had two other portraits/paintings on copy paper, Lady Nada and Archangel Michael by the same artist. None of them was inscribed. I took a photo of each and printed them on photo paper. I framed them and have them in my office and above my altar. Magdalen is also framed behind my Shabbat candles.

She became my new companion. Almost every morning, the message would come from her. They still do. Occasionally it is The Christ or another. Or both of them. The Voice mostly address itself as "we." The messages are always encouraging, affirming and filled with love and support. Sometimes slightly more severe, tough love, telling me to drop it or stop worrying. Never judgmental.

Then came the invitation, unexpectedly.

I have known Flo Aeveia Magdalena for many years. I received channeled sessions from her, attended gatherings and trainings, learned Circuitry Alignment and HeartThread® and 'met' John Henry, the source of HeartThread.® She has always been a support and inspiration for me and the messages she channeled from The Ones with No Names[1], The Council of Light and John Henry brought great comfort during some of my hardest times. I co-edited a Hebrew translation of her book *I Remember Union, the Story of Mary Magdalena*. And in 2020 I edited transcriptions of a year-long course with The Ones with No Names I participated in. At the end of July 2020 each one on the course received a brief channeled message from the Ones. In my message I was asked to receive 12 voices, one each day. I had no idea who would show up, but each morning during my journaling time, a different 'voice' would bring me a message. The 12 voices then channeled messages and answered questions during a weekly online course I was asked to facilitate. Towards the end, it became apparent that there was one more voice who wanted to add his energy as part of The New Earth Council.

It also became apparent that this material needed to be shared with a broader audience and had the makings of a book. The process of transcribing and editing followed. After many edits and rejections from publishers, I finally found someone in the UK to produce a color copy of the book. However, I was not satisfied with this edition and its formatting. Despite all the editing, it needed a more thorough rewrite. I also realized that, in fact, the title of the book needed to reflect the intention of the New Earth Council to provide a practical training 'course,' a path for evolution, transformation and ascension, *The Path of the Spiritual Warrior*.

Each voice offered a message in the first hour. After a break they answered questions. Each entire 2-hour session is a separate chapter of the book. It is my hope that as you read you will join the process that the participants experienced, as if you yourself were present as part of the unfolding. There was a progression as the course evolved and the participants became more open and connected as a group. As the recommended practices began to have an effect, the voices seemed to reflect a deepening vibration and power.

I am grateful to the students who attended the course and brought through their wisdom, and often brilliant questions and comments. Their semi-anonymity is represented by their initials in the Q&A sections. I use a hyphen when there is back and forth dialogue in the comments and Q&A.

As you will read in the final message from The Ones with No Names, there may be a sequel on the way, for there are many other voices who seek to be heard, and, as they amalgamate, they become One Voice.

I would like to emphasize the importance and simplicity of some of the practices recommended by the Guides in this book, such as the breath, examination of all thoughts and beliefs, time in Nature, to always seek the silver lining in every situation, and trust. They may seem simplistic. It brings to mind the words of Docusan, a Zen monk I met in Jerusalem many years ago, since then, I believe, a Zen Roshi, "Zen meditation, very simple, but very difficult." Sitting facing a blank white wall, focusing on the breath will convince you of the truth of that statement. Such is the path of the Spiritual Warrior. It requires commitment, dedication and fierce impeccability. If you are about to read this book, be aware that this is the journey, and that it is well worth the effort.

As you read these messages and the answers to the questions, please allow for the idiosyncrasies of capitalization, unusual wording, sentence structures and grammar. In this reworking I have altered sentences that ran on without adhering to correct grammar. Because their words and ideas flowed, they had a life of their own. I tried my best to remold the sentences, so they would make clearer sense. In many cases, I reframed the sentence and shortened or broke it up into its component ideas. I was not entirely consistent in the use or disuse of capitals for words like "Soul," "Love," "Light," "Pillar," "Sphere," etc. It was not always possible to distinguish when "light" was just that little ol' light that we all carry, or the Great Light of Creation. In the same way, I sometimes distinguished between "God" or "Goddess" and "god" or "goddess," "Creation" and "creation," "Essence" and "essence." I am sure you can understand what a challenge some of these choices would be like, acceptable grammar notwithstanding.

Often during the channeling sessions, I would have to bring a part of my awareness back to the figure or "identity" of the voice or personality I was channeling. I, or they, seemed to default to the pronoun "we." So, I found myself reminding the messenger that the voice was representing a mythological or historical character such as Pan, or Joan of Arc or a deity, or the Christ, and then they would return to an "I" statement. It is something I have now become rather relieved about, almost as if I, (or "they") was faking it or pretending to represent a particular being. I have come to realize that it does not matter. The message is what is important. The One Voice continues to speak through me. It is humbling and a constant challenge to maintain humility in the face of the wisdom, love and beauty that flows forth in words, colors and images as "We" answer people's questions or bring forth the messages from people's cells in a HeartThread® session. There is only one voice. It is the voice of the Heart, the voice of the One, the one voice, the still, small voice.

I am grateful to Flo Aeveia Magdalena for our connection and love over all these years and to The Ones with No Names (TNO) for the incentive and invitation to receive the 12 voices. My gratitude extends to my faithful guides John Henry[2] and Old Chinese[3], who have been with me since time immemorial, to my friends like Isis and Mehernaz Madon who encouraged me in the process of publication, and to Jessica Manley whose editing and formatting assistance was so vital to the reworking of this book.

Blessings and peace to you all.

June, 2022

Raphael Weisman, Santa Fe, NM
www.RaphaelWeisman.com

The Invitation

"So, as you know, you have been tapping the secrets of the ages. You have been tapping into wisdom from many corners of the universe, and that is going to continue in a more direct way. It feels as if there are voices that would like to utilize your consciousness for primarily bringing messages during this time of de-structuring; you know, we could call it destruction, but it is de-structuring and that's actually what it is. You are a builder. You build consciousness, you build friendships, you build community, you build the essence of water, you build the mountain. You build many things; so in that building consciousness, what seems like it is now yours to do is to ask for, each day, a message that will build the structure of consciousness on the planet, build the frameworks for the New Earth and begin to add voices, information, guidance, instruction and focus to what others can do to assist in the building of this New Earth.

Your voice and the way that you are connecting with many beings at the moment, seems to be requesting answers, you know, ways in which people can find more solace, depend more deeply on the essence and connection with truth versus the world, and turning inward, as it were. And so, your opportunity in this lifetime right now is to add (we're trying to get you a number here) 12 new voices to your consciousness, and these 12 voices are in a group, but they're also individual, and they are ones who you have known about but not necessarily brought forth. These 12 beings want to create a new kind of council, and you could call it The New Earth Council if you would want to do that, and they're going to be from different times of the story of humanity, and they're going to be from different locations, and they're going to be from different walks of life, you know, what pertains to them in a way that opens the consciousness of each person that will then offer a suggestion or an understanding for the world because they have this different perspective. And because you're calling forth all these different opportunities for interlacing wisdom, it will be as if, when you're working with the information and guidance, as if what's happening is you're weaving a new journal of reality or truth as you go, and you'll be feeling as if what you're doing is, it's not prescribing or is not instructions really, either one, and yet it is, you know. It's that feeling of "This is what we do today" or "This is what we do this week" or however you want to do it. It is probably by the week, but you want to say, "This is what we do this week to hold the vibration frequency of a balancing and truth in this time, and this is how we're going to build within ourselves a structure that can hold us when the outer structure is gone."

So you're working with the affirmation of building in the process of things falling into disrepair or shattering or going away or being, you know, in some way annihilated; and you're bringing that consciousness in, and it's going to be needed, every week, starting at the end of this week. It's very rough times ahead. So you're going to be looking at where are the 12 beings that want to come together to form a group that's unified with building the consciousness of the human being into the New Earth Council consciousness of the avatar energy, into the consciousness of the Earth, into the consciousness of the truth of Creation itself, so all those things. So, it's got creation in it. It's got the story of humanity and where humanity has been and where it's going; so there's evolution and there's a feeling of Earth energy and human energy and expanded energy, and it's all coming so that the words and the ideas and the instructions or prescriptions or suggestions are offered in a way that's relevant to what's happening, provide an opportunity for people to feel that their presence is able to stand in the midst of whatever is happening and feel comfortable and safe, and that whatever action is instructed through this group of 12 is going to be consistent and coherent for everyone; so it's as if there's a kind of, the word we got was "blanket," you know, blanket prescription, but it's much more than that. It's as if what you're saying applies to each person and their situation and their perception; and so what's really happening here is that you're moving into the consciousness in a way that allows for the acceptance of what you're saying, no matter what the perception or experience of the person has been or is (which is amazing) and then you're able to fully bring the resonance of that capacity for truth and knowing where we're going into this, so that people feel steadied, inspired, creative, connected, and as if they're ready.

They're ready to take the steps, so this becomes something that you do probably through your newsletter or, you know, some way that you expand it for people so that they understand that this is kind of a 12-week process, and you're going to be establishing this group, working with this group and bringing this forward. And of course then after the 12 weeks the 12 is there for you and there are other rides they will take you on and other things they will open for you. Old Chinese seems to be part of this. There are many beings that want very much to instruct the consciousness of humanity so that it feels ready to take on the challenges that outwardly are experienced, so that inwardly there is calm and there's a structure of oneness that's extremely profound and opened out to, with excitation instead of fear. So you're moving in a way that opens the doorways for people to celebrate what's coming and to know that, in creating it, they/we all are going to benefit because all of that is moving towards this Heart of the One experience that you carry so deeply within yourself.

Thank you."

TNO Message, 2020 Action, Year-Long Class, 30th July 2020

The New Earth Council
Introduction

All considerations melt in joy. Joy is the highest level of consciousness. Period. The longing for enlightenment or awakening is an illusory, imagined state that the mind puts out to delude us into thinking that whatever challenges we have as human beings will be dissolved or resolved by becoming "enlightened" – full of light. It is true that being filled with light will resolve all issues, can resolve all issues, but this experience has to transcended the realm of the mind and become an aspect of your Essence – which it already is. So, in fact, being in light, full of light or enlightened, is actually a state of "mind" where the mind itself has dissolved. That state is the state of joy, the word "state" meaning "to be." So being in a state of joy means being free of the constraints of the mind's judgments, projections and assumptions. It is a return to innocence, to an inner Remembrance, on an ongoing basis, of being pure, of being free. We use and define or redefine and examine all these words to bring to your attention how much the mind, the thought processes, the ego, uses words to escape from feeling or to feel safe or secure or OK in the face of a deep sense of disillusionment – another word to express being caught up in the illusion of separation, for when there is no illusion, reality becomes the experience of joy.

So, in some way, I, Joy Weisman,[4] have been "chosen" to offer an introduction. In introducing myself as the 12th Being or Energy of the New Earth Council, I represent the energy of the child. I left this plane at the age of nine, having completed my Earth cycles and contributed my greatest gift to the world, by dying. For, in my departure, I set in motion in the hearts, minds and lives of my parents, siblings and those who knew me, a transformative process that altered their lives tremendously. You could even say that my release from form was the impulse that set in motion a transformation that allows these messages to come through this one (Raphael). It set him on an accelerated path towards joy. The byproduct of his ability to have an empty mind, facilitates these transmissions, and permits the higher dimensions access to a level of communication that is intended to assist, guide and heal those who are ready for their own journey towards joy. It brings them clear communication with Spirit and communication with their own inner voice – the voice of their innocence and purity.

I represent the child. However, there is also a reflection on the part of my father that relates to personal and collective realizations that are accompanied by definite, though vague memories of abuse. There is therefore a strong correlation and understanding about much of what underlies the current situation on the entire planet today. People face lock-down, mask wearing, "social distancing", death and illness, loss and economic hardship, and great fear. This is a result of an orchestrated pandemic stemming from the development and release of an engineered "virus" on the populations of the world. This is enhanced, supported, and reinforced by the effects of 5th Generation[5] (Five-G) and the prevalence of electromagnetic and sonic frequencies that generate symptoms of radiation poisoning, mistaken for "C-o-vid[6]" symptoms. This is propelling your civilization towards the greatest destabilization and de-structuring it has known since the Flood, the great final sinking of Atlantis[7].

The forces behind these initiatives have been active on your planet and in your star system for extended periods of time. They have been allowed a certain amount of free rein to affect duality and separation-consciousness and have affected the evolution of humanity and life on Earth. These energies emanate from distant "systems" and have long since been banned from access to your dear Mother Earth. However, during their long sojourn and control over your populations and their life force, they have influenced and generated a vast network of human beings and energies whose consciousness has been overtaken by density to such a vast extent, that they have fallen into great darkness. They have embraced what you could call "evil", which is the reverse spelling of live.

This energy is anti-life, selfish and blind to consequences. Their reign has been a factor in the learning and evolution of the souls that have been incarnating on this planet for many eons. This includes "perpetrators" who serve Karma by creating the suffering through which many souls have to experience their learning on their journey towards the Light. This has generated greater levels of soul awareness and awakening from the great illusion of separation consciousness.

All things work for good. As Old Chinese teaches, souls are eternal. Your true nature is immortal. You are infinite and universal. Death is a transition. Suffering has been an instrument of evolution and transformation.

So, where are we now at this juncture of time and life on your dear Mother Earth? There is so much to tell of the story of humanity. We could say "man"kind, but that is an anachronism, for it is an expression of how the masculine has come to dominate the consciousness and has used the objectification of women, children and "the other" as a means of domination and control.

Objects only have value in this mindset because of their usefulness. They are not recognized as having consciousness or sentience, and therefore can be disposed of and treated without respect, recognition or honoring. Objects have been transformed into possessions, and within the consciousness of darkness, black New Earth Council 18 magic and the manipulation of energy, they have been used as fuel to create control and the misuse of power over the world and life on this planet.

It is with a heavy heart that we even bring up the subject of the abuse, torture and murder of children and women, of trafficking and slavery and such vile insensitivity. We are not implying that men or male children are not also the victims of this widespread horror. Nor are we suggesting that this phenomenon is perpetrated by males solely. On the contrary. Its extent is pernicious and vast.

The power structures that control your world depend on and run on the energy supplied by ritual cultic practices and cruel sexual abuse that feed the dark powers. These energies, practices and abuses are at the root and the base of all the infrastructures of power that run your world, your governments and corporations. They have been the foundation that underlies the control and authority over your personal and collective lives. They have determined how you think and act and feel in the world and have become calcified and entrenched into the very fabric of the matrix of what you consider "normal". Knowing this information is important. One must not hide from the truth, nor fear it, as fear feeds it.

Dismantling this edifice and restructuring society based on the model of love, cooperation, unity and non-judgment is y/our job now. This pandemic is actually the greatest opportunity being afforded all life to shake off the reign of terror and fear and separation. Your species has endured millions upon millions of years of existences in civilizations throughout your galaxy and universe. Your soul has the power to completely transform this reality into unity consciousness based on love and light and joy.

We are the New Earth Council. We have asked this one to be a vehicle for our transmissions, teachings and messages. We are here to assist in, not just the dismantling and de-structuring, but in the creation of structures that will replace them. It is our intention to provide the foundations for your return to joy and self-realization; to freedom from fear and the re-establishment of your self-authority. We wish to restore your power to have your life accord with your highest and purest intentions, and to give you the encouragement and tools to reclaim your innocence and freedom.

The members of this council are 12 in number. We represent a variety of wisdom traditions, viewpoints and perspectives and are aligned and associated with all the Councils of Light, Holy Beings and Masters of Wisdom, all the avatars and angelic guides, and with all the realms of the Living Spirit that is in All Things.

We are:

Seshat

Thoth

Apollo

Pan

John Henry

Ashtara

Old Chinese

The Druid

Joan of Arc

Ganesha

Padma Sambhava (Guru Rinpoche)

Joy

We encompass a broad spectrum of wisdom traditions and lineages, and each of us will explain what we represent and bring forward as we share our individual and collective messages with you. We will provide instruction, suggestion, formula and guidance over the next weeks and months. We begin to share these messages on the 16th August 2020.

The complete course with the Introduction, the 12 Messages, Q&A from participants and a thirteenth voice will all be transcribed and published as a book.

We love you. We are the 12.

Joy Weisman
12th August 2021

Voice One
Seshat

16th August 2020

Let us put our right hand on our hearts and left on our right, feeling that stillness beginning to pour down from above, filling us, filling this column of light that we are with a sense of stillness and peace as it enters into our hearts and as we begin to feel our feet or our seat firmly connected below. We connect to Mother Earth below us, feeling a column of light that surrounds each one of us and this whole group, expanding out to connect all of our hearts together as we feel the depth of Mother Earth, feeling our roots deeply entering and penetrating into her very essence, so that we feel grounded and present. And as we do this, the column rises up towards the heavens, and we feel the connection with Mother Earth below us and with Father Sky above us, connecting to the Source, the origin of All That Is, our connection to the ones that watch over us in the heavens.

And as we feel this connection of above and below, we begin to bring it all into the very center of our hearts, where that source and that origin resides.

As we do this, we also begin to feel the threads of our hearts beginning to reach out and weave together; the threads of each one of us weaving together with the threads of all those on our call, beginning to create a fabric. The fabric grows bigger and bigger as it extends and connects the threads of the hearts of our loved ones, our friends, our families, our neighbors, our pets; reaching out further and further afield, across this whole continent, reaching outward across the oceans and all the continents, reaching towards the very edges of Mother Earth, surrounding the planet with this beautiful grid work of light, of love, this connection with the One Heart, with all time, and with all space.

So, we welcome you to this place. We ask you to fill your hearts now with this beautiful, golden light and with this beautiful weave of HeartThread®8 energy that surrounds each one of us and weaves us all together into the Heart of the One. As you rest your hands now, let us call upon the first of the twelve new voices, of the ones from the Council who have gathered us here together to weave a story, perhaps a new story; a story of all time, of all space; a story of origins and a story of truth, a story of our true connection, one with the other and with our purpose here on this planet at this time. We have gathered you together, those who have answered the call, in order to prepare you for your work in the world in a much more powerful way. We have called you to answer your own questions that dwell within your hearts, to find that source of your own truth, to find that place of your own power; because you are now ready to embark upon the creation of structures that are at the heart of why you have come here.

All of you who have been drawn here have come because you have been from the beginning. You have been watching, and you have been participating in the evolution of consciousness on this planet. And you have done so out of a strong desire and of longing to be of service and to bring your special gifts to the world and to help with the evolution, this new 'Event', so to speak, that is happening on the planet. So, each one of us 12 that has formed this council will bring to you our own special message; but understand that, just as you are actually one council, so are we, and each one has their separate identity throughout time, throughout space, and in the realms of Light, that which goes beyond the form, beyond the structures of the world and the third dimensional realities that you are currently engrossed in.

I would like to introduce myself as the first one to show up in this one's consciousness. My name is Seshat. You may never have heard of me, which is not surprising, because most are familiar with the one Thoth, who is known throughout the ages as Hermes Trismegistus, but not Seshat. Thoth was one of the original avatars who came to this planet at the very beginning of the immersion into density that began the cycles you are now reaching towards the end of.

Seshat is regarded as the consort of Thoth; And it is because of this understanding, because of this presumption on the part of those who write your books and your history, that Seshat was "merely" a consort, merely the so-called woman behind the man in power, that we wish to address you initially from this place. For Thoth was regarded as the god of learning, the god of magic, the god of numbers, of language and of bringing to the Earth all the aspects of civilization that you are needing and using in order to have a society. Seshat, is the *goddess* of magic, of numbers, of writing, of wisdom. For Seshat is not a separate entity, in the same way as Thoth is not; in the same way as the many other reincarnations upon your planet of the one Thoth. And this is also why we have chosen to begin our sessions with you, coming through as the one Thoth and the one Seshat; because we could have chosen to come forward as the Christ and the Magdalene or as Isis and Osiris or as other energies that have been with your planet as guardians and as these over-lighting energies.

For, in essence, within the many incarnations upon your planet, within the many eras and phases of your civilizations, going back to Atlantis[7] and through Lemuria[9] and even prior to that on this planet and on other planets and in other star systems, the energy that we bring, is not a separated energy of male or female, but it is essentially a united field that encompasses masculine and feminine in a wholeness. So, we wish you to bear in mind that part of what we have come to do, what we have come to bring, is a tearing down, a dismantling of all assumptions and all the ways in which you have been thinking and have been taught to think and perceive over the ages. Everything has shifted back and forth from a male to a female, to a male, to a female-dominated society and civilization over the many ages that you have been in existence upon this planet.

For essentially, the energy of god or goddess is one, and so it is important that you begin, not to analyze so much, but to pay attention and to notice the ways in which you use your language, your way of thinking, feeling and seeing. We want you to question every single aspect of your consciousness, so that you become the authors of your own self-authority. You will hear from the one John Henry ahead. He is a master of bringing through the energy of self-authority, but, essentially, we wish to begin by opening your minds up to the possibilities that the ways in which you think, the ways in which you see, the ways in which you regard what you are told, are not as they appear.

We are planning in the time that we share with you, between this time and the ending of our 12 sessions, we are planning that you will have a brand-new way of seeing everything from the perspective of the power within you, so that truth, for you, becomes an energy that is not a belief system. It is no longer something that you have been taught or told or has been imprinted upon you through your conditioning, through your education, through your upbringing and through your ancestry and lineages. For you are in a new world; you are here because we are all together as a Oneness energy to create the New Earth, to bring it into being. You could say, at some level, that it has already been created in the mind of God or Goddess. We are asking you to tear apart each concept, like the word "God," and consider how you might rephrase it for yourself in a way that relates to a new way of seeing reality. Because, in the mind of the Creator, in the mind is All That Is, all that has been and that does not serve the Oneness energy, the arrival of the unity upon your planet and the ending of separation-consciousness; everything that does not serve it is now ready to be dissolved away.

And so, in this process, we will be asking you to review much of your life and much of your ways of thinking and seeing. We will be asking you to review your habits and concepts. We will be asking you to review your past, and align with only those energies that serve you, that serve the whole, and that serve the higher purpose of your evolution as a species and an individual soul. You are here to express this fullness. Essentially, you are here to experience and express your own inner beauty without any judgments, without any diminution of anything or any aspect of yourself, and without voices in your mind. You have inherited these voices that say that you are less than perfect, less than beautiful, and less than magnificent. And we are intending that by the end of this series, you will think and see your reality without judgment, and re-mold it into a brand-new way of perceiving everything.

This is important because the world, as you are very aware, is harboring a giant cloud of illusion, is harboring a deep sense of fear, which is counter to the very essence of love and which is, in many ways, inhibiting your ability to understand Truth. All the energy of what is called truth that you are receiving is coming to you from the outside, from your media, your peers and authority figures. We are not saying that all of them are untrue, but that it is a conglomeration of information and energy that creates confusion in the mind, because the mind is not engineered to make sense of it all. It is the heart, that inner power within you and your intuition; not the mind, that brings the awareness of a field of guidance, of light and protection. We are asking you to start to dismantle what you believe. We're asking you to go into that place of your heart and begin to ask "What do I know, what do I trust and what can I change that will shift how I believe something, even if it does not feel good for me in my body or emotions. Instead of running on belief, I begin to go inside and ask, 'What do I know?'"

You could begin by saying "What do I feel?" and begin to sense what sensations appear in your body, because most of you dwell primarily within the mind which you use so consistently to make your choices and to decide what you believe or even what you feel. It is vital that you create a relationship of deep love, of deep companionship and communication between yourself, your higher self, your lower self, your ego self, your mind self, whatever you call it, and your body. We are recommending that you recognize the importance of feeling, through your body, with your body. Whether it be a sensation of fear or sadness, there is going to be a location, a place in your body that has a physiological response to an emotion that arises when it is triggered. For most of your emotional experiences and belief systems, what you think is your truth, often is a triggered response from your conditioning. It comes from your ancestry, from the imprints within the cellular structure in your DNA. Your childhood and your past lives all create triggers that elicit an emotional response in the body. Unless you have a healthy relationship with your physicality, you will become confused as to what is real.

It is important for you to create this relationship with your body, to feel what it's like to ground, to anchor yourself into Mother Earth and sense your connection to the life force. Even though you are a soul with a connection to the angelic or the divine realms, you still are a breathing, heart-beating energy of flesh-and-blood. As a human animal, you are connected to that life energy and to Mother Earth. You serve her as she serves you, and in the same way that we would ask you to establish a deep relationship with your own body, we are asking you to contemplate what it would be like to have that same depth of relationship with Mother Earth. You are comprised of the same elements as the soil beneath you, the trees, the water, the air; with the bacteria and viruses, the birds and the insects, and with the unseen populations of life-force energies that are part of this tremendous living library, this Garden of Eden that is Mother Earth.

This relationship, that we are asking you to develop, is the key to the survival of the human species with Mother Earth as its host. For Mother Earth is fine. It is humanity that is in jeopardy; and yet, because you are surrounded by guardian angels, by benevolent extraterrestrials, and by holy beings that watch over you, Mother Earth will be okay. Humanity will also be OK in the long run, or perhaps even in the short run, because this opportunity that has arrived at your doorstep, is to co-create the New Earth. The old Earth must disintegrate. This is not news to you. The aspects of the New Earth that wish to come forward depend on you loving yourself unconditionally.

Old Chinese's definition of "love" is "the unconditional acceptance of another's reality." If you put that in your hat, and you take it personally, what it requires of you and implies, is that you love yourself, personally and unconditionally. I suggest that you make every attempt, on an ongoing basis, to not judge anyone or anything whatsoever. Do this, even if you decide they are dark and not deserving of the light and the love energy. On the contrary, those who are lost within the darkness require this light and this love to be surrounding them so that they can wake up. This will allow a greater number of people on your planet to achieve the mass expansion of consciousness that is required for your Earth to transition, for humanity to transition into the next dimension with ease and grace instead of doom and gloom, cataclysm and fear. This is not necessary.

Seshat is the divine consort of Thoth. Thoth is one of the early incarnations of the Christ, and as a corollary to that, Seshat would have been Mary Magdalen. The original incarnations of the feminine wisdom energy have been on your planet from the beginning to bring you divine guidance and a new way of seeing your connection with Spirit for the evolution of consciousness, and what's unfolding on your planet. One of the things, therefore, that we would like to bring to your attention is the understanding that, within the current construct of how you think, 'past lives' is a misnomer. In order to consider lives linearly, as past or future, one has to be in a mindset of a very specific and limited approach to that which you call time and space.

We have shared in other ways that the energy of the heart is a quantum field, a quantum energy, which allows for everything to be in the same place at the same time. It allows for the holographic nature of the Universe to be understood in a way that the mind is not accustomed to experiencing. Even a cycle or a spiral is a way for the mind to grasp reality. In this approach that we are offering and insisting upon for you, in which you question everything, and we mean everything, for your mind, your being, your consciousness to expand to the level of the Fifth Dimension and beyond and be an example for what is needed in the world now, it is essential for you to dismantle *all* of your constructs.

The New Earth will be based upon the energy of building structures. We do not necessarily just mean organizations and activities, we mean structures of the mind, of the heart, of the psyche and of consciousness. They will not necessarily be ones that you are accustomed to. Essentially, you are joining this one in becoming builders of new structures, however that works for you. That will be something that you will determine as you find what resonates for you. And then, as a result, you will begin to find what is the way in which you express your truth. The ultimate truth is "Union;" It is the truth of Oneness.

So, we are suggesting that you hold *that* truth as your mission, as your guiding light. Let your practice be the questioning of everything. For most of what is regarded as reality is the Maya, the Illusion. Your mission and your task in this world is to uncover Truth. You do this through that guiding light of the truth of Union, of non-separation, of non-judgement. And you come into an alignment with it in a very simple way; by connecting with Mother Earth beneath you, with Father Sky above you and with your heart in the center. Coming to that place of stillness. You open yourself to that alignment with the truth of non-judgement, no longer listening to the voices that are put downs, that say that you are unworthy, or that you are not good enough. As for you, so for everyone.

This is your work now, to release from your field, from your mind and from your heart all these imprints. And you do it through your willpower. You do it through your discipline, through your practice. This becomes your practice. When you meditate, when you take your daily walks or whatever practice you have that aligns you with Heaven and Earth and your heart, send out that column of light in a spiral, clockwise Christ Consciousness[10] energy to touch the hearts of all with light. Make no distinction as to who should receive it and who should not. Send it out as an extension of just being in that column of your own light, of your own power. Surround yourself with a sphere of bright, white, golden light to maintain a field of love and energy that protects from fear and judgment.

By standing in that column of light, you are realigning your whole being with your inner truth in Oneness and connection with all of life. For you cannot have union without respect for all life, without having respect for Mother Earth and all of her creatures. Indeed, it is necessary to have respect for the struggles, for the hardships, for the sadness, the losses and the pain that human beings experience within this field of illusion. You are asked to hold a field of compassion through finding that place of love within yourself.

Seshat, as the "divine feminine" aspect of Thoth, is part of humanity's encounter with wisdom, with writing, with letters, with magic, with agriculture, and with the arts. You associate these aspects of culture as the foundations of civilization - communication, connection, an understanding of the world within and around you.

These secrets were imparted at the beginning-less beginning by the unified energy of Seshat and Thoth. All of you here were there in the very 'beginning,' when there was such a thing as a 'fall from grace' or "The Fall". Divine souls entered into the density of the Earth field and became trapped. These divine sparks wished to experience themselves as individuated energies. This first wave forgot their divine origin as aspects of the Oneness.

And so it was that a second wave chose, and were chosen, to descend, shall we say, to the Earth plane in order to retain the memory of their Divine Consciousness as they entered into the domains of density in order to save those who had become trapped. There are many stories within the mythology that talk of this. Edgar Cayce[11] has talked about creatures who were a combination of human and animal forms. There was a need to heal these of their appendages and the consequences of the mating of this first wave with the humanoid life forms that were developing upon Mother Earth. And so, this second wave was led by the forces of Seshat and Thoth, whom you are more familiar with as the Magdalene and the Christ. The Christ and the Mary energy, the energy of the so-called "Savior," is like a combination of Mother and Father, Above and Below. The energy of Christ and Magdalene has been in your field, most of you, who have had an experience of working with Flo Magdalena, the Ones with No Names and the Councils[12].

And so, this energy is also an extension of the energy of Isis and of the goddesses, who were the feminine aspects of the gods. Isis was with Osiris, and all the different incarnations of the energy of god and goddess over the eons on your planet. So, I am coming, as this feminine aspect of the bringers of wisdom, language, writing and communication, and agriculture and architecture to your planet. Seshat was the one who appears on the stelae and the walls of the Egyptian monuments, as being the one who recorded the span of years allocated to the pharaohs. She was depicted wearing the leopard skin with many eyes that could see everything. She was the one who knew how to measure and lay out, along with the king, the alignments of the temples, of the pyramids, and the structures that were created in Ancient Egypt, and prior to that, in the lands of Atlantis, and in Lemuria.

These buildings, like the Pyramids, were aligned with the stars, especially those in the Big Dipper, with Sirius, the Pleiades and Orion. These stars were regarded as sacred, and sources of guidance and communication with your early civilizations. And so it was that Seshat and the king would lay out a cord and make sure that it was aligned with the correct star within the correct constellation. And in the beginning, many of these were part of what you call the Big Dipper. So it was Seshat along with Thoth who laid out these alignments so that everything on your planet, would be in a divine alignment within time and space and sacred geometry that underlies all cosmologies. There was this understanding that they needed to be aligned with these planets, and with particular star systems. Many of the visitors, and intelligences that have been watching and guiding you, and some that have been misusing you, are from these systems.

I, Seshat herself, would like you to feel, and you can do your own research, but we would like you to understand that the energy of the divine feminine, the undercurrents and foundation of your civilization and your understanding as human beings with human minds, was established in the same way as the laying out of the cord did for these structures. The energy of the divine feminine laid out and established the creation energy for your planet. And for your own alignment with your own divine feminine. For each one is a combination of the masculine and the feminine within, which is not really dividable, even though the mind has a way to separate the two and say "There's the left side and the right side and this one has these characteristics and that one has those." In essence, just as with mind, with body, with emotion, with spirit, you are a Wholeness.

The mind is accustomed to partitioning and trying to make sense by dividing things so that you can understand. However, the heart carries within it the understanding of Oneness, of Wholeness; the understanding that there is not a separation, even within the internal structure of your being human. Being a divine human angel, a combination of divine and human, you are of Earth and Sky, of Mother and Father. All these dichotomies are aspects of the dualism, the energy of masculine and feminine, positive and negative. Polarity is necessary in order for energy to move. And there is no judgment on the energy of the electron and the nucleus, positive and negative, on good and bad, or right and wrong. For everything within your plane is based upon that movement of energy from one polarity to the other, and is just energy in motion, what you call emotion.

We are bringing you this understanding to help you find ways to dismantle your thinking, your ways of seeing, especially yourself. We want you to understand the power of your own pure essence that dwells within your heart. And when we say it dwells within your heart, we are pointing to the deepest and most central part of your field as an energy system; that part of your connection with the divine spark which is manifest within the world of physicality. However, it is a place you have access to, and you must find access to it. You must find your own personal way of connecting with that space of your inner beauty, your inner wisdom and your inner truth. We will, throughout this course, be reminding you that this is your work in the world, though, we do not like the word "work" because we are all about ease and grace, and we wish this for you. We want you to know that the end of the struggle has come and that we do not want you to experience struggle any longer, but rather ease and grace, abundance and joy. For this is the true nature of your divine essence. And we wish it for you, as much as you wish it for yourself.

As we embark upon this journey together, 12 voices will bring messages to assist you to reach this space. You find this alignment with your inner wisdom and come to know what you know by being your own self-authority without question, without judgment and without giving yourself away to anyone or to anything outside you.

We suggest that you begin by creating a journal for yourself. Write down and note every single thought. Be aware of, question, and replace any that no longer serve you with a new thought. We are asking you to notice each time you do something that you have always done in the same way, and make a determined choice to do it differently. Notice what words you use. Write down what that word meant in the past and how you are now able to redefine it to make more sense within the structure of Oneness.

We are asking you to pay attention to the health and well-being of your body, your mind, your emotions and your thought processes. Then you will begin to eat healthier food, to drink lots of water and find ways to implement a discipline of exercise of some sort that specifically suits you. We are asking you to become Spiritual Warriors[13], who hold the Sword of Truth, and find ways to interrupt the assumptions of others and their judgments, without interrupting them, just through being and holding the field of Truth within yourself.

We are, in fact, asking you not to share your truth with everyone, through words or proselytizing or a need to influence others by what you uncover as your truth. In the process of these 12 weeks, we will be delving deeply into much of the illusion, into much of the facade that is being expounded on your planet. We will take you to some places that you might find extremely enlightening. In the meantime, we are asking you to use this energy of self-examination, of self-love, as your mission. It is your exercise, so that you become more and more grounded in self-love, in self-non-judgement, in the experience of non-separation, as best you can without ever putting yourself down when you notice that you, so-called, 'slipped up.' Instead, notice and say, "Oh, I did that, or I said that. Interesting! I can now do it differently."

We wish you to experience the deepest levels of joy and satisfaction in your lives. We wish for you to find ways, and we will assist, to experience the fullness of health, well-being, vitality and clarity. We ask you to examine everything. What agreements did you make or did you not make? "How can I go back and revisit those areas where I was not clear and generate structures of clarity for myself, within my own life and the lives of those I love and those that surround me? And how can I do this in a way that comes from love, that comes from acceptance, and from that space of peace within my own heart?"

So, I welcome you to join us in this adventure that we are all embarking upon. Just as you are encountering us, we are encountering you, and we are surrounding you with our love, with our light and with our blessings.

What you do now, essentially, is train to express your wisdom and your learning, as teachers, by practicing with each other and with yourselves. So, communicate with each other. You have that inside of you, the ability to listen to another and to respond from your heart in a way that allows them to receive another level of clarity. Choose somebody and ask them "Hey, would you like to be on a call together, I'd like to talk to somebody. I've got this issue, and I think you would be someone who could help?" Trust what feels right. By the time we reach the next class, there will be an opportunity for others to listen to the recording of our afternoon together, which will allow them to get a better sense of what they are diving into.

We want you to share with one another, to support each other with your questions, and be able to guide each other through your own wisdom. You can do this for each other and there is no harm as long as you are in the space of your heart when you begin and end this particular kind of experience. It's part of how you get to transform your consciousness in a period of 12 weeks, so that by the time those of you who are on the course with Flo return after your pause, you will be empowered to take the sharing that comes through her from The Ones with No Names, to a whole other level.

We wish to expand and accelerate the Awakening, so that there is a greater amount of light on this planet and the energies of dark will be able to uncover the truth for themselves that, truly, at the very core, they too are light, and it is time for the New Earth, beyond anyone's agendas.

Sheshat Q&A

Q. (AY) I am very moved. I have wondered whether the wisdom schools and teachings from Lemuria and Atlantis might be reinstated, and when Seshat worked with these to be aligned with the star systems. Was this in the first wave? How did these people lose their connection, when all this was in place? Is this going to be in place again, or is it still here, some of this connection with any of these sites? And will they arise again in some way, for teaching?

A. The ancient wisdom that is part of your complete consciousness is known in the Akashic Records. It is something that is available and will become more and more also as your consciousness allows it. It is definitely an energy that will return to Mother Earth, through the consciousness of those of you who again carry your own truth and expand and open it. And teach it. You are the teachers of the new wave. You are the ones who are going to recreate the structures, who will bring back the teachings. They did not come with the first wave. They came in with the second wave. The first wave were the ones who were lost, who became trapped in the density. Many of the waves of avatars and teachers that have come to your planet over the period of these vast eons of civilizations, have come to remind you and to rekindle in the lost ones, the memory of their origin as divine. And so, what is of value in creating Heaven on Earth will reappear in a way that is aligned, structured and in accordance with the way in which it needs to be expressed on the planet at this time - through the consciousnesses that are awakening now.

It will become part of your job, your work, your mission, to be one of these teachers, to hold the beauty and value of the goddess energy, to gather around you the circles of the young women, and the older women, and bring them together to dialogue, to share their wisdom and their teachings for each other. And then, to also do this with the energy of the men, so that the divisions of male and female and the separation dissolve in the necessity of creating safety for those that have experienced great suffering. All of this will be part of what unfolds from you stepping into your, and this is "Your" with a capital, for all of you, stepping into your own power as teachers, as leaders, as guides, and as able to be in tune with us.

Whether we be this particular configuration of 12, or the other Councils of Light or Federations, you are connected to all these realms and to this wisdom. As you work on these simple exercises to unravel the ways in which your thinking is limited, and you begin to experience life outside of the box, you will find your mission unraveling before you without effort. It is important to remove the effort, the push, and the sense of angst or urgency, and allow your heart to follow its pace with ease and grace.

That will also allow you to tune in to your guidance and your intuition, because you won't be rushing and thereby miss the significant meeting that you would have missed if you had rushed or sped and arrived too late, or too early. Instead, when you are not feeling any urgency, everything will be in its perfect timing and its perfect alignment for you. So too will be the unfolding into your wisdom, your teaching and the creation of circles that we are asking you to bring together. We suggest that, when you feel ready, you gather around you those with whom you share, heart-to-heart, face to face, woman to woman, man to man, man to woman, child to adult, to elder. All these separations wish to be dismantled. Does that answer your question?

- More than that, thank you

Q. (CR) I am wondering if the immune system is the answer to the virus?

A. The immune system is the answer to everything about your health, because, if you have a strong immune system, you will not be affected by extraneous energies. Recognize that most of your genetics is not dependent on your genes, but on your environment. Your DNA is programmed by your belief system, not by your genetics, except in certain rare cases. In the same way, your immune system does not believe in germs or viruses, it only believes in following the path of your energy and organ systems being in harmony with the life force energy. The particular virus you are referring to, whatever it is, or is not, cannot impact you if you have no stress, no fear, no belief that it can harm you.

So, the answer to health, the answer to well-being, to clarity, to your emotional, physical and spiritual well-being is: make sure that you have a strong immune system. Do everything that you can to create a strong immune system. Do not believe energy, or words, or ideas, that are counter to life-force energy. Do not trust everything you hear or see, especially if it comes from mainstream media. This is especially so if your heart does not resonate with it, and if it is counter to your intuition, and what you know to be true. This is why you have these 12 weeks to polish up your ability to intuit your own truth. You achieve this by letting go of anything that impinges on your ability to be clear. Clear about what is true, for you.

We've already said that The Truth is Oneness, non-separation; therefore anything that separates is going to be counter to the truth of honoring life, of honoring all beings. Once you digest the understanding that you create your own healthy immune system through your beliefs, you begin to look at what your beliefs are telling you and creating for you. You will become aware that the possibilities of living within a quantum field allow for instant healing, allow for the healing through prayer at a distance, allow for hands-on and energetics to heal your system, even to regrow organs or teeth through entrainment with frequencies.

Many of the things that are possible are held outside of your box, because you have not entertained their possibility. So, this long answer to your question is "Yes." Life depends on viruses and bacteria. You have millions of them within your body. They are not "good" or "bad." By building your immune system, you will keep yourself safe from any virus and from any infection of negative thinking that is directed towards you. As you put a sphere of golden light around you and live within that sphere, or you draw over you the "golden mantle," or you sit within your column of light, none of that will impact you any longer. You will be safe because you will know that you are safe, and that you have all the guidance in the world at your disposal. Peace.

Q. (KM) My question is specifically about the assignment. Can you give an example? I'm having a little trouble around writing down our thoughts and replacing them with different ones. Are you specifically choosing thoughts of duality and replacing them with thoughts of oneness? The other assignment was writing down a word and thinking about how that word has affected you in the past and the present. I just didn't understand. Could you give me some examples of each assignment?

A. Essentially what we are asking of you, is to pay attention to your thoughts, to the ways in which you use words, to the ways in which you see the world, to your belief systems, to the ways in which you pay attention to those voices in your head that come from the past, from your conditioning and the imprints of everything you've experienced or suffered in this or any life. All these are in your field and impact how you experience life. Recognizing that you are the creator of your reality forms the understanding and the basis for what we're asking you to do. It is to track everything about how you have been, and how you have been creating your reality, and then shifting it. So, when this one here for instance thinks, "Oh God, I'm not going to be able to do this or that" or "Here I go again, I screwed up," you immediately notice that thought, and you interrupt it. You say, "I am doing my best. I no longer pay attention to these old voices. I'm absolutely good enough. Everything I do is fine and perfect. I love who I am. I love how my life is unfolding."

We're giving you an example of that which undermines your experience of union, because they are separative ways of thinking, seeing and feeling. When you are not coming from a space of union, we recommend redirecting what comes from the mind, so it comes from the heart, from the field of Union. In other words, bypassing the mind will allow you to live in the moment with your heart open, without being subject to those internal voices that come from the past or from your conditioning. It will empower you to let go of your entire story, your entire past. This is necessary in order for you to embrace your coming of age, shall we say, you're coming out as a teacher, a healer, a leader, as one who is creating new structures in the world that are foundationed on love, cooperation and unity consciousness. Does that make sense?

You would need to go back and listen to the list. Keep a journal, and write down everything you have been doing that day, the thoughts you have. If you catch them, notice them and replace the old with a new one, you are doing your work. If you decide to exercise when you haven't been and make a decision to do it consistently, write that down so that you can share it. Then others can see that each one is struggling, so to speak, with a similar propensity to think from within a box. And you're being asked to open that box and breathe the fresh air without the mask and look through different eyes. Look through the eyes of heaven, through the eyes of the angels, instead of through the eyes of the little child that somehow was not loved enough, or was told that they couldn't.

So, we are asking you to just educate yourself in how to replace the old ways of thinking, being, and seeing with new ways. You do not have to be, and we don't want you to be, caught up in restricted thinking, "I have to do this, I have to do that." We want you to flow freely from the heart in every way of expression. We also want you all to experience music, art, and culture. Open yourself during these times, where you have plenty of time for reading, for drawing, for playing music, and take it to another level, where you're opening up new vistas of experience for yourself.

Comment: *(MSG) I want to say how touched I am. I met you five years ago around the Medicine Water Wheel[14] with Marshall, Golden Eagle. It's only recently that I've discovered your beautiful channeling and teachings, and I am so touched. For the past year, I have been working with a Kogi Shaman from Colombia. The Kogi People are the ones who are very connected to the original wisdom. They hid away for 500 years in the mountains when the Conquistadors came, and they recently came down to warn the world that we're out of balance with Nature, and we need to come back in. I just spent 10 days with him in North Carolina, and the teachings and the sharings that you're doing are so in alignment with their teachings. It comforts my soul to hear everything that you're sharing: doing the writing. He calls it recapitulation, changing and releasing our negative programming. So, I just want to say, I'm so grateful to have discovered and stepped into this Council for The New Earth. I'd love to support and help in any way that I can.*

Q. *(NB) This was just so beautiful. I could literally feel energies around, and very, very powerful. So, I just first want to say thank you for taking the time. My question is specifically: Everything that she said for us to do, it makes total sense. How can we get more support on taking care of health and exercising, with being home all the time because of lockdown? What are some of the things, some of the practical ways we are able to do that for ourselves?*

A. A very good question. We would like you to share with each other, to pair up and talk on the phone with each other and to view and support each other in your progress, in your sharings of where you have been with these choices, and these ways of working with yourselves, so that you can reflect for each other the love that you begin to see in each other. We also are happy to offer our own guidance for you, so that you can connect with this one here and ask questions.

The energy of Zoom is a very useful and powerful energy, but it is extremely draining on Mother Earth's resources. It is part of a vast network of energies that cause a deep amount of suffering to the creatures and the human beings that are required to maintain this kind of network of communication. There will be in the future a much more benevolent way of communicating, because the amount of bandwidth gigabytes that are required for streaming all these faces and voices for these periods is extremely unsustainable to the planet. We are going to recommend that you try to use this method as infrequently as possible.

In spite of this, we still recommend that you access all the amazing resources that are available for doing yoga, for dancing, for sharing other ways of moving, and exercising, and emotional release by accessing the various offerings that have now become available through this technology because of lockdown. It is really, at some level, up to you to decide that you're going to follow a disciplined practice on a daily or twice-daily or weekly basis, where you do yoga, where you dance, where you do some kind of movement or energy; that you align yourself with others who are taking care of their bodies and are discovering various supplements, or various methods of creating health within the structure of your body and of boosting your immune system.

We want you to understand that when you realize what you know, you will know that you are safe. You will know it because you will feel the energy of your angels and your guides around you, watching over you. You will know it, because you will be more attuned with your intuition, so that everything you do will be in alignment with your best practices, with your best health, and with your safety. There is quite an extensive field that we will explore. We will explore a few very fundamental practices that will allow you to feel more safe. We will help you to understand better what is happening and what you are facing, that will allow you to relax and let go of any stress. Because, of all the aspects that impinge upon your health, fear and stress are your greatest enemies. We want you to replace them with love and faith. As you trust your guidance, as you trust the serendipity and the ease and grace, and the synchronicities that begin to show up in your life, you will recognize that you are blessed. You are guided, you are loved, and you are held in the palm of God's hands or Goddess's hands, as the case may be. We hope that has answered your question

.   -Yes, thank you so much.

Q. (SL) I am a rebel. I have been a rebel all my life. I do not accept this lockdown as something that I need to participate in. I wonder what your thoughts are on civil disobedience.

A. We could say the same thing that we have just shared with you. Everything that you do, every aspect of decision-making that comes from you, must come from that place of knowing. It must come from your heart. It must come from that place of compassion, of non-judgment. It is fine, within the structure of your self-authority, to call yourself a rebel. However, you must also be aware that there is a balance of holding a certain space of truth within yourself and trying to beat others up with it. There is a place where invisibility can be a great asset.

Instead of rubbing people the wrong way, who are not ready to listen to your truth, we are asking you to revisit all of your constructs, including the ones you have just shared with us. We are not saying you are right or wrong, or that you should do this or that. We are asking that you examine every thought, every process, every assumption, and that you come from your heart, wherever you come, so that you are clear that you do not have to be in lockdown. You can go wherever you choose to go. No one is stopping you at this point. You do not have to do everything that's required of you. When you walk around your city, you can wear a mask or not, and you can do it as you choose. If it makes for more invisibility when you walk into a store, instead of trying to create a ruckus and stand out from the crowd, it might just be easier to stick that silly old mask on your face, do your shopping and take it off as soon as you get out.

You have a lot of freedom of choice within your current lockdown system. You do not have police breathing down your neck, yet. It may or may not come to that. Just know that you are not alone, within the bristling that you feel, of having to go with the dictates of what is being forced upon you. But most surely, we are asking you to examine each and every concept, each and every thought, each and every feeling and assumption and then come to a place of peace within yourself, before you take on the world and start raising banners and organizing. Make sure that whatever you do is done from the space of the spiritual warrior within, who only draws the sword from the scabbard when it is absolutely necessary to uphold their own truth. Do not strike another with your truth. Peace.

Closing Meditation

So, let us put our hands on our hearts again, and go back into that column of light, feeling Mother Earth beneath our feet, feeling that beautiful connection; allowing ourselves to enjoy the experience each day of being able to feel Mother Earth beneath us, and feel that rising of her love for us and through our hearts and up towards Heaven, up towards the galaxies and the stars and the Cosmos, to that place of Divine Source; so that our hearts are the connecting points between Heaven and Earth, and it is part of what we do as we are in our essence of connecting Heaven and Earth, in bringing Heaven to Earth and Earth to Heaven. We bless you. We surround you with our love. You may talk to us anytime by going into your heart and asking us your questions and listening from the depths of your stillness to the answers.

Blessings and peace to you all, and thank you.

Voice Two
Thoth

23rd August, 2020

Let us put our right hand on our hearts and our left hand on our right and take some nice deep breaths, just to settle in and relax; beginning to feel that this stillness is encompassing our whole being. Breathing in a sense of stillness, we allow it to wash over our entire body, fill our minds, fill our hearts, and, as we breathe out, we let go of all thoughts, feelings or sounds; just letting it go with the out breath, feeling our feet or our seat connecting to Mother Earth deep beneath us, allowing ourselves to feel our gratitude for Mother, that sense of connection, of being anchored, of having roots within her very core; Allowing that feeling of centeredness, being settled in our bodies, fully present, feeling the column of light that surrounds each one of us. And the column reaches all the way down to Mother Earth, down to her core. It is filled with a beautiful, golden, healing light. The column reaches up toward the Heavens, up to that place of Origin, of Source, that Divine Spark, allowing ourselves to be connected above with Heaven and below with Earth. Allowing the breath to breathe us from Heaven to Earth and from Earth to Heaven, feeling that breath and that centeredness within our hearts. And then we begin to feel the threads that weave around the planet to connect us, creating a fabric made up of the threads of our hearts that weaves its way into the hearts of all of our loved ones, our family, our friends, our neighbors; reaching further and further, weaving a beautiful fabric of the hearts of all beings, all creatures, all humans; that reaches its way all across the whole face of this planet, encircling Mother with a web of heart essence, of love, of connection. It reaches into all worlds and all universes, into all Time and all Space.

As we feel that stillness present within us, we can rest our hands.

My name is Thoth. I have had many names over the great spans of time. I have been known as Thoth the Egyptian, Thoth the Atlantean, Djehuti, Hermes Trismegistus (Thrice Great). I have been regarded as the god of wisdom, of knowledge, of language, of architecture and of all benevolence, of the gift of Heaven to the people of the Earth, of the foundations of culture, of civilization.

My name is Thoth. I have had many names over the great spans of time. I have been known as Thoth the Egyptian, Thoth the Atlantean, Djehuti, Hermes Trismegistus (Thrice Great). I have been regarded as the god of wisdom, of knowledge, of language, of architecture and of all benevolence, of the gift of Heaven to the people of the Earth, of the foundations of culture, of civilization. soon as one leaves that space of innocence, one becomes subject to the influence of that which no longer resonates with the heart and with that intuition, with that sense of knowing deep within you what is true. Even if there is no 'right' or 'wrong,' there is an alignment for you that you know is right or wrong, for you. It does not have to be right or wrong for another, for it is not our place to judge anyone.

Of course, when you call magic benevolent, it will be that space of the heart that is pure and innocent and open. One of the main reasons why we have asked you to be so vigilant about your language, your use of words and about the way in which you see, experience and think about things, is because there is a place within you that knows. There is also a place within you that has been overridden by the desires, impressions and imprints of others. You have been influenced by your ancestral patterns, by your cultures and religions and your peer experiences from schooling. You are indoctrinated by your particular cultures, especially the ones that exclude connection with other cultures. They say, "You must be like this or that. You cannot do that or this." This keeps you separate from others, and encourages you to see others from a different viewpoint as 'not-you.'

The Truth that takes you beyond the mind and beyond your linear ways of thinking is "interconnectedness;" for, if there were one Truth, and we would say there is one truth, that truth is, not that there is one god, but that God is One, that All is One. Everything is a part of a whole and this whole is made up of many interconnected parts that, like the hologram, are all reflections, one of the other. They are like the different sparks that are all part of the same flame or fire.

So, when you start to think holographically, you are beginning to shift the old ways of seeing things as separate, as fragmented, as divided up into pigeonholes that your mind needs in order to be able to understand them because understanding has replaced knowing. Belief systems have replaced your inner knowing, and it has made your lives so much more complicated. You are free to act from the harmonious place of your intuition, that which is free-flowing, that which is aligned without restriction but is spontaneous, like the child. All these ways of being have been put into a box and been labeled, and so we have been left with these ways of seeing and feeling and behaving because the mind has become so dominant.

The mind, the body, the emotions and the spirit are also not separate. They are all part of a wholeness and the more you are able to deconstruct the idea that you are made up of parts and that the parts are separate from each other, the more you come to recognize and feel what it's like to be whole. Judge less, because in order to judge something, one must put it at a distance. If it is within you, it cannot be at a distance; and so, it is important to gather all the shards and facets that have broken off over time through the stories, through the conditioning, through the traumas, the hard knocks, and experiences where you had to leave aspects of yourself behind or separate them out in order to survive. Otherwise, you would be in such a fraught and tortured place within your psyche that you could not function.

This is the time to look at structures for the New Earth. It is the time to brin back all those parts, to allow them to be here now, to recognize that you are no longer at the mercy of your story or belief systems that do not support that beauty of who you are. When you look in the mirror, see beauty. For, no matter what you think you look like, no matter how beautiful or not-beautiful you think you are, nobody knows what others see. You must begin to look through new eyes to recognize that everything and every choice was always perfect for you, for that moment, for that time. Right now, you are experiencing a brand-new moment, a brand-new time, where the story is no longer relevant because it's only a story. It's very fine to use it as the foundation for a novel, for a book or a memoir that shares something of your journey and perhaps teaches another who might read it. They may find value in what you have experienced and where you are now as you have contemplated your story and found the joys, the treasures, and the beauty. You are aware of those spaces of pain and loss, sorrow and agony, and how much you have grown as a result of each time you faced that agony and came through a little bit stronger, a little bit wiser, and more peaceful.

This is essentially the most vital thing to find at this time, during what we call the 'Great Deception.' Find peace within your heart, equanimity, that place of non-judgment, whether it be of yourself, of another, or of somebody else's truth. Or, of the great story that you are living in. Only six months ago there was a very different story, and now it has changed, and within 6 months it will change again, and you are being asked to look inside to find the truth that, for you, transcends the stories, all of them.

For the new story that you have had thrust upon you, not only is it a grand deception, but it is in many ways the pivotal point, the pinnacle of all the deceptions that were written into all the stories throughout time. The stories, the gospels, the "truths" and the histories were all written by those who usurped the old stories and converted them to their own ends. This applies to your Bible, your holy books, and the mythologies that you have grown up with. They were distorted by cultures before you, and then they were transferred into your own culture.   You   can   rest assured that all the stories are deceptions. There may be kernels of deep truth, of great mystical power, knowledge and understanding within them. Some of these have survived within the mystery schools, and some of you perhaps have been involved in those in this lifetime in some way or another. However, all these insights were later written about or told about, and then put into a format where it was, so-called 'inscribed on stone.' It then became the 'gospel truth,' and it has been passed down all the way from generation to generation as something for you to believe in, something that you must call "the Truth." The ways in which you must behave have been chiseled into these tablets, even if the tablets were stolen from a previous culture and changed. For this is really the greater truth of all your truths, of all your stories from all your cultures and civilizations.

New versions were rewritten or re-sculpted, mostly by men, over the eons of time. History is different from her-story, and has been engineered, in the same way as your current, what we call 'Great Deception.' Everything about your culture and your civilization, everything within the society, within your politics, within your financial systems, has been engineered for the power of the few, to manipulate and to have dominion over the many. This is one of the main reasons why we are asking you to explore, to investigate, to examine, and to change the patterns of belief, of behavior, the habits and the words you use, because all the words you use in your current daily life have components based on emotion. By this, we mean they are used as a basis for manipulation, based on meanings that allow room for misinterpretation, and for the creation of misleading understandings about them.

So, it is important that you do these assignments, that you focus on using your little book every time you have a thought, and you notice that you had the thought. Perhaps it makes you wonder whether that thought is accurate, true for you, or not. Does it perhaps reflect a mythology or a psychic reality that you no longer subscribe to? That you now call in question because you are the ones who have been called. By answering this call, you create new structures and develop new patterns of behavior based on love, cooperation, honoring, and respect for all life.

We want you to consider sustainability. That which is no longer sustainable will not be able to maintain itself. This applies to every thought, word and behavior pattern. In order to create structures for the New Earth, you cannot build on unsustainable foundations. You cannot build a New Earth on an 'us-vs-them' mentality, disrespect of life and greed, or accumulation at the expense of another. It is not sustainable to treat humans and living beings as objects and possessions.

You are being asked to shift from unsustainable thought patterns to new ways of seeing from outside the box, beyond the left-brain way of experiencing the world. We are not judging the left-brain way, but giving it its rightful place as a co-creator with the right-brain. For, male and female need to be co-creators. In the past session we shared Seshat's wisdom, guidance and beauty, the feminine 'aspect' of Thoth. She represents the goddess of wisdom, letters, magic and measurement of time. These are attributes that are shared in common. In order for the mind to understand this combination of masculine and feminine, we were divided into a male god and a female goddess with almost identical attributes. You were told by your (mostly male) 'experts' that she was my consort, or we were father/daughter, because this is how humans have pigeonholed energy and wisdom.

So, I come to you as the one, Thoth. But, I also represent a combination of Seshat and Thoth, of masculine and feminine, without excluding the one or the other. Because we wish to bring you this perspective, we chose to be the first two of the 12 voices to appear before you. Part of the learning is to recognize you have had many incarnations as one or the other. However, in essence, you are a unity that appears to have been divided up.

As we have said before, we also represent the sun and the moon, the male god and the female goddess. We have the cycles of the sun rising and setting and then rising and setting again, engendered by the 12, the planets, the Zodiac. This spawns mythologies that go back to the very beginning and are essentially the roots of your religious practices and beliefs systems throughout the many cultures and civilizations. There are cycles based on the sun, and cycles based on the moon and their interrelationship.

So, in reference to the sun, we have death and resurrection, rebirth and decay, Solstice and Equinox, and the changes of seasons. The moon gives us the rhythms of the tides, eclipses, cycles of emotion and menstruation. We have the movement of the Earth around the sun and the sun around the center of the galaxy. The 'wobble' of the Earth's axis generates the grand cycles called the Precession of the Equinoxes[15], where each of the 12 signs of the Zodiac 'rules' your civilizations over a span of approximately 16,000 years, apparently going 'backwards.' These are the underpinnings of all of your religions.

We (Seshat and Thoth) also represent for you the energy of Christ and Magdalene, Isis and Osiris, and all the other god/goddesses. In addition, we represent the threefold nature of 'Divinity,' the Trinity - male, female and child. For, of this masculine and feminine "god-ness" is born the child that you are. Your divine parents, the male and the female energies, have created a unique newness, a new birth, the consciousness that you represent.   Your true essence is the place of innocence we referred to, of the heart. It is a space of inner knowing. The child is still alive and strong within you, the child who was told not to do this or that, told to behave in certain ways to fit in to society. The child is conditioned into social behavior that benefits the whole. We are not saying this is completely inappropriate. However, it socializes you to not question authority. It is taken to unacceptable levels, as with social distancing and hiding behind a mask. Your beautiful eyes are all that can be seen, and you are barely recognizable or acknowledged as a human being. Being forced to live in separation is really a way of manipulating you to stay separate, to maintain the unsustainable 'you-versus-them' attitudes that denigrate the 'other,' because of the color of their skin, their religious beliefs, how they worship divinity, or because of their age, gender, or perhaps some disability in their physicality.

We recommended the assignment to notice when you regard another person as an 'other.' Even those who have created this Grand Deception are to be treated as if they are souls that are immortal and eternal, and have within them a spark of divine consciousness that can still become illuminated. Thus, the flame of truth and consciousness, that spark of God's love, the root of all interconnection may eventually become recognized through an awakening. And so it is important not to even judge those who are behind the control element. They are hungry souls that need love, that need light and not judgement. For they were suckled on judgement.

We shared the definition of Old Chinese from long ago that 'love is the unconditional acceptance of the reality of another.' The foundation of non-judgement is an understanding that your judgements are only a reflection of aspects of yourself that you are not comfortable with, that you do not wish to see or acknowledge as within you.

Old Chinese once remarked that many of the drunks among the indigenous peoples were, in their past lives, the souls who, as the US Cavalry, despised, mistreated and attacked the indigenous peoples so viciously. Each one of you has been on this planet through numerous cycles of lives, and you are here today because you have experienced the entire gamut of what it is like to be a human upon this planet. You have all been murderers and rapists. You have all been slaves. You have all been beggars. You have all been disabled. You have all been everything. And within that process, your soul has learned the many lessons and grown to experience what it means to be awakened or awakening to the greater light of God's love, of Consciousness.

And so, it puts you in a position where you no longer have the right, where you no longer give yourself permission to judge another, to separate. This is similar work for you, if you are in the course with the one, Flo and the Ones with No Names. Your 'work' is to interrupt any aspect of separation-consciousness that rises within you. This is also why we are giving you this assignment and asking that you put pen to paper. When you do so, it actualizes it and makes it real, visceral. It is a recognition that you, shall we say, 'made a mistake;' or that you erred in how you perceived something, be it a word or judgment, and it takes it through the hands into the heart and imprints it there. So, it becomes easier to shift the pattern. It is no longer necessary to express it ever again.

We are asking you to demolish your entire unsustainable infrastructure, so that, hopefully, by the time we are complete with the 12 sessions you will have been able to look back on the thought processes, the words, the concepts and behaviors, and you will be able to say "Oh, I have certainly shifted. I have moved. I've grown. I am so grateful that I was given this assignment to examine everything with a fine-tooth comb, with that flashlight, that torch, that shines light upon every aspect of being, for it is my intention to be an expression of God's love." You already are this, but you will be able to experience yourself as being so, which will enable you to see everything through the eyes of non-judgement, through the eyes of divinity.

Perhaps at the top of your list, you should probably place the word "god," for it is a concept that evokes great confusion. It puts into a pigeonhole that which cannot even be comprehended; for the truth of Divinity or of Creator, or of Creation is: The All That Is, encompasses all that exists and all potentiality. It is the consciousness that you call God. It is Infinite, Immortal, it is Universal and Eternal, just like you are. For, as we said, you are an aspect of that consciousness of Divinity. When you leave, you will return to oneness with that All-That-Is-ness, but you do not have to wait that long, or that short! You can do it right now. You can experience yourself as that aspect, as the Light, as the Love of God, or whatever you want to call it.

We are not asking much of you. (That is meant to be 'tongue-in-cheek). We are asking you to be the Spiritual Warriors, to be the vanguard of the New Earth, to be the teachers, the way-showers. We are asking you to live your lives impeccably in the fullness of ease and grace and abundance. We are asking you to live your lives in joy, in peace and equanimity, no matter what is going on around you. We are asking you to imagine that your feet are firmly planted in Mother Earth, grounding into her very core, connected to all life, connected to the roots like the trees, connected to the trees, to the birds, the waters, the creatures, the insects, to all of life.

Understand that 'this too shall pass,' whatever it is that is going on in your world, in your family, with your job, your housing situation, whether or not you have a partner, or a bank account. Everything is undergoing a change. As you recognize that everything is flux, like the river, is moving constantly and there is no point in clinging to the bank. Just as the Hopi have suggested, that you look around you and see who is there with you. As they say, "You are the ones you have been waiting for[16]." And here you are!

It seems that there are twelve of us gathered here, a very apt number for this program. For you will gather around you your own 12, your own 144, until you become 144 thousand[17]. For, as we said when we began, the energy of Thoth and the energy of Seshat is about magic. It's about the power of numbers, the power of writing, of ideas, of hieroglyphics. The hieroglyphics were not just ways of writing words and letters, but they carried within them magic, as does every letter of your own alphabet, as does every word, for words have power. And as you use them wisely, as you use them to express the power from within you, you begin to get a sense of who you are throughout time.

You begin to use magic, you begin to recognize that you have the right to experience miracle and that miracle is a part of who you are, now, in this time. You are an ascended being, still living within a body. John Henry calls himself a "once human angel." So, too, you are a human angel. You are on assignment from the Councils of Light, from the Federations of the Galactic, from all the beings that watch over you, that have the care and love of this planet in their hearts and who are helping you in every way to experience magic. Like serendipity. Like the joy of knowing that you are not alone, that you have companions on the road and that you have support systems. Knowing that you have ones who can bring messages, but that actually, eventually, you do not need even them. You can access the entire body of wisdom from your own source, your heart, your own access to the Akashic Records; so that you know everything you need to know, and it is within.

For the grand illusion of a divinity outside of you is one of the major concepts that needs to be on that list. For God is within. The one, Christ said, "The Kingdom of Heaven is within," and as it becomes true for you, then you can build it on the outside, like the Field of Dreams. You show up. You show up with your heart open, which means no judgement. You show up in the moment, fully present, which means you no longer need to be dependent on substances, on habitual patterns of ingestion, whether it be alcohol, hallucinogenic substances, food, drama or gossip. Whatever old patterns have been in your background are ready to go now, all them. You are being born again, like that innocent child that you once were, and that still dwells within you. It's called the inner child, but it truly is who you are and who you were, all come together in a oneness that is expanding and opening and blossoming.

This is the time of blossoming. It is not permitted to you any longer to give power to fear. We will say that again. You are no longer allowed to fear! That does not mean you are not allowed to feel fear. It means that whenever fear arises within you, you recognize it, and you let it go. You replace it with love. You replace it with Truth, the Truth of Union. You recognize that you are immortal and that nothing can harm your immortal soul or spirit. And that nothing matters. You are just inhabiting this body for a short time, and you are on a mission. You are wearing your Star Trek uniform and exploring the many outlying regions of the Universe on behalf of your civilization, on behalf of humanity. You are preparing humanity to expand its own awareness, so that one day soon you can greet your sisters and brothers on their ships as they come to celebrate with you the freedom, the release of the fear, the release from the control, the release from what we could call "The Façade," the "Grand Illusion" that you have been taught; "The Grand Deception."

And so it is that we wish you to know how much you are loved, admired and respected that you chose, once again, perhaps for the last time, to enter into the density to explore what it's like to forget the true nature of your consciousness as light. And that you will begin, somehow, to remember how to recreate your divinity once again; knowing that you have come to share this understanding of being light with others. You are already looking, as you look at your list, you are already contemplating "What will be my contribution? How can I bring this understanding of wisdom, of magic, of culture, of the wisdom of the ages, from the beginning? How can I bring it into my life and into the lives of those who will begin to feel the shift in me and be drawn to ask me how is it that in the midst of all this fear I have such calm, such equanimity. I don't seem to take things personally. I don't take them so seriously. I take them with a pinch of salt or two, or perhaps a pound of salt. I look after my body. I take care of my health. I choose to exercise every day or every few days. I do yoga and stretch and swim and walk. I play and sing and dance, and that I find joy in everything and everyone. I love to communicate, even if it is mask-to-mask instead of face to face. I don't avoid people because, perhaps, they will shower the plague upon me through their very out-breathing of words. And so, I look at everything. I investigate. I ask. I share. I explore, and even with all the many ideas of what is what, I never take anything as truth until I have digested it in my own heart to see if it is palatable; to see whether this is a sustainable way of living my life, of experiencing my truth, of sharing my words, my thoughts, my concepts, my beliefs."

There is an understanding that you are not controlled by your genes but that the genes are a result of your environment, of how you think and what you believe. There are such things called "molecules of emotion[18]" within the body. One organ does not keep itself separate from the others, but relies upon the entire system to function as a wholeness. Just so, you are creating structures for a new world that is interconnected. As you build community, you build it around you through family, through friends, through those of like mind, and eventually you create living communities where you can create new structures that are based on cooperation, on peace, harmony and respect, for Nature and Mother Earth, and for your fellow creatures and fellow humans.

The communities that you begin to develop, they become your vehicle of expression, of teaching. You gather around you those who are willing to create their own lists, that are willing to examine, that are willing to operate from the heart. You will find out what your steps are as you visit your heart, as you listen to your intuition, as you recognize that the truth is within, not without. You realize that the whole gamut of gods and goddesses that have run the show for millions of years are merely externalizations of something precious within the heart; and sometimes it was nice to see it on the outside. It is delightful to hold the gem and admire it in your hands. So too it is good to honor your children, your parents, your friends, your spouses and each other, as gems that have come to teach you of the multi-faceted diamond that you are and that they are; so you are reflecting that which we call God's love with all its many facets. You recognize that within your own blood is this expression of the true nature of divinity, that you were created in the image of God or Goddess, whatever that means for you. It means that you were created according to a DNA structure that was orchestrated by beings of great intelligence. They engineered your DNA to have the capacity of 12 strands and the capacity to access multidimensionality, and to experience an understanding far beyond the limitations of the pigeonholes and boxes that you have been taught are 'reality.'

So, we will leave you with these words for the time being, and answer questions. We want you to know that we love you, all 12 of us, along with the angels, the guardians, the Beings of Light and avatars that surround you. We are present with you, eager and willing to help you and answer your questions, so that you listen in the inner 'still small voice' for the answers.

And if you have an issue, you ask us to take care of it on your behalf. You use your soul to communicate with another soul that you are having difficulty with, and you choose to see them as soul and communicate with them: "This is what I am experiencing. I wish to not separate. I wish to see you through the eyes of love." Use your ability from within to communicate soul to soul, soul to tree, to bird, to creature, to insect and to human. Understand the vastness of who you are. Then you take on the role of teacher, of wise one, of leader. For you are the one you have been waiting for, and you are here to create structures that are sustainable. Consider, doodle, write, paint, draw, create bracelets as that one, LB, has offered to do. Be creative with all these thoughts, with all these words, with all these ideas. Find your own special, unique medium of expression and begin to share it. You/we all on this journey together. We are so honored that you have chosen to join us, for we love you dearly. It is our desire and wish to see you thrive, to see you live and experience joy, the bliss of knowing that you are one in the fullness of experience and expression. Blessings and peace.

Thoth Q&A

Q. (AY) I want to know more about all you had referenced: genetics and DNA coding and how that relates to health; and because you referenced emotions being part of that, can you expand on that a little bit more?

A. Certainly. A woman called Candace Pert, wrote a book called *Molecules of Emotion*[18]. She was one of the first to demonstrate that the physiology responds to emotions and that it can change according to the nature of the emotion, so that you actually can change your physiology or biology through the very shifting of your perspective. Also, the geneticist Bruce Lipton, in The *Biology of Belief*[19], has shown, through his studies of genetics and through looking at genes under the microscope in a Petri dish, how the influence of the environment can actually change the nature of the genes. He has shared that very few illnesses are actually at the mercy, shall we say, of genetics. As you change your belief systems, you can actually change the genes, so that if you believe that you have a genetic disposition for a particular cancer or illness, you will reinforce that genetic code. If you no longer believe it, but you believe in health, in miracle, and you believe in your ability, by changing your belief and your thinking, and by doing affirmations, you are no longer subject to that particular genetic disposition and it will start to crumble. It will shift. It will destabilize and will no longer be a factor in the running of your genetic systems.

When one replaces old thought forms, the patterns of the firing of neurons within the brain that have created habitual pathways, can be altered. Through repetition, they are replaced with different pathways that, over time, generate a brand-new storyline. This establishes a shift in how you think, how you feel, and how you experience your existence. So, there are many ways to approach the subject of how belief can affect health, behavior and well-being. Affirmations, when spoken aloud in a deep state of meditation or by accessing Alpha or Theta brain wave patterns, penetrate deeply into the body and subconscious mind and shift thought patterns from old ones that are deleterious to you, to benevolent ones. Does that make sense?

-Yes. I was also wondering how that common 12 strand DNA comes in then for what we're doing now.

- There are 12 strands of DNA. Essentially, it's like looking at the fact that you employ maybe 10% of your brain power and that you have access to another 90%, which is interdimensional. Your science suggests that you have two strands of DNA, but there are other layers that are in other dimensions, and, as you shift your consciousness, you are activating these other strands of the DNA. As you are aware, it is not by chance that this one was asked to receive 12 new voices. The number 12 has been a factor in your cultures and civilizations from the very beginning. It is a particular alignment with the world around you and other cosmic energies. The number 12 and 12 strands have been touted for a long time as an underlying part of the wholeness of who you are. There is also an alignment, within the structures of the Divine Feminine, of the number 13. This can be seen in the term "baker's dozen," the 13 moons, and the idea of the Christ surrounded by the 12, forming an energy of 13.

It may be possible, through current Quantum Science, through Kirlian[20] photography, to view something happening within the structures of DNA so that they are no longer just interdimensional or extradimensional in terms of your 5 senses. There may be ways to actually "see" some of these patterns of other strands of DNA actually becoming more manifest in your consciousness. Your psychic abilities are opening more widely now. Many of the children that are growing up today, that are incarnating on your planet now, are being born with more of these strands activated, whether they are visible or not. Certainly, those who are clairvoyant or medical mediums will be able to perceive some of these differences in their physiology and biology.

Q. (SL) I was wondering. I have always had my head in the stars, and I was wondering what you think about what I need to let go of as far as my belief systems about extra-terrestrials is concerned.

A. We would say that we don't know what your beliefs about extraterrestrials are, however you should give up other people's ideas about what they aren't! We would suggest that you await with open arms the arrival of those benevolent ones who have been watching over your planet for eons and who hold you in the dearest light and concern for your benevolence and well-being. We would like you to know that we have put a curfew around this planet from ET dark energies that have dominated you and influenced the minds of many humans, still caught up in darkness. It is this element who dabbled in the dark magic, who are still manipulating your minds for control. The extraterrestrial energies that instigated much of this are no longer allowed access to your planet. You can still send them light and love, however, because they too are on the path of evolution.

Know that your space brothers and sisters exist, and that there are many races and species that are involved in communication with your planet and with individuals. We recommend that you maintain an open mind with regard to these, in the same way that you would to all beings on your planet. Do not judge those that are off planet, and hold space for what is called Disclosure[21] to come sooner rather than later, even though it may be a jolt for some of your fellow humans to understand that they are not alone in the universe.

It is important to recognize that much of the negative associations that have been orchestrated around the connection between human and extra human, or extraterrestrial, has been generated in order to amplify fear, often on the part of your 'secret government,' or Deep State. The only ones that you would want to have communication with, are the ones who have benevolent intentions and can help you. In fact, they have already done much to prevent any possibility of another use of nuclear weaponry that could threaten your planet's existence. They also will help you in the reconstruction, in the creation of structures upon your planet as that which is unsustainable falls away. Does that make sense?

-Yes, thank you. Could you define 'structures' a little further for me? That's sort of an abstract term. I was thinking of inner structures as what was meant originally but can see that some of those are external structures also.

- We understand, and in fact, if you hold to the idea that the word "structure" was the word given to this one, in essence, when you look at the structure of the universe, it is foundationed on patterns, sacred geometric matrices that build form, like scaffolding that is upheld by divine intelligence. In many ways, the essence of what Thoth and Seshat bring, is this understanding of structure, of how sacred geometry is behind the forms of creation. These are the invisible powers, the interdimensional forces that create 'structures,' so that in your world you see objects, you have societies, there are civilizations, and you have families. These are all structures.

The energy of that word can denote a vast range of understandings. When we talk about you creating structures for the New Earth, it will come from your creativity as to what that expression will look like. So, you are correct to ask and question what the meaning behind it is. Essentially anything that is in existence for you to interact with, will have some form of structure. And so, the creation of an organization, an association, an alliance or group would be a structure. Or, it could be a mental structure, a plan in your mind of how to move from A to B to Z. There is a vast scope of what a structure could look like, and we are hoping each one of you will determine what yours becomes, through your creativity. Does that make sense?

Q. (NB) I grew up with astrology and there is mundane astrology that SL was talking about, and UFOs. And that's one thing that they're saying in Astrology: that there is an X Factor, something they predicted January, February, March, the way the planets were aligned something was going to happen, and then Co-v-id hit, and they're saying something else is going to happen which is going to be an X Factor, probably another couple of months - October timeframe, around elections, and that probably it could be something like either civil war or UFOs attacking us. I don't know, but this is what information is coming. I would love to hear from you what your thoughts are, and how we can sustain ourselves as we look at a total new challenge differently and stay above the fear and protect our families.

A. As with the question of DNA, it is important to understand that everything is connected. The 12 strands, the 12 dimensions, the 12 or the however many understandings of reality that are not quite in alignment with the way humans normally think when they look through linear eyes. So too, within Astrology and within the many varieties that are available, as in Vedic Astrology, and your standard Western, Chinese and others. Everything is there because of its connection with everything else. You have tools. There are ways, practices, understandings that can take you one step deeper, one step higher, or one expansive field broader than what is seen through the normal waking eyes of your standard consciousness. The reason that we are encouraging you to trust your guidance, your intuition and your heart, is, so you can stay safe, no matter what is going on around you. Yes, of course, as everything is becoming de-structured, there will be periods, and they can be alluded to and understood within the timeframe that can be visualized through the alignments of planets, and understandings of different numerologies, all the sacred arts that came to your planet, mostly through Egypt, but not only. Many of the sacred wisdoms and teachings were about the numbers and how to understand the underlying structures that we spoke of in answering SL.

So too, with Astrology, as you look at dates, whether it be the Mayan or the Gregorian or the Plieidian calendar, there are so many levels at which you can view and understand. Through which eyes will you see all these connections and interrelationships? Yes, you have known for a while that there will be other phases of this unfolding.

It is necessary. We are going to give you a little perspective on the current situation that you are in. It was necessary that the dark energies that orchestrated this grand illusion of vi-r-us and danger and expansion of fear and separation on your planet would come up with such a diabolical plan, because without their assistance - can you imagine what else it might require to de-structure all the constructs of your civilization that we have called unsustainable. So, in many ways these dark energies, in thinking that they will affect control over humans, over society and life on this planet, have unwittingly become the agents of the transformation that is required to effect the New Earth. And so, within that holographic understanding of how everything is connected, what they put into place, what they orchestrated, and engineered, will have the effect of destabilizing, de-structuring, and essentially destroying the very foundations upon which your unsustainable universe is based. And so, yes, there will be markers within the linear time frame and October, November, around your elections will be an extremely pivotal time.

It is important to recognize that you will have these phases, you still have testing, you still have the vaxseen coming, you still have many challenges within the intentions of these dark forces to establish ways in which they can establish world domination and control. And yet, you will find, and they will find, that each step of the process enables a new destabilization and a new disintegration of each aspect of that which, up to now, you have regarded as "normal." Those who think they will be able to go back to a previous 'normal' before the pandemic are very much in illusion, because there is no going back.

This is another reason why we are recommending that you investigate your past, personally, globally, and cosmically, to glean from it the nuggets of truth, and to understand that the continuum of existence that you have been in, is coming to a very pivotal turning point. It is a cosmic event, as it has been referred to by some higher beings, because it is happening not just on your planet, and generates a ripple effect throughout the Galaxy. Because everything is interconnected.

These alignments of stars, solar systems, planets, and cosmic mythologies, or cosmic symbologies, are all available for those who can read the signs, even if they don't quite understand the full meanings of these markers in time. Just as the end of the Mayan calendar did not mean the end of the world, so it is with these signposts. One should prepare as best as is possible within what is available within the establishments of your society, in terms of food, water and survival elements. Every day, surround yourself with that golden mantle of love, of protection. Surround yourself with your teams of angels, with the Beings of Light[22] that have been placed around you for your protection and for your guidance.

We are asking you to examine everything, so that you have more clarity. For when you examine, and you find that there is some fog or smoke that you need to penetrate to get to the clarity, you will find that you will breathe a little easier as you recognize that everything is changing. However, you are eternal, and you will be okay. You will survive, and your loved ones will survive, because of your attitude, because of your practice, because of your love, because you connect with Mother Earth and Father Sky and you focus on the heart; and love. And you understand that this is your work, and this is what will help you to go beyond fear, and to go beyond worry and concern that feeds fear. So, we believe we've answered your question. Does that make sense?

Q. Absolutely, it does, thank you so much. Can I just ask you one more question? My last question here is that ever since I joined the last Sunday, this Sunday, and you know the session that I had with you, the HeartThread®, what is this energy that is so sustainable? It's so palpable. I'm feeling it inside out. It comes and goes, but the way it sustains itself, what is that? It is incredible, I'm not doubting it, but I'm curious.

A. It is an alignment with the highest vibration that is possible for you to experience at your level of consciousness at this time. It is what is called "coherence," a congruence that you have, that all of you have with the Higher Realms, with the Beings of Light that watch over you. You are actually experiencing the feeling of being in their presence, of them being in your presence, within you. It is as if you have been through a transformer and had your vibration amplified and expanded. This is part of the intention, for all who are waking, to experience themselves as an expanded vibration, at a higher and higher frequency of existence, so that love becomes who you are. Love is this expression that you are feeling and experiencing as vibration. It is like light. Light is a simpler way of seeing Love in motion as a frequency, and as the frequency gets faster and is higher, it encompasses a much broader perspective. You are experiencing this movement viscerally, through your connection with this one, and through the connection with this group, and this teaching. You are experiencing in real time, real terms, the expansion and elevation of your vibration. Does that make sense?

- *Thank you. Thank you for putting words to it.*

Q. (CZ) *My question relates to this oneness that we are recapturing. On a personal level, there has been confusion with boundaries on the Earth. I have experienced people that have vampired my energies. I know on the other levels that I see us all working to help each other grow, but on the physical level I do have problems putting the oneness and the personal boundaries on the same page.*

A. We understand. We recommend that you surround yourself with a field of immense power of Goddess energy, the kind of energy that Seshat represents, the fierceness of the warrior; that you surround yourself constantly, every day, with a sphere of protection, of light, golden, white light, and that you constantly reject any thoughts of being victimized or of being less than. We recommend that you move. By actually physically moving your environment to a new one, you're able to cut those ties as well as the ones that have linked you to these negative energies. Use a piece of Obsidian and cut the ties in ceremony.

Smudge your area, your home, your surroundings, and your person often. Ask that the vibrations that are attempting to impinge upon you be cleared. Send lots and lots of love, light, blessing and forgiveness to your parents and your ancestors. Ask to have all of your ties, all of your oaths and contacts severed. Do this for any of your ancestral connections who are not in alignment with the highest vibrations of light and love. Actively find someone to help you to cut these ties. Someone you trust, who has very strong shamanic power. You will perhaps need to see them three times, so that you work with it layer by layer. Build up your self-esteem by looking in the mirror and seeing your beauty, and by remembering your childhood innocence and your little one. Carry her with you. Carry her with you in an embrace of deep love that has her feel safe. Let her know she is always protected from now and forevermore more, Amen.

Q. (ZS) *My question is regarding the timelines and the understanding of time. I know that there is a lot of wisdom shared about how we are on the Gregorian calendar, versus the Mayan calendar and how to better manage time, or allow time to manage me. I guess it's hard for me to even ask, but in regard to time management, daily time management and carrying it forth with the different visions and projects that I have coming forth. Also concerning other studies that I have been involved in. I know that it's interesting to lean into and be a part of both timelines, if that makes sense.*

A. We understand. We could go on forever with this subject, so we will touch the surface now, and perhaps later, some of the other voices will take us deeper. This relates to the question of Astrology, to the multilayered, multidimensional realities that are behind the scenes in the invisible. Time, when one approaches it from a linear perspective using the mind, that left-brain way of seeing things, is a string. It's a one-after-the-other kind of experience. Whereas Mayan time and other times, Cosmic Time, is instantaneous, is spiral, is multidimensional and doesn't exist. The Ones with No Name say "I am Light and Light I shall remain. There is nothing but Light, and there is no time." This has been the mantra from a very long time ago. What does it mean that there is no time? It means that you are fully present in the moment, in your body. You keep your body clean and clear of all substances; you anchor your vibration with Mother Earth, so that you are fully present in the body, in the moment. Time does not exist in the moment. Time can be stretched or can be condensed by the very factor of enjoying yourself or being bored to death.

As you understand and know what I mean, you will realize that time is flexible, is fluent, even within the linear understanding of the structures of time. Time is multidimensional. It is important to also consider the subject of "clarity." What does it take to pare away all the smokescreens and diversions, all the places in which your energy is being pulled to do this or that distraction? How can you bring it into a clear focus of "What is important for me to do right now, at this moment? How can I bring myself back to the moment when I notice, just as I do with my assignment, that I am getting distracted, my mind is wandering, and somebody wants my attention. Perhaps I can't say "No! I'm doing something important for me. Perhaps I am becoming a doormat for somebody because I did not have clarity, and did not say "Here is my boundary." Perhaps I did not expect that I would receive a clear agreement in writing from someone, and I did not put my foot down." As you see, there are many layers in answer to this question, but we are highlighting the key points for you.

This week your assignment is to write down on one side of the page, "What am I clear about" and on the other side, "Where am I not clear," and then you draw a line below these, and you start writing your intentions for how to become clear, how to have clear agreements. Write down your intentions for caring for your body and your mind and for how to live being fully present, in the moment. What will you do to remind yourself to take a breath every time you notice that your mind is going astray.

This would be a very good assignment for each one to do, as part of your ongoing work with yourself. As we progress with the 12, we will offer other assignments that will help you to create greater clarity. For, when one looks at the grand illusion that surrounds you, it is vital that you bring your energy back to yourself, put it back within that sphere of protection that you have around you and that you reinforce every day. Ensure that you have a practice you do every day to align yourself with Heaven, Earth and your heart. Make it your practice to become centered within your own knowing and guidance and intuition. Be aware always of the help surrounding you through voices of guidance and intuition. And pay attention. For if you are distracted, and you are not listening, you will not hear the answers. Does that make sense?

- *Absolutely, thank you.*

Closing Meditation

Let's take a deep breath again and connect with Mother Earth, with Father Sky, and with our hearts, breathing in that stillness, and beginning to feel once again the threads of our hearts reaching out, and weaving together with each other. We are reinforcing our connection, this beautiful tapestry that we are growing together, that we will eventually weave into all the ones that we know and love until it reaches the edges of the Universe and fills itself with the Great Light of Creator. Full of Love, so all beings may know what it means to be children of The One. And so, we leave you with our love, with the light of the Great Ones, with the Christ energy, the Christ Consciousness that permeates everything and is an aspect of the Thoth and Seshat energy. We will be with you again next week, and it will be Apollo's turn to share with you. It will be very interesting to see what he has to say. Blessings and peace.

Voice Three
Apollo

30ᵗʰ August 2020

Let us put our right hand on our hearts, our left hand on our right, and taking some deep breaths, feel a downpouring of light, a downpouring of this golden energy that is filled with stillness. It enters down through our crown and reaches into our hearts. And as we breathe in, we breathe in that fullness, and it begins to expand our hearts and open up a beautiful sphere of light. And it gets fuller and fuller as a beautiful gold, soft energy of love and stillness, peace and balance. And as we breathe out, we breathe down through our feet into Mother Earth, connecting with her through our love, through our gratitude, so that this sphere is like a column of light that connects us with Heaven and Earth. Our hearts are in the center, expanding out to create this beautiful sphere that surrounds us and protects us. It is full of our guardian angels, of the Holy Beings that watch over us, and our particular team of angels. And we feel that Presence surrounding us and filling this sphere with light, so that only the highest vibrations are allowed in this space.

We invite any ancestors who wish to appear, to come only in love and light for the highest calling and the highest intentions for healing, or to witness. We call upon all of our angels and guides as we weave together into the oneness. It reaches out and connects all the hearts on this call. The threads of our hearts weave with the hearts of all of our loved ones, with all those in our world, our creatures, our pets, our neighbors, our friends and our family. This weave of heart essence begins to spread its beautiful fabric all the way out across our cities and continents and our oceans, reaching out to surround the planet with a beautiful network of heart, love, and a golden energy of light and protection. It weaves its way into all time, and all space. You can rest your hands.

We are coming to you today from what we call the Great Central Sun; that place that is the origin of life in, not just this solar system, but in your galaxy. Apollo represents this beautiful energy of Sun, the energy of the Solar Logos[23]. I am that which shines upon you, sends its rays into your hearts, into your lives and into all life. I bless all beings upon your planet, sustaining it in its orbit, holding it in a perfect alignment, in a perfect sacred geometry that allows you to have the conditions for life to exist. Gaia is a Garden of Eden, a place of great beauty, a place for the celebration of all life; the magnificent diversity of life forms. It belongs to all creatures, cultures and beliefs, all who share the experience of living on Mother Earth. She is your home for the duration of this lifetime and for the many other lifetimes that you have been here.

Each lifetime, you have felt the warmth of the same sun. You have felt the energy of rebirth in the spring. You have felt the dawning of the icy cold of the winter, the snows, the rains, the clouds. You've experienced the fullness through your many lifetimes, through each season as it comes and goes and changes. You have experienced the fullness of life on this beautiful planet, and it is because you have this appreciation, there is within your heart this resonance with the sun. The beauty of the rising sun in the morning and the sunset with its magnificent colors as it illuminates the clouds and changes from bright to reds and purples and pinks. Then comes the indigo as it morphs into the darkness of the nighttime. We want you to remember the appreciation you have for the energy of the sun.

Apollo is a mythological name from a particular culture that has been given to the energy of the sun. It is at a perfect distance from the Earth. This makes it possible for its emanations to support life. It is not just the warmth of sun. Many kinds of rays are emitted that reach your heart, your skin, the soil and the creatures within it, and the life forms that have been created on the Earth. So, we are asking you to focus for these next few days, on your appreciation, on your gratitude, each time you experience the warmth of the sun upon your skin. It will hopefully remind you that you have had this experience in numerous lifetimes, and each time that sun was there. It was a witness to your triumphs, to your tragedies, to all the experiences of what it is to be a human being upon this planet.

One of the energies of Apollo, of the Helios energy of the sun, is the laurel wreath; that which is regarded as the sign of the victor. The laurel crown represents the greenness, the energy of heart, the energy of Mother Earth and the growing things. The energy of life. We want you to imagine it upon your head as the sign of one who has victory over the illusions. One who has not succumbed to the entrapment of emotional entanglements, whether personal or planetary. One who has obtained the distance that leads to clarity. We are also replacing the symbol of a 'crown of thorns',[24] that was supposedly placed on the head of Jesus during the crucifixion, regarded as a symbol of suffering, with one more compatible with life and triumph.

Clarity comes from being able to divest yourself of emotional involvement, attachment to that which you always thought was true. Perhaps you have identified a belief system that is now just possibly under fire; that is now being examined, taken apart, and is being felt in its fullness. You are teachers and way-showers for the New Earth. This is why you are here. This is why you have been drawn to these messages and the energies we represent.

We represent a vast array of different embodiments. We come from a variety of time periods and walks of life. We represent different belief systems, cultures and civilizations. As we express the unique energy of each of the 12 through these 12 weeks, we are hoping that you will receive an expanded experience and an array of understandings and recognitions. We want you to find greater clarity for yourself and for your purpose. Clarity for what you are 'unpacking;' those folders you have created, full of many files. Each time you open one up, have a look and see whether you still need to keep it on your desktop, or perhaps you can discard it. It may no longer have any purpose. And you have not looked at it for so long, that it may as well go into the trash.

The house cleaning, the housekeeping that we are asking of you, is very basic. It is to examine *everything*: every thought, every feeling, every belief system. It is why we invite some of the ancestors to join us today, so that they can also witness for themselves some of the old patterns. What were some of the old requirements they had of you? Perhaps some of the vows and contracts still control you, because you committed to them. It may now be the time to let go of them. They may have served at a particular time, in a particular cultural or religious mileau, but today everything is up for grabs. Everything is sitting outside in the yard sale. You are giving it away. You are getting rid of it because it does not contribute to clarity. All the clutter in your mind, in your garage, in your closets, has become a diversion.

As aspiring Spiritual Warriors–those who carry a sword of truth--it is vital that you understand and have the clarity to know what is truth and what is illusion. You must be willing to cut through the web of illusions that make up the matrix of what you have believed up to this point. There are many who choose to remain within their box because they feel safe there. There are also many of you who are now ready to expand your box, so you can 'swing your cat by its tail' and have more space to breathe. Your boxes have been encroaching upon you. Your mind pigeonholes information in order to grasp concepts, trying to make sense of everything.

So, we are asking you to expand your boxes, your rooms; to open up the doors and the windows and let in the fresh air. We want you to feel the warm sunshine pouring in through your windows, feeling the breeze, hearing the birds, rejoicing that you are alive. You are alive at this special, special, special time. You are here because you have been called. A long time ago, before you left the Swing Between Worlds, you considered what it would be like for you to come back to this planet. What agreements would you make? You designed your blueprint and your destiny. It is time to ask, "What is my mission?"

You are now ready to visit that place within your heart and your Soul Seed,[25] where your ribs come together. That is where you can feel the connection to your soul. You are ready to examine your purpose, not as a mental construct, not as an idea, but as a container that is filled with light and blessings. It is asking you to embrace the possibility that your life is no longer a struggle. This can apply to your ancestors as well. They have the same opportunity as you. When they embrace the light and receive the healing, they will no longer want you to suffer, to have it hard, to have it rough, to have to watch your back, or look over your shoulder. For you are surrounded by angels and guides who are protecting you now.

We are asking you to open your hearts to a new reality that is not an illusion. Your life can be full of ease, filled with grace and plenty; full of everything that your heart desires. May your heart's desires come from that place of your innocence, of that little child within you that is pure and who knows, and has always known. You are here to fulfill your calling, to express and experience love. You are here now to experience what we will call God's Love or the love of the Christ or of the Goddess. We use the term "god." It is short and sweet. We remove all the connotations that have been accrued upon it and just keep it simple. If you look at "g-o-d" backwards, it is "d-o-g" and, if you like, you can consider the Great Being that watches over you as the loyal energy of "dog." It does not matter what you call it or him or her. The energy of Creation, of the greatest intelligence that is, the source of everything that is, is shining love and light into you, through you and upon you. And you are an expression of this deep, pure and beautiful love.

We want you to experience this in the same way that you experience the warmth of the sun's rays upon your skin. We are asking you to feel that they are expressions of God's love, filling all space, filling all time, going backwards into every single life of yours (seen from a linear or parallel perspective). All of your lifetimes, all of your experiences in any dimension, are now being filled with the beautiful rays of God's love. We are asking you to take a deep breath and allow yourself to feel it in your body, in your heart, in your mind. Do not try to make sense. Just feel it. Every day, when you do your practice, ask to feel this love. Express it through your actions, your words, thoughts and feelings. Transform everything that is not love into this beautiful, magnificent warmth, this golden light and energy. That is one way of seeing and feeling that which you are. For within this beautiful radiance of God's love, you are all melting into each other. And as you do this, you melt everyone into the same vibration of Oneness.

You are here to establish structures of Oneness. They are structures of the energy of coming together, of resolution, of finding ways to live in peace and harmony and cooperation. They facilitate letting go of the struggle for survival, the struggle that requires you to think in terms of competition, scarcity and limitation; seeing yourself as limited or diminished. You cannot diminish God's love, and you are it. You are it! The buck stops with you! You have to be God's love in action, in motion, in expression, because that's what you are. This is beyond the illusions. For everything that is not God's love is the illusion.

It is a long stretch perhaps for your mind, but your heart knows how easy this step is. Your heart will now direct and instruct you how to dismantle the illusions. Your heart will guide you to dismantle the belief systems that do not work, that create separation and dissension. They have established the idea that there are 'others' that are to be feared. Each human being, no matter how dark their experience, has this connection with God's love. Within their heart is the same spark, the same sun, the Solar Logos energy. Embedded in the very center, within the heart of each being that has consciousness, is God's love, that spark of Divine Fire that you are.

It is written in the Bible that you were created in the image of God. What is more true, is that humans, have created "God" in the image of "Man." This creation myth is perhaps the greatest illusion of all, when taken literally. Many truths are hidden in the annals of all your sacred works. Only that which is of the heart is sustainable, as we have said before. Only that which resonates with Oneness is allowable any longer for you who are on this path of the Spiritual Warrior. Only love, only light, is your reality now. Each time anything else pops up in your mind, a voice from the past, from your father, your mother, your peers, your teachers, that says you are not good enough, that you can't, that you do not deserve, that you are too small, too large, too old, too fat, too skinny, too whatever; you take these concepts, and you throw them away. You do not allow them to occupy your mind.

You begin to look in the mirror. You begin to see beauty. You begin to create beauty around you in your environment, in our homes, wherever you go. Whatever you do, you establish beauty as part of your container. You establish beauty as the blueprint for your structures, because beauty is an expression of God's love. It is a feeling of being at peace and harmony. It is a feeling of everything harmonized. It is an experience of the sacred geometry of the structure of all of Creation at peace with Itself. There is nothing sticking out that you need to pull back in. Everything is laid out in a perfection that is constantly in motion so that you are not stuck in some idea of a perfection that is not real.

You are now in the season of Virgo. There is a great challenge to leave the mind, to stop trying to figure everything out and put it in its pigeonhole. So too, you will have the full moon in a day or two, in Virgo. What is the energy of Virgo? We are looking at Apollo, the energy of Helios, of the sun as the center of the Zodiac, of the 12 energies. The 12 represent a wholeness. Like the Zodiac, the numbers on your clocks and the seasons and the months, each has its course, that creates the precession of the equinoxes, within these cycles of time.

Throughout time, humans have worshiped the energy of the Sun, the rising and setting, the riding across the skies in chariots and descent into the ocean of darkness below the horizon. You have had these glorious beings: Tammuz, Dionysus, the Christ, Adonis, Osiris, Helios, Apollo. You had all these sun gods and goddesses, but mostly the male energy that has come and gone, that has had to die and be resurrected upon the Tree of Life26. These cycles are what run your life, what control your biorhythms and all life on your planet. They have been turned into mythologies to teach ancient wisdoms and to control your lives, for the good and for the not so good; to create dogmas and doctrines.

You are now facing one of your greatest moments of the grand illusion, that which we have called "the grand deception." This great illusion is pressing you to seek out and find your truth. You must find the inner wisdom and guidance that is like the sun energy. The sword of truth, that reflects the sun, has two sides like a coin. There is an aspect of good and bad mixed up into a oneness that is neither. That is why a sword is sharp, and it has two sides to it. A coin has heads and tails. Everything is upside down, topsy-turvy, so you must find clarity for yourself and for each other. For there is resonance in truth. There is knowing in the heart what is true and what is not. As you become the Spiritual Warrior and face your illusions and beliefs, you must use your intuition, that inner truth that guides you.

We help you to see and steer the boat. We invite you to communicate with us on a regular basis. Ask us your questions, and take the moment of silence, of stillness, to listen to the answers, so you know within the very depths of your being, what is right for you, what is true for you. It could be about food or people, or belief systems. It can be about what you are told or shown or instructed. We are supporting the one John Henry in helping you to attain this sense of self-authority, of being your own authority. It is no longer the time of the monarch, of king and queen, of emperor, of pharaoh, of guru. Even the wise ones had their flaws and their illusions. Merlin was trapped into the stone by the nymph.[27] She drew him in with the wonderful promise of re-attaining his youth, but he lost his power because he followed an illusion.

Many of your mythologies represent this kind of accounting. They are featured in the great dramas of Egypt, Persia, Greece, Rome, and modern times. These plays relate stories, of famous historical characters, who had their Achilles heel, their fatal flaw that misled them, whether it was their ambition or blindness. It led them to disaster because they could not see that which was their great "pie in the sky," their grand illusion; that if only they could obtain that throne, they would be happy. They ended up on a throne of blood. Shakespeare (Sir Francis Bacon) was a genius at portraying this kind of weakness in his tragedies. These stories offer many lessons to be learned.

It is time to look at your life story and ask, "Is this story worth keeping? Is there value in my story? Is there value in focusing on my pain, on my loss, on my sorrow, on my anger, on all the rejections, abandonments and betrayals? Why do I hold on? Why can I not let go? What must I do to forgive, to forget, to give it all to God or the Goddess, to give it to Mother Earth, to give it to the water, and the air, and the clouds? To let it waft away and be gone, so that I can begin again with the brightness of this beautiful golden light shining around me, filling me. And as I embrace this, I embody this gold, this beauty of God's Love, these beautiful expressions of the Solar Logos, this love that shines and radiates unconditionally."

The sun does not care what color you are, what you wear, what you think. It does not care where you hide, or who you are or what you have done. Nor does it withhold its light from whomever you think you are or are not. It radiates its golden warmth and God-given life energy, like the rays of the Aten,[28] into the nostrils of the worshipers indiscriminately, without judgment, and without limitation.

We invite you each morning to wake up and visit the rising sun, to begin your day giving honor and gratitude that that sun is always there, that it rises like clockwork and that it sets in the same manner. Go and see and pay homage to the sunset. As the sun leaves your day, you are blessed with the brightness of color and the beauty of sleep and dream. Your dream time is a busy time for many of you. That aspect of you that is not conscious is very busy in service and in working out all these crazy dilemmas that you experience in the daytime. Your subconscious mind is assisting you as you try to figure it all out. It puts it into symbolism for you, and causes a harmonization, so that you can rise the next morning to see a new day, feel a new sun and see its beautiful warmth and color.

Let us take a nice deep breath once more. I invite you to feel Mother Earth beneath us. I invite you to feel your heart open and soft and tender. We are requesting you be tender with yourself. Allow yourself to be vulnerable, to be "not so cool" all the time. Allow others to see all aspects of you. Admit that you are human; that you hate, that you lust, and that you have passion. You get jealous, you feel competition, you have grudges. You get angry, you are absolutely furious about something, and, also, you are peaceful, joyous and loving. Experience the full gamut of humanness, and see it as a great treasure; see it as the pot of gold at the end of the rainbow. Perhaps it is always receding, but it is always there.

It is like a chalice within your heart that you can put everything into. All your stories can go into your silver or golden chalice, your heart, for Spirit knows what to do with it. You can put your anger and your jealousy and your hate and your longing, all into that beautiful chalice in the center of your golden heart, and you can give it, give it to God, to Goddess, give it to the Great Priestess, give it to the Great Mother, to the Great Ocean. Allow it all to dissolve, the good, the bad, the ugly, the sweet, the sour, the bitter. Everything is a treasure house. Everything has beauty in it, even the hatred, even the lust.

Each chakra of yours is an energy system, an energy point, an energy wheel that gives you access into the world of experience of that specific energy, with a specific color. It is part of the full gamut of the 12 colors, like the 12 tones. There may be seven colors, but consider how we also have the halftones, the sharps and flats. So, too, there are chakras that extend above and below. Open your chakras each day so that you are in full awareness of your energy system operating in balance. Begin by connecting with the root down to Mother Earth. If you have Shungite,[29] you can hold a piece of it, or sit by a tree with your back against it or lie down on Mother Earth. Connect to her through your rootedness, your 1st or root chakra, grounding yourself.

Connect with the RED energy of the ROOT chakra. Spin it counter-clockwise. When you are done and feel it is open and balanced, move up to the SECOND chakra: This is the energy of creativity, of creation, of sexuality, masculine/feminine in union, the beginning of the rising of that Kundalini energy moving upwards, the snake. Allow it to spin clockwise in an ORANGE-colored motion. Feel this energy, the orange. Feel that energy of the juiciness of the orange as you peel it, as you taste it, as you pluck it from the tree and peel it. Enjoy the succulence of your second chakra. Do not disparage or judge it. It is merely energy.

Once you feel this harmonization, allow your SOLAR PLEXUS to spin in a counter-clockwise motion, again, the beautiful YELLOW of the sun energy. It is not called Solar Plexus for nothing. It is the place of your energy of self, your sense of who you are. Open it, allow yourself to come into the full presence of who you are without diminishment or comparison to anyone else. Allow yourself to tune in to "Who am I? I am here. I allow myself to be fully present in this place of power, this expression of self-ness. My self is my higher self, is my lower self, is my energy of knowing who I am. It is me in my body. It is me connecting to my next alignment as I move through the Soul Seed, that place between the ribs, as I move up toward the heart."

"I feel my blueprint, my connection with my Soul, right here in my very center." It spins clockwise, connecting my solar plexus energy of physicality with that place of my HEART. It spins clockwise with the beautiful GREEN of life, the beautiful laurel that we have mentioned; the growing things, the beautiful color of spring. "My heart, as it opens, embraces all life and allows my being to rest in that simplicity of stillness. It expands into a fullness. My heart, as it expands, is filled with the green and also the gold that has been poured into this chalice, there in the very cave of my heart where I sit. As I allow my heart to open and expand, it begins to spiral in a clockwise fashion, extending that golden light of the Christ consciousness, of God's love out into the world, to all places, to all people. It brings comfort, succor and hope where there is none. As I send out this ray, the spiral motion of God's love, I feel my heart expanding. And as it expands, I feel that sphere of golden light around me coming in closer, surrounding me, protecting me, filled with these Golden Beings of Light."

"I begin now to spin my THROAT chakra, feeling the BLUE energy, like the beautiful sky of blue. My voice opens to its full expression in the expansiveness of SKY-BLUE as it circles anti-clockwise. I feel my throat opening, freeing itself from all encumbrance, from all the voices that said 'you may not speak, you have nothing to say.' My voice knows it has its own unique power. My voice is pure energy. It is here to express Truth, and as my throat opens and the blue energy spirals counter-clockwise, the energy moves up toward my THIRD EYE, the color of INDIGO. The beautiful clockwise, spiraling awareness, of knowing all, of seeing all, expands out into the Akashic Records, giving me access to All Truth, cutting through the illusion. I see into the hearts of the people. I see into the body. I know what is beneficial and what is not."

As the beautiful indigo-colored chakra of the third eye opens, we rise up to the CROWN, that connection with the Ones of Light and the counter-clockwise spiraling motion of the VIOLET Flame of Saint Germain, which purifies any negativity. As we feel this shower of the Violet Flame, we rise up to connection with the WHITE LIGHT of Source, of Origin, that which we call Heaven. Golden Beings of Light watch over you, the planet, and all life. This is the energy of the Great Central Sun.[30] This connects you to the Galaxies, the Cosmos; for it is so that you are Immortal, you are Eternal, you are Infinite and Universal.

As you drink the water of immortality each day with your chakras open, you are ready to ride forth upon your stallion, upon your steed, your sword at your side, firmly planted in its scabbard. Perhaps you are riding a unicorn or a dragon or a tiger. Your own unique expression must now go forth into the world to create clarity, beauty, peace and harmony. You work in cooperation with all the Beings of Light that are here upon this planet, like you, the Lightworkers that have come. You have heard the call and are gathering to bring the Earth back to its pristine purity. Remember your childhood innocence and that childlike wonder. Remember your purity of heart. We surround you with our love as we leave you in this beautiful space to take a few moments to sit in peace and stillness.

Apollo Q&A

Q. (ER) When you spoke, especially in the beginning, I cried a lot and I just couldn't stop. At the end, I was more peaceful. Why is this happening to me?

A. Why are you crying? Because your heart is opening, and when your heart opens, there is a flood of emotion that has been kept suppressed. You're feeling the love vibration of the angels pouring into you. It is not a mental thing. It is beyond the mind. It's like the heart just says, "I can finally let go of my armor. I can allow myself to be loved." And that's what they want. That is what we are asking, for you to love yourself because without that you will not become the world teacher that you're intended to be. We are asking you to gather around you the people that you are to lead and co-operate with, because, you must learn to model what it's like to be a heart-centered being. And in that space, there are tears from years, lifetimes, eons of pain; suppression, loss, abandonment, and betrayals. And all of that comes up when the heart opens, and it's OK. The more we cry, the more we let that flood become part of the ocean of All That Is. So, rejoice, because it's essentially an opening. It's a softening. It's allowing yourself to be vulnerable, and it is precious. It is part of the gift of humanness, and if all of us were able to do that and be that, the world would already be transformed. So, thank you for that question.

Q. (LS) I worked with someone earlier this week to clear contracts out, old vows and ties within my body to my anxiety and my physical symptoms, and what I came to discover is that I definitely agreed in this life to experience, release and heal through my physical body. But it has been causing me so much distress and so much illness. And it's gotten so hard to move everything through my body. So we rewrote that contract and I felt better for about a day; but then afterwards I realized: if I don't have my body and physical illness as an indicator and messages for me on how to process, release, grow, heal, I almost don't know how to afford a life, and process and heal. I've been trying to use my imagination as to what it would be like to not have to experience life through my body so strongly, but I don't know where to go with this, and it brings up even more anxiety, the thought of being healed and being healthy.

A. Thank you, it is a very interesting perspective to recognize the role and the connection between your soul and your body and your mind. What if you could let go of the need to suffer in order to heal? What if it were possible, with one breath, to let it all go; to place everything, the entire story, in the balloons, in the receding ships and send them out into the distance, loaded with every single aspect of struggle you have ever known? What if you could take a breath and let them all go? How would it be if you could feel your body loving you, feel your body as your friend, as your lover, as your beloved? Could you feel that there is no space, no dichotomy, nothing interfering in that space between your body and your mind? How would you feel if your voice, that pure energy, that sphere of beautiful blue between your head and your heart, were full of clarity, and emptiness, and truth? Your truth, your voice, has no limitations upon it and does not have to become a go-between. Between the heart and the head, between the body and the mind.

What if you can absolutely love yourself as you are without the need for that biofeedback loop? You do not need it, but it is your friend. It is not necessarily the pain that is needed. Before the pain, before the distress, before the anxiety, there is a very simple message, one that you can hear, can listen to, and then you do not have to let it go any deeper or any further. You have such amazing access to guidance, and Beings of Light that are surrounding you. Give it all to them. We would like you to imagine this golden light pouring down through your crown, all the way through your whole body, down through your feet, like a beautiful shower of gold, just washing it all away. Let it be simple, let it be easy. It is only the mind that has the attachment to the difficulty. This is your time. You do not have to struggle. We do not want you to struggle. We want to help you. I want you to know that you can let it all go with one breath. Do you think that might be possible?

- *Yes*

You are powerful, are you not?

- *Yes*

You are scared of your power?

- *Yeah*

You're terrified?

- *I am a very powerful healer.*

You are terrified of your power. What would your life be if you allowed yourself to adopt the fullness of your power? You would be like a dragon. You would be so overwhelmed. You are scared that you would overwhelm people with your power, but it is not so, because your power is in your heart. It is not in your mind or external to your body-mind-spirit-soul being. It is all a oneness. For so long, you have torn them into shreds. You have created partitioning, like your hard drive. It is time to reset, it is time to reset the program, the software, so that you become one with yourself. You can be a dragon, as long as people are willing to experience themselves in your presence in the face of a benevolent dragon, that knows how to love and has tenderness; has a soft, beautiful, radiant heart. Allow that soft, radiant, tender heart to dissolve everything. Allow yourself to be powerful. You are holding on so tightly to the fear that if you expressed your power, you would frighten everyone away, and would be lonely and lost. You can have it all, your power, the love, the tenderness, the softness. You will be such a healer beyond what you have accomplished to this point, when you are no longer the wounded healer. Your kingdom will thrive. There will be green. Spring will return, and all things will thrive and celebrate your coming out as a free being.

Q. (LB) I am a heart-centered being. My question is about those who come into our life who are projecting the opposite of who we are. I did not choose this person, but she holds my granddaughter and is carrying her. I receive back from her an energy that's very opposite of who I am. I've been working with new agreements on a soul level, and I'm not certain what is mine to do with this. I'd like your thoughts on it. How do you be with that kind of energy in the Oneness knowing it's part of you, but not, and it just feels like it's completely different? I don't know how to. She rejects me, she really rejects my energy altogether, so I'm not certain.

A. We are understanding. It is a part of human experience that there are those who do not like us. There are those who do not understand or see who we are. They are our greatest challenges, for it is they who provide the grist for the mill. They provide us the opportunity. It is like you are the Samurai facing that mortal combat, a matter of life and death. You will either survive or you will not. It is where the rubber meets the road. This is your work. Your work is to embrace this soul without judgment, to talk to the soul, to send love and light and blessing and to recognize that you have an agreement. You have an agreement that each of you will help the other to find that place of ease, of love, of non-judgment. It may be that you will not have great fondness for each other, but just accepting. However, it is yours to do the work no matter what is on the other side of the coin, no matter what the responses or the reactions are. It is for you to also examine those places in your wounded child, where you were hurt, where you faced this kind of challenge of non-acceptance, of somebody who judged you, scorned, or rejected you. Perhaps they spoke about you to others and were vindictive. And you felt as if you wanted to die because it was unbearable. It is necessary for you to go to those deep places within your woundedness and find a way to bring light.

Your mind cannot do it. It must be done through the heart. You can use shamanic practice, because, at the same time, there is a component that is connected to past lives, to ancestors, to agreements and contracts. You can seek assistance from someone who has no attachment, but knows how to help you to cut the cords, to cut the ties. You do not ever have to like this person. Love is not liking. Love is the unconditional acceptance of someone's reality. Perhaps, even for a moment, you could glimpse the possibility of what it might feel like to be in their shoes. Perhaps there is something in you, you are not necessarily aware of, which triggers them. How do you find the compassion to recognize that somehow you trigger them, and it is their problem, not yours? They feel this way towards you, they project this stuff upon you. We can help you to place around you a sphere of light that creates a protective environment that cannot be penetrated.

We would recommend that when you wake in the morning, and each time you think of this person, you surround yourself with this sphere of light and that you do not allow anything that is not of the light to penetrate this sphere. Ask your guides and your angels to assist you with this. We will help you to create this structure. For you, this is the first structure to establish, so you feel, in a real, palpable way, that you are surrounded by protection. Whatever is being flung towards you will bounce off the protective coating of this sphere of light. It would be beneficial, too, to share with someone you trust, to share your feelings and allow them to arise.

This is why we are asking you to pair up and share with each other. It gives you a platform to express yourself, as human beings with feelings, with anger, with frustrations. If you can express it, then it is not unconscious, within your cells. Do the HeartThread® work. If you are a HeartThread® practitioner, we would recommend that you find another practitioner to do an exchange with. This will help release some of these old patterns. There is a sense; we are feeling it in this one's body, that on the left side of your upper back, there is a deep wound. You were perhaps stabbed in the back, betrayed by her, and this is your opportunity to face this betrayal, this murder, and find a way to release it from your field, from your cells, and from your heart.

Recognize that each one travels their course across the skies in each lifetime with their individual challenges and each with their childhood wounding. For it is only woundedness that allows one to judge and target another. We are holding space with you, and trust that you will find a beautiful resolution to this issue. Does that answer your question?

Q. *Thank you from my heart, and I would ask for that structure, that assistance for my son, because he's in a relationship with her, and he is trying very hard to find a path forward for him and the baby.*

A. It is important for you to assist him to create his own sphere and for him to understand that there are those who express their woundedness as a way to receive what they are hungry for - love. One can love in a way that does not suck energy from another. We need to stay detached with compassion, recognizing that they need our love, even if we have to summon up a tremendous amount of courage to give it to them. You are a Spiritual Warrior. This is your path, to face each challenge with fullness, directly; to face your demons and call in your dragons, all of your guides and angels, your helpers in all the realms. Thank you.

Q. (AY) What's just been said, I'm trying to identify how that is operating in my experience in this lifetime with my son. Which of course is a bit different, because I have great love for him, but not much like. And I understand some of his wounding, but I seem to be the last person who can address it, at least on the surface. Of course, behind the scenes, I can do all those things of creating love around him every day. But when we come into contact with one another, there's usually great ruffling of the vibrations and great sadness. So, I wondered how I might address them.

A. Thank you. We are feeling that there is a deep need for you to shed many tears. You brought through the idea of sadness. There is great grief, and it is difficult for you to see any clarity around this. It is difficult for you because of your love and not-love relationship, to have clarity. It is important for you, too, to have someone who can listen and help you talk through your feelings. It is essential for you to be able to work on the inner planes with yourself, and to have distance. You require the space to see things from a different perspective, as if you were watching a past life or movie. Can you be an observer, observing, even when you are engaged with him?

You might also address this through hypnosis, through the assistance of a practitioner, who can do past life or early life regression work. It's vital for you to recognize, that this is not about 'figuring out,' using your mind to deal with the issue; for the mind is not the right tool for working with this. It requires you to go into the heart, and within the heart there's great suffering, there's great pain, a sense of loss, and the shielding that you use to keep yourself safe. It is understandable. It is why so many default to the mind more and more.

So, it is important, we would say, for you to also to work with the HeartThread® or some form of heart energy healing work that would allow you to cry, and cry, and cry like a river and let it all go, because behind and beyond the tears, there is a joy. There is a place of resolution, of reconciliation. You have agreed, both of you, to be this trigger for each other, this challenge, this warrior that you have to face, with whom you have to come to terms. Perhaps to slay in whatever way you understand that to be, for sometimes it is necessary. It does not mean literally, but figuratively. You might need to kill him in a way that is symbolic, that releases you from an old embodiment together, in which there was great pain and great suffering and perhaps also betrayal. There may have been some kind of enmity that went beyond the blood ties that you have now, or perhaps even deeper and thicker. There were essentially blood ties that were not treated in an honorable and respecting way.

So I recommend that you to find some practitioners who can help you with this work. Do not feel that you have to go it alone. Do not feel that you are lost. You can ask for help. Certainly do the practice of surrounding yourself and your son with spheres of light, and direct towards him love and light, the golden energy of sun, of heart. Flow it towards him without any attachment that he receive it, but as a practice for you, to direct that energy of your heart outwards in a giving way. This will open the spaces within you that are closed, so you can receive love. For you do not know what he is doing on the inner plane to work towards a resolution from his perspective. You may not know what has been triggered in him. In each childhood is encapsulated all the triggering, all the restimulation from other lifetimes, so that we have the opportunity to heal in this life, all the previous ones and to clear all karma. Is that making sense?

- *Absolutely. Yes, thank you.*

Q. *(NB) The messages that you gave today; I was taking it all in and there was one place where you said "forgiveness" and "letting go," which I work on. It's really, really hard for me to sometimes hear my mother's voice. There is that wounded child and there is betrayal. There still is betrayal, and I can hear it in her voice; and I've been doing my work and I know I've been separated for a good reason. Forgiveness is one side, the message that you gave, and then you said that anger, that it's all welcome, it's all an emotion, and it's all good. Where is the balance? Sometimes, when I feel that I can't hear her voice, I feel guilty, and I don't want to feel guilty, because, in some sense, I feel like I'm keeping myself safe, but then I get confused. Could you shed some light on that, please?*

A. Forgiveness is the other side of the sword of truth. You can cut and cut and cut. You can cry and cry and rage and rage, but in the end, you must come to that space of forgiveness. And all the work of the warrior, all the work of the spiritual adept, all the work that you engage in, when you follow a spiritual path, is to come to that place of forgiveness, for what is forgiveness but detachment. The ties that bind, ties connected to emotions that were caused through harm, through damage, conditioning and imprinting and through our childhood and past life wounds, are being released. It is the ultimate challenge for the Spiritual Warrior to embrace the energy of witness, observer without emotion. And it is easier said than done. However, for each one who is human, this is the challenge. If you wish to be, so called, enlightened, if you wish to live in peace and tranquility, if you wish to have a calm, satisfied mind, you must find that place within you where it doesn't matter anymore, where it's a story. It does not bring up emotions. There is no triggering left.

One way that we are feeling, is to work with the Emotion Code[31] to release trapped emotions from within the body. It is a very simple process. It is even something you can find out for yourself how to do and do for yourself, or this one here can do it, even at a distance. It is very quick and easy and brief. And there are many emotions that can be released in one mini session.

It is also good to have a punch bag, to have access to a way of expressing anger and frustration and bitterness safely. You can scream and shout, and you can call whatever names you wish for all the harm that has been done to you. You do not do this in order to reciprocate or harm the other, but just in order to release the emotions that are still trapped within yourself. It is also why we advocate the use of HeartThread® as one of the most powerful modalities for releasing emotions that are within the cells that one regards as there forever. They can be released in just a second, by saying the words. This is the work of John Henry.

So, there are many techniques that you can use beyond what you are already doing, and we highly recommend that you find a room where you can scream and shout. Get yourself a punch bag or a pillow, do whatever you feel necessary to do, as long as there is no intention within that practice to bring any harm to another. It is only done in order to release from your cells these emotions. As we shared about the work of Bruce Lipton and Candace Pert, *(Molecules of Emotion)*, the biology holds memories, holds emotions, holds the stories. They can be released with ease and grace through the intention to release them. All the techniques, all the systems and modalities that do that, are avenues for releasing those ties. You can also consult a shamanic practitioner who is an adept observer with no attachment whatsoever. They can help cut the ties, cords, and any agreements.

You can ask for your ancestors to be present, and we will call them here now. We will ask them to release any attachments to anything that was ever agreed upon, any contracts or vows, any oaths that you ever had with them. We are asking their consent to release them. As you take a breath, you can let them go in the moment, allowing them to dissolve through your feet. For this work can be that simple, and within the framework of HeartThread®, this work is done with ease and grace and simplicity to restore you to your self-authority. You can call in your ancestors. For the ancestors are also those who are in your family who have been with you before, and are now incarnated into this lifetime. You can ask that the ties and bonds be released, by calling them in with love, to witness and to heal for themselves as well as for you.

And you can talk to your mother's soul, and ask that she change her story or your story or whatever is necessary, so that you speak soul to soul and say, "Look, this is what I am experiencing. Can we find a place of love beyond all these old stories, for we have known each other before this life, and in the Swing Between Worlds[32] we agreed to take on these roles? We agreed to play out this movie together, and that episode is now over. Can we start a new movie that is based on love?" Use your imagination, use your writing, drawing, use any techniques that engage the imagination to heal yourself. Call on your guides and angels to assist you. Use your dream time and recognize, on your waking, the importance of the dream and write it down and examine it; not so deeply but just surface, to feel and see what it is bringing for you. Perhaps you will experience a release in that way, because the subconscious mind will listen to what you ask it to do while it is going to sleep, and it will do what is necessary to assist you. Is this helpful?

-Very much so. Thank you so much, thank you.

Q. (SL) Are there any special procedures to process unconscious or subconscious stuff that was created and brought forth from past lifetimes?

A. We would recommend the use of affirmations. Go into an Alpha brain wave pattern or state of mind, by breathing deeply and meditating. Once you are in a meditative space, begin to tell yourself aloud affirmations of what you want in your life, in your consciousness instead of the old voices that are running around in your mind, the old affirmations. Self HeartThread®, you might call it. So that's a very simple technique.

Closing Meditation

Let's put our hands on our heart and feel Mother Earth beneath us and Father Sky above, allowing us to also feel that beautiful weave of heart connection between all of us, growing and expanding into that beautiful golden sphere that we have experienced together. Allow yourself to let that expand out into the edges of the Universe, sending out your vibration and your intention for this life and for all the benevolence of the Universe to expand into all beings. And as you breathe in, breathe back in, that benevolence of the Universe and of all the guides and guardians who surround you. May your life be filled with love, with peace, with great honoring for the magnificence of who you are. We thank you for this day. This has been your message with Apollo, even though we speak with the voice of all the angels. Blessings and peace to you all.

Voice Four
Pan

6th September 2020

Let's place our right hand on our heart and left hand on our right. Today we hear from Pan, as part of the New Earth Council.

As we put our hands on our hearts, let us go into that place of stillness, allowing ourselves to feel that stillness pouring down through our crowns and filling our whole being as if golden liquid is being poured into our hearts and then percolating its way down through our feet into Mother Earth. Allow that breath to fill us with the light, allowing that golden energy to penetrate into every cell, feeling that there is a column of light that surrounds us, a column that reaches down into the very center of Mother Earth.

Allow that breath, that stillness to completely fill your whole being, allowing all the thoughts, feelings, any sounds, to melt away with the out breath. Giving it all to Mother Earth, giving her our thanks, our gratitude; connecting with her from our hearts. Allowing ourselves to feel that Mother Earth too is sending her love up through this column to fill our hearts, to rise up towards the Heavens as the column reaches up toward the stars, up to the Cosmos, up to that place of origin, up to Father Sky, that place of the divine spark that animates this body and allows us to be here as souls and spirits, fully embodied in this presence.

And then we begin to share the threads of our hearts as they reach out to weave together with all the threads of all of those hearts gathered here together, and those that are part of this group, weaving those threads into a fabric. And that fabric grows bigger and bigger as it weaves more and more hearts into this beautiful tapestry, into the hearts of our loved ones, our friends, family and neighbors. The fabric reaches out like a wave, moving out further and further across our cities and our states; weaving more and more and more threads of hearts across the oceans and the continents. This beautiful weave grows bigger and bigger and spreads further and further afield; reaching out to the very circumference of Mother Earth, surrounding her with a beautiful weave and web, made up of this heart essence. It reaches into all worlds, into all universes, into all Time and all Space.

We call on all the energies of the 12 and all the Golden Beings of Light that watch over us to surround us with a beautiful sphere, each one of us and collectively, a sphere of golden light to hold us in its safety and protection, to carry us through whatever may show up, to create a safe space that allows only the highest vibrations possible. I call on all the angels and guides of those that are here together with us to be present, to surround each one with their guidance, their love, their blessings and their healing energies. You may rest your hands.

I welcome you to join me in this place, this magical time in your life. The energy of Pan is the energy, not of Mother Earth as a global being, but of that which rests upon her, that which you may call the Garden of Eden, this beautiful library that is made up of all life, all the great diversity of what Creator has allowed to be and blossom upon this planet. As Pan, I represent the energy of naturalness, that energy of the heart expressed through love of the growing things, of the creatures, of Nature and all the magic, all the blessings that Nature has brought to this planet. It is a living energy that is extremely potent and that expands in vibration to encompass all life, not just on this planet but in this solar system and all the Universe. It is not as the ones that no longer have atmosphere.

For this energy of life is the greatest gift of the Creator for each one, and for all in this expansion of consciousness that is now reaching into new dimensions and spaces of being. This life energy is the energy of what you call free will, of the ability to be fully present here and engage from that space of individuality, with all of life. There is no limitation on your ability to communicate with all the creatures and with all aspects of life. This includes the plants, the trees, even the breeze or the stars, or the moon at the changes of season; all the magical arenas that surround you on this beautiful planet.

This planet was always intended to be a Garden of Eden. It is now a time in the evolution of your planet and of humanity in which we are engaged in what you might call the final battle for Life. This final battle has long ago been won, to allow life to flourish once again in freedom, in peace, in harmony and in the way that within your own heart there has been a longing, ever since you can remember. You all yearn for the waters to be pure again and the air, and for people to be happy, for people to live a life filled with joy and celebration. This is possible. It is not a pipe dream. It is not just another illusion. We have asked you to examine your own illusions, to look at those things that you postulate would make you happy if only you had them, felt them, or were them.

And so, it is important on this journey together, that you allow yourself to continue this process of examining everything, because it is necessary, at this time especially, for each one of you to uncover your place of truth. It is called the inner truth[33], that place of knowing, that place of being, where you penetrate everything with an understanding that comes through the heart rather than the mind. We have said many times, "The heart knows it all." It is in fact within, within the heart, that you have your answers. It is in the heart that you understand and know the interconnectedness of all life, and are therefore able to celebrate. It is also within the heart that you have that place of softness, that place where there is, perhaps, a deep sense of loss or sadness. Perhaps there is great rage because of the injustices that have been laid upon you, not through your own reason or cause, but because you were born into a particular situation or because you have accumulated these times from the past that have come up for you now to clear, to deal with, and to rectify or resolve.

This is the time of facing everything that you are not complete with. It is necessary to find resolution within your own personal life, because every step that you take personally becomes, as is said, a great giant leap for mankind, or humankind rather. Each spirit, each soul, must penetrate the illusions they have created for a sense of safety. As you penetrate through this veil, you contribute to the greater truth that surrounds you. Cut through the deceptions that are placed upon you and that run the lives of many of those around you, and perhaps even generate a certain amount of fear within your own person. Actually, this is an aspect of the challenges that you must meet every day in some manner; because you are human, not because you've done anything wrong, are fated, or there is anything that is missing in the fullness of who you truly are.

The external experience is seldom the truth. There is a place of sensitivity on the inside that is being reflected and externalized as a mirror for you to see and question, "What is going on for me? Why am I feeling this way? Why do I have this particular challenge that I wish would be over?" And, of course, there is that place where it is your destiny. It is our desire as your guardians, our greatest desire, that you should experience the fullness of ease, grace, joy, peace and abundance in your life. It is your birthright as a human, especially for one who is regarded as a lightworker. You have come to this planet, not just to experience a personal, 'selfish' kind of growth and enjoyment of life (though there is nothing wrong with that), but you have come with a mission. It is to be an example, a model of what it can be like to live with complete equanimity.

We would like to invite you to take a breath for just one moment, to go into that place within your heart, within that stillness that we all brought in at the very beginning. Allow yourself, just for a moment, to experience that equanimity; as if you are a duck and the water is splashing all over you and as the saying goes, everything that bothers you is 'like water off a duck's back.' It has no place to adhere. There is within you a calm, a space of simplicity, a space of satisfaction. "I have enough, I am blessed. Everything that surrounds me has come to me for a reason, and the reason is for my highest evolution, my greatest good. As it is for me and for mine, so too it is for all beings and for all life. For each emotion that I honor, is a small step that I take as a human being. I feel and recognize the message and allow it to be. I allow it to dissolve away, and it becomes a minor, or even a major triumph for myself, my life and my family. It is also so for my ancestors and my progeny. It becomes a gift for the world."

This relates to your connection with Nature, with life, with growing things, with the creatures in the forests and the fields; the ones within your homes that have a different environment of consciousness. Still, you are able to love them and communicate with them. An aspect of living within the natural world entails and encompasses a relationship with your body and your chakras. There is nothing wrong, no good and no bad. The energy of your bodies, of being human, in and of itself, poses a certain challenge to your minds. You judge yourselves by your appearance and how you *think* others see you. You assume and project that they judge you as too big or too small, too skinny or too fat, too old or too young. The "too" is always a judgment that says, "I am not good enough the way I am."

This also concerns the deepest levels of your sexuality. In many ways, the energy and the mythology of Pan has been associated with the natural expression of sexuality, 'natural' meaning beyond social mores, an aspect of the world of Nature. As the cultures have changed and shifted, there was laid upon the energy of naturalness great judgment and severity, a kind of Victorian, 'nose in the air' attitude that says, "You are doing something that is not okay, Madam!" Naturalness can be expressed in many ways, be it nakedness, be it sexuality, be it the ways in which you move your body in a sensual manner to the music, to the beat. When you dance upon the earth or play music, you are engaged, and have always been, in the celebration of human life through ceremony, ritual, and the deepest level of honoring and connection with Mother Earth.

Whatever practice you do, when you go to your altar and light your candle or incense, or you smudge; when you sit in meditation or gather with others in ritual for the new and full moon, the equinox or solstice, you respect and honor the natural order, as part of the unfolding of the cycles of time, the ways in which life progresses in a spiral motion. If you gather around the ancient stones in alignment with the stars, the heavenly bodies or the Galactic Center - all these things have been done in order to communicate and connect with the Beings of Light and the Devic[34] kingdoms that oversee life upon the planet.

It is because of this that Pan, or the Green Man, has been represented with the horns of the Aries Ram, with hoofs and the pan pipe, the pipes of Pan playing the music for the celebration. For Apollo, when he was talking with you, did not mention that he was the god or the energetic divine being that brought music and oversaw the experience of music in the life of a human being. Music is an experience of the soul's connection with the stars and with all Creation in a way that bypasses the mind and allows the body to have free movement as a natural outpouring. So, we encourage you to gather around the trees and the circles of water and the circles of stone; to gather with your fellow beings and do ceremonies. You will have an opportunity at the autumn equinox, which is a very pivotal time in the cycle of the year. It is a time of transition, energetically, in terms of weather, in terms of movement of air and water and moisture on the planet. This is a very special time that was celebrated throughout the ages. It is an important time for you personally to connect with Mother Earth, with your fellow human beings in the open, if possible, to experience the sensations of Nature, of the sun, of the breeze, of the warmth, of the coolness, of the strength of Mother Earth beneath you.

It is critical that you honor all aspects of body. It is extremely important to honor and bless the water that you drink, and that you drink copious amounts of water, and that you drink the highest quality water you can access. Much of the water commercially available in plastic bottles is nothing more than recycled water from your metropolitan water systems; tap water that has been placed in bottles, perhaps purified with chemicals, and is essentially dead. In order to be in touch and alignment with aliveness, find life-giving, structured water. Always bless your water.

It is extremely vital for your energy, because your field is amplifying itself. The consciousness of your cells is expanding in frequency. The vibration of your body is rising, so, in order that the vibrational increase be more fluid, and because your body is made up of mostly water, pay very strong attention to the water that you drink. If the water that is accessible to you is not of the highest vibration, bless it and put your own light energy into it. It is important to grow your own food and purchase food that is organic, not GMO,[35] nor artificial, or processed. We recommend that you eat healthy, organic vegetables and fruits. Do not be afraid to eat as much fruit as possible. The sugars that are contained within the fruit are extremely benevolent for your body, and are highly absorbable. The fluids that most people are drinking are not life-enhancing.

It is also vital for you to move, to dance, not just for the exercise but for the joy of moving, moving in a fluid motion that allows your emotions that are tied up within your cells to become free and to be expressed. Find a way that you can express through vocalization, through making sounds, through screaming and shouting or whatever is necessary to release those trapped emotions within you that have no place to go. Allow them the freedom of motion, and they will of their own accord begin to leave your body and create more space for light to penetrate into those places where previously the emotions had been trapped.

It is wonderful, is it not, to spread your arms in great gratitude to Mother Earth and Father Sky and to feel the breeze in the warm sun, to feel the rain upon your face and head and allow it to pour all over you in exhilaration. It is good to feel like a child again; to play in the sand and the dirt and not worry about having muddy feet. The child does not worry about whether their face is smeared with the food that they eat, full of wonderful nutrition; "strawberry face forever."

Allow yourself to remember what it's like to be a child, what it is like to go outside into the yard and talk with the Little Ones that you were able to communicate with when you were still an innocent little one. Remember what it is like to have your so-called 'imaginary friends,' some of whom, most of whom, many of whom, are still with you right now. You can almost reach out and feel them. You can almost bring them to your breast like a teddy bear and cuddle them. And we would recommend, right now, in your own way, that you hold your little child, the true 'you,' and bring them close. Give them a reassuring hug, letting them know that everything, all the fear and all this craziness is just an illusion. It will fade away as surely as the spring will turn to summer and the summer to fall and the fall to winter. Everything is so precious according to a Divine Purpose, a Divine Order. Your heart knows the truth.

These little ones, like the child that has just climbed onto your lap, know the truth. It is good for you to communicate with them, to talk to them, to remind them how much you love them. Remind them that they made it through, no matter what it was that they had to deal with. Here they/you are, fully grown now and still remembering the beauty of childhood, of innocence, of purity, that space within the heart that is so precious. When you trample the Earth with your bare feet, you somehow re-evoke it. When you gather around the tree and hug it and give thanks for its presence, for the roots that penetrate down into Mother Earth, it allows you to feel your own connection through that beautiful tree.

The tree does not require anything of you. It is just there, and yet it loves to experience your gratitude. It loves to feel that you honor it and that you can come and sit beneath it, put your back against it, go into the stillness and the silence. Perhaps to hear the rustling of the leaves, the birds, the waters and the breeze. If you are fortunate to have water, trees, stillness and Nature accessible to you, go often. And if it is necessary for you to travel, do so. Find a way to go into that space of Nature at this time in the current annals of your herstory of Mother Earth's evolution. It is vital for you to spend as much time as you can, allowing that stillness to penetrate into your being, allowing the sounds of the rippling of the waters, of the soft breeze and the feeling upon your cheek; to allow your hair to blow in the wind, hear the rustle of leaves, the beautiful singing of the birds within this encapsulated energy, that is outside of time, outside of stress, outside of the belief systems that have taken over your planet in the Great Illusion.

Allow yourself to breathe again the purity of love. Allow yourself to feel that the energy of god/goddess pouring its divine love and lotion upon you, is fully present within you and is wafting around you and penetrating into every cell of your being. So, when you are sitting at your desk staring at that screen, and writing an email to someone with whom you have difficulty, you can take a moment's pause before you do so. Remember that moment in Nature, the last time you were there, and felt that peace and remembered your child. Ask your little one, "How would you answer this person? What would you say?" For a child's mind is often very simple and very clear and extremely direct. Perhaps they would say, without compunction, "I don't like you, go away," or something that you are totally desirous of saying but are not willing to, because you have been conditioned to be 'nice.'

It is important that you communicate with that deep place within you that knows Truth. When you meditate, when you spend time in your practice, it is important to constantly examine the thoughts that run through your mind, especially the thoughts that diminish you. You see yourself in some way less than perfect, less than good, less than right. There is no such thing. There are billions of souls on this planet. Each one is unique. Each one is an aspect of the Divine Creation, of Love in expression, and many have forgotten this truth. It is your job today, and from now on always, to remember that you are an expression of the love of the Divine.

We are comfortable saying "God's" love, but there are some who prefer "Goddess" and we use these terms even though they are so incapable of expressing the true nature of that which is the Divine Intelligence that creates All That Is. It is not possible for the mind to comprehend divinity, and so humans have encapsulated it in a word. We have asked you to examine your words and the meanings behind the words you use and their associated thoughts. The belief systems that are based upon these words feed the illusions. We ask you to be fully aware of how you use language, of how and what you think, and how willing you might be to let go of many of the belief systems based on the associations with the words that you do use. The concepts and assumptions are the boxes through which you approach the reality of that which is outside of you and that which is within you. They reflect each other, and as you shift the patterns within your cells, you shift the experience of the realities, so to speak, outside of you. And if it causes a few feathers to be ruffled, that is just one of the casualties of your ascension process, of the expansion of your consciousness.

Are we all in the same ballpark, enjoying an experience of Nature, of the breeze, of the trees, of life on this planet, beyond the mask, beyond the limitations that would be placed upon you to keep you in fear? If there is anything that you can do each day that will shift our planet into its new vibration, it is to face your fear with courage. It is to face your fear with love, to recognize that you are not a victim, that you are a living spirit, that you are the Living Spirit incarnate; an immortal, eternal, infinite and universal soul expressing through a physical, mental and emotional body, and that you have the power to rise above whatever fear presents itself. You have the power, through your free will, to just say "no" or say "yes;" to embrace that which you feel is of love and to reject that which is not; to allow yourself to feel the warmth of human contact in a hug, to have communication heart-to-heart, face-to-face with another; to not allow the authority of others who do not carry that vibration of heart, to direct how you behave, how you feel, and how you express your love.

You also have the Sword of Truth at your side, and as you use it sparingly and wisely, you invoke what we shall call the "invisibility" of the Spiritual Warrior, who knows when to keep silent, even though s/he is bristling at the idiocy of those around them who are spouting nonsense. Sometimes the wise one will simply smile and leave the sword in the scabbard and allow them to have their opinion and allow yourself to have yours and let it be at that. And, as necessary, in order to do your shopping, you put on that silly mask, and you pretend to be 'normal' and then you are able, when you come out, to become the true normal human who is not that distortion.

We do not wish to be hard upon you or on those who live in fear. However, it is true that you are being controlled and have been for thousands upon thousands of years, and this is why it is vital for you to examine every thought, every feeling, every injunction, every directive, and especially every authority figure. You must become your own self-authority, at peace within your own heart, and aware of what you *do* know deep within you. It is important for you to reach out and communicate with those of like mind so that you form circles, that you gather in some ways to support each other and remind each other that you are facing the greatest challenge of any lifetime and that you are here because you have everything you need to face these challenges. You are surrounded by teams of angels, of guardians, of extraterrestrial energies, of galactic energies, of the energies of devas, of fairies and elves, and of dragons.

You have the power to be in your own truth, and we are asking you to do so. We are asking you to remember that Nature is the greatest gift to human beings and to all creatures, and that it is to be honored, respected and loved. It is part of the structures that you will create that will allow humans to once again re-establish a bond of love, of communication instead of fear. Even with the snake or that insect that you may have feared would bite or harm you; if there is no fear in your heart, there is an ability to communicate in a loving manner with these beings, these creatures and have a different experience. They are part of this divine energy of Nature, that I, as Pan, represent.

I wish to give you my special secret, my name, and you may call upon me as you reach into the worlds of Nature to expand your own consciousness with her. It is "*Ri-Mi-Sha-Ha-Na-Pan.*" It was given by the one Herman Rednick,[36] and we honor him, and we honor this special connection. *Ri-Mi-Sha-Ha-Na-Pan.* When you invoke the energy of Pan, that presence of Nature, the overlord, you might say, (we do not like to use masculine form, however it is how it is expressed), the oversight, the oversoul of life on Earth within the fields of Nature, you invoke my being. I will bring you and your heart a deep connection to all the beings of Nature and that space of expansion and freedom that Nature represents.

We are going to ask you to examine your belief systems and what you were taught around the free expression of all aspects of your physicality; of each chakra. We have given you an exercise to open them. There is an association of each chakra with an emotional component. It is especially the second chakra, which has received an extremely bad rap because of its power and because of the great fear that authority figures have had around free expression of sexuality. If you look at the dolphins, they do not have any moral judgement about who they engage with sexually. They celebrate and experience it in a way that is free, that has no restrictions upon it. It's important to examine this in your own heart, in your own way. The power structures that have controlled your lives and of your ancestors for thousands upon thousands of years have imprinted severe taboos into sexuality. They have distorted the natural truths about this into the so-called gospel truth that so many believe to be true. This is one of the most potent techniques of the great deception of control and domination that has been used to keep you from your freedom all of this time.

You cannot have a New Earth without the freedom of expression of your heart, mind, body and soul. Your higher self and self-authority can be trusted totally to know the right from the not-so-right, for you, and what is good for all. The expression of your physicality can be allowed free play when your higher self and self authority are aligned with your innocence. This is our parting thought for you before we take a break and answer your questions. Thank you.

Pan Q&A

Q. (EM) You mentioned the importance of drinking water, live water. First, tell me what is the right water. How do I get that right water, the alive water?

A. There are many ways. It is probably important for you to do some research and to find something that resonates for you, because in this day and age with technologies, there are so many energies, companies and beings who have been working with structuring water through vortex technology, or through the use of a triskelion,[37] a device made up of three copper spirals. You can make one yourself from a single strand of copper, or purchase one to put underneath your jar of water. The one here, we have been directing him energetically and encouraging the expansion of his vision for providing the use of Shungite for purifying, amplifying and energizing water. There are other devices. There is a company called Vibrant Vital Water,[38] owned by Randy Hatton, a colleague of this one, who works with vortex technology and magnets to structure water. He offers various technologies, some of which incorporate braided copper, based on the work of the late Slim Spurling[39] as well as vortex systems for structuring water. He also sells a simple device which connects two bottles of water you can rotate to structure water.

The best water you can drink is the water that comes from fruit and vegetables. Fresh, organic fruits and vegetables, whether it be juiced or consumed in great quantities, is the most bio-absorbable and beneficial water that you can possibly get. The one Anthony Williams, who wrote *Medical Medium*,[40] advocates drinking celery juice first thing in the morning and in quantity. This will give you that kind of water, the water that will immediately be absorbed into your cells and is harmonious with the water within the body and all life. It also stimulates the secretion of hydrochloric acid in the stomach, so important for digestion.

We can direct you towards a number of sources, however, there are so many technologies on the planet available today, you must find a system that fits your budget and works for you. A device like the triskelion underneath your jar of water or a few nuggets of Elite Shungite placed within the water, and a way to test when it is ready, constitute a few simple methods. Shungite charging plates placed beneath your water container will structure the water. Perfect Science™[41], a company currently in Florida, produces a range of healing, living water formulas. This was originally the work of Ayhan Doyuk in Turkey many years ago. His formula converted toxic substances into organic fertilizer as it purified and structured the water.

We would like to recommend that you do some research on all that is available, and that you find a way to test for yourself through Kinesiology,[42] using a pendulum[42A] or through tuning in to your own higher self to feel which of these many alternatives would be the best for you. You can always connect with this one to get the information that he has access to. There is so much more technology available today, with new devices and systems. So, essentially, we are recommending that you feel into what is best for you, and start simple. It does not require more than you blessing the water. Each time you drink it, put light into it.

If you purchase water that is purified through a filter system or reverse osmosis, add some trace minerals to it. You can use a few sprinklings of Himalayan or Redmond salt. They add some trace minerals as the filtration process removes the naturally occurring ones. You want to drink water that is not dead but has living energy, through structuring or vortexing the water. On some level, it is enough that you put light into the water each time you drink it, each time you use it in your cooking, in your tea, or in your bath. You can also get filtration systems for the whole home which would allow you to have the water that you bathe and shower in purified, and many of these can be found through the Internet.[43]

It is not just the water that you need purified. You also need to have some kind of protection from the EMFs,[44] the harmful frequencies and radiation emitted by devices like your smartphones, Wi-Fi antennae, modems and the base of your portable phones. The radiation that is emitted from this technology has a negative spin or torsion field, which is harmful to biology. One of the benefits of the Shungite is that it reverses the negative spin into a positive spin, and therefore offers a level of protection for life forms. It also helps to counter the negative spin of synthetic clothing, processed foods and products made with artificial ingredients as well as toxins.

Have we covered enough territory here? We trust that you are very good at research, and therefore perhaps you will share with this group what you uncover. It would make life a lot simpler for everyone to know that there is someone who is good at uncovering the true nature of what would be beneficial. Thank you for the question.

Q. (CR) *This is kind of a perfect question for Pan today. I have a sacred mother/ father tree out in the yard that has the ability to communicate and has accepted the responsibility of being kind of in charge of the other trees around here. So, I was curious about some of the tree order, of how they interact with each other and things that aren't told to us. What kind of purposes do the trees have, that are kind of like their secret world?*

A. You have touched a subject that is dear to our hearts, dear to the hearts of me, as Pan and the 12 who are blessing you all. Our presence is here in order to bless your lives and bring you into greater alignment with joy and peace, ease and grace;

"easy-peasy," as they say. The trees represent the interconnectedness of all life. We have some recommendations for reading material[45] for you. The biologist Diana Beresford-Kroeger, an Irishwoman who lives in Canada has written extensively about the interconnectedness of the trees and the vital importance of the Boreal Forest around the planet. It is a ring somewhat like the tonsure, the ring of hair around the head of the monks. It circles the planet and includes the great expanse of forest in Siberia, that sustains the planet and extends across Canada and Russia. This vital energy keeps the planet alive and is being infiltrated and destroyed at an alarming rate.

You already probably understand about the world of mushrooms and mycelia and the way in which they form a giant web of interconnection, communication and life-sustaining energy beneath the soil. In the same way, the trees weave with each other a web of roots, as do the leaves. The canopies of the forests are alive with pheromones, the very, very fine mist-like emanations. They are filled with these very fine vapors, molecules that are emitted through the leaves, extending out and communicating with each other and other life forms. They contain substances that are extremely beneficial medically. Science has only uncovered the very tip of the iceberg of what is available so far. Many of the substances that are produced by trees contain healing compounds.

Trees do communicate with each other. They establish a network and interconnectedness that is not visible, but it is palpable on an energetic level. It is similar to the ways in which there is an interweaving of root systems. If you consider the Aspens, they are not separate trees, but a community of trees that are all interconnected by their root systems. It is as if the trees are the fruits that come from the soil, in the same way that mushrooms grow from the mycelia. Little threads weave a mesh of white that you see when you cut through a side-section of soil. You can see the way in which they form this incredible network.

The trees have this way of connecting life to life. They also communicate vertically, between Heaven and Earth. They bring up the nutrients from the soil, the minerals and the water and the flow of liquid, up towards the canopy, towards the leaves and then send it out as a kind of mist or spray into the atmosphere that connects to the clouds, connects to the heavens, connects to the mountains and the eventual downpour of rain. The hydrological cycle. The roots manufacture substances from the minerals within the earth. They provide food through their fruit, bark, wood and leaves. They provide shade, medicines, energetic and emotional support and communication.

In relation to your friend in your back garden, there is no hierarchy within the system of trees even though there is great respect for old age and for the veterans, for those that have been there a long time and have seen much through that long lifetime. The wisdom encapsulated in the energy of trees can be transmitted through the communication from your heart and your desire to talk with them as you hug the tree. You can feel the messages, and sense that support upon your back as you lean up against the tree, be it grandmother or grandfather tree. And they do often have a masculine or feminine energy that you can sense.

When you approach a tree with respect and love and wish to communicate, from the stillness, the still small voice in the heart; the tree will respond and bring you messages. Silence the mind. The tree will even assist you in your healing process, for you or for others. You will develop the ability to sense an answer or a direction around a particular healing substance, as you cultivate this relationship. The Native people, when they harvest the Osha from the roots of the plant, they ask permission, and they leave a little tobacco or offering for the spirit of the plant.

When you plant seeds to grow food, you can communicate with the spirits of all living things. The one Anastasia from Russia who is featured in the books of the Ringing Cedars[46] series, teaches a most beneficial form of gardening, of food production, by communicating and by connecting the energy of your planting with the energy of the stars and the cosmic radiations that are present in the environment before you sow your seed. She teaches how to mix some seeds with your saliva, so that it is imbued with your own DNA and present them to the heavenly bodies to receive their vibrations. You're then growing food that will benefit yourself and your little ones.

There is much to be learned from books about the secret life of plants, the secret messages from plants, the Boreal Forest and the way in which trees produce substances, communicate and are connected, written by the biologist Diana Beresford-Kroeger. There is also a movie about this woman that is very important and very special, about her work with the trees[47]. There is a novel called The Overstory[48] that was written and inspired because of this woman and contains oodles of information about trees. We post some of these references for you to explore in the end notes.

We honor, respect and encourage all of your desires to communicate with the trees, with the plants, and with the living things, because, not only does it enhance your lives, it enhances the connection and the consciousness of all life. There is great joy in the tree when you approach it in love, with a desire to communicate. For, like Mother Earth, all that is a living being has consciousness even if it is not the same as yours, and rejoices in the communication of heart-to-heart. So, we believe we have answered your question.

Q. (CR) Can I just ask a tiny one more that's related? I have always thought that perhaps trees are visible in the fifth, the same tree that we see in our third dimension is also visible in the fifth dimension and beyond.

- Why not? Why would it not be so?

- Good. OK. I believe that they are, so, that's what I wanted verified.

- Everything is actually aware at a multidimensional level. It is only the consciousness of limitation that stops the ability to penetrate through the veils and be in communication at other levels of dimensionality. It is not right or wrong. It is just the way things are, and one can experience life in the third dimension and find great joy within that without any need to go beyond that, for surely when you leave the physical you will return to being a part of the Whole in a much more expanded way. Peace.

Q. (LB) I have an affinity for labyrinths. My son built a labyrinth on our land about seven years ago, and I was wondering about the healing for the Earth, that energy that's used with that symbol and that space, that sacred space. If you could talk about the labyrinth, how that can assist the Earth and how those in Nature can use the energy of that, and if there's anything that I could contribute more in the space of our labyrinth that I hold very sacred and dear to my heart?

A. It brings us great joy to hear that this is an honoring that you do; that you have a ceremonial space on the Earth that you walk and honor and that you use it as an energetic tool, a portal, a ritual and a place to do ceremony. The labyrinth, the Medicine Water Wheel that this one creates, the sacred Medicine Wheel of the Native people, the circles of stone of the Ancient Ones and of those who are recreating all these structures upon the earth, all carry a vibration. They amplify the vibration of your prayers, of your intentions, of your love and of your blessings for Mother Earth. They open up portals for interdimensional communication. They can open a portal or a wormhole into other dimensions and other locations within the galaxies and within the systems of all life. The energy of the earth beneath you will produce a life-enhancing feeling, that will communicate with you and bring you closer to the hearts of living beings. The birds will respect and feel your energy of ritual and devotion, and they will show up; they will fly over you. This happens frequently, that the Nature kingdom responds and feels this energy of the portal that you are opening.

There are many ways that you can use this energy. For one thing, we highly recommend that you gather others with you to do this at specific times, like the full moon, the equinox or the solstice and that you use a space of contemplation that is inviting you when you are walking into the labyrinth. It is almost as if you are walking into the inner planes, into the womb. It is a very feminine space, and it is very much like going within. One goes into a place where the mind is still, and the heart is opening to receive messages, to receive the stillness. You go into a field where you can receive answers to your questions or responses to those things that you are not clear about or that trouble you in some manner. You will receive clarity.

It is also part of the nature of the labyrinth and the way it is structured, that it incorporates a counter-clockwise motion that then opens up to a clockwise motion, depending on the direction that you use. Normally, the anti- or counter-clockwise motion will gather to you or concentrate the energy of your prayers and intentions or questions, or even the energy of negativity. It will gather it into the center and then the motion of the clockwise energy, moving outwards will reconfigure it into a positive, clockwise, spiral motion which is an alignment like the Christ Consciousness. This is the same spiral we talk of when we consider what we call The Pillar;[49] the energy of connecting above to Heaven and below to Earth. This generates a vertical flow of alignment, which builds and modulates into a clockwise spiral motion, which amplifies the energy of prayer and blessing and radiates it outwards into all space and all time.

So, you can also actively and consciously call to you, not in order to hold, but in order to release, all of those aspects that trouble you or the negative vibrations that may have shown up that are coming forth in order to be transformed. Because, as you gather them in the counter-clockwise motion they will come into the center of the labyrinth, the place where you place the altar, enhancing its vibration with stone or crystal or flower or energy of celebration and honoring. This will then purify all of those negative energies, and send them back out as a healing, as a release and as a return back to the Light. It can be felt and can expand out to bring benevolence into the Universe, even if you are not conscious of how far it can reach. For you are not necessarily aware of the great benevolence that each positive thought or activity creates in the world as it ripples forth.

Know, too, that it is highly beneficial for the energy of labyrinth to be officiated or facilitated by the energy of priestess or goddess or feminine, because it is a very feminine kind of energy. There is a drawing within, a gathering inwards, before the sending out. The expansion, the movement outwards becomes an active force that is very male directed, but the energy of the center of the labyrinth represents that space or energy of the divine feminine. It represents the chalice, the Holy Grail into which you can place all your concerns, your worries, your questions, and all your prayers. The chalice, through the very nature of its receptivity, will purify and create an energetic re-connection, a restoration. This resourcing energy allows the purification to be drunk in a way, to be imbibed, and shared, almost as one would consider the sharing of the bread and the wine in communion. This is not a Christian, religious activity, but it is a ritual, a participatory activity of those who gather together in honoring of Mother Earth and of all life. This practice of ceremony and ritual blesses Nature and is a form of devotion. You could consider it a Pagan practice, but it is a universal one. Are there any further aspects to the question?

- *No, thank you so much.*

- We recommend that you do this practice with other people and invite them to join you, for it amplifies all their energies. It is also your work in the world as priestess, is it not?

- *Thank you.*

Q. *(KM) Pan, I just want to say thank you. There are so many things that you have said that have resonated with me, but my question is actually for Apollo, if possible, is that something I can ask Apollo?*

A. Yes, of course. We talk in terms of "we," so there is no real distinction necessary between the names and the mythologies that we represent as we come forward. Primarily, we are intending to represent for you a vast array of perspectives. We 12 are an alignment with the 12 aspects of the Zodiac and the moons and the signs of the months and all the various ways in which you have used the number 12 to represent a wholeness, so you do not need to be concerned to distinguish. We will answer your question in the highest way we can.

Q. *Well, based on that answer, the question is interesting. I have been recently told that this sun consciousness would like to work with me, and there are many things that resonate with me. So, in a sense, I have learned that my role here at this time is to bring in light and also, I have a huge affinity to working with music. My aim is bringing healing music to people in the hospital. So, my specific question is: Is the Sun consciousness or Apollo actually seeking to work with me, and, if so, how can I learn to work in the future and learn?*

A. Beautiful! Go for it! The energy of Apollo or Helios or the Aten has been with humanity ever since it saw the first sunrise. It is the energy of light. It is the energy of life-giving force. We receive it here upon this planet in the form of Pan or the form of Nature, as the life-giving rays. Apollo represents not just the sun, but also music and also the Archer. He also represents this interesting balance between masculine and feminine through his connection with Artemis, the other hunter or the huntress, because, as we began our series, all energies are essentially not a dichotomy between masculine and feminine, but a blending, a coming together and a way in which there is a higher aspect beyond any polarization between positive and negative, or masculine and feminine. So it is that you have sun and moon as representing this. However, it is the sun that represents the Great Central Sun of your Galaxy. This, in many ways, is also the dark hole at the very center of every Galaxy, the connection to the potential for creation. So, always be aware that there is a unified field behind all polarity, be it the positive and negative aspect or masculine and feminine or light and dark, that truly transcends any kind of polarization or limitation.

Having said all that, the energy of light is the greatest healing energy, for it is love. The vibration of love is transmitted through the frequency of motion that you call light. You cannot see light except in contrast to that which is not-light. However, you can feel light as a consciousness, as a healing energy, a life-giving energy and also as a protection energy. This is why it is so vital at this time that you embody light, that you repeat the mantra of the Ones with No Names, "I am Light and Light I shall remain. There is nothing but Light, and there is no time." Consider that light is the energy you are made of, that everything is made of. When you focus it, it forms around you this protective column or protective sphere or protective healing energy that you can direct like the golden glow of the sun's radiance. You can feel it within your own heart as a radiation from within you, and you are, in fact all of you, being asked to represent and even to experience, that you are this radiance of Love, of Light that comes from your very central sun that is within you. It is within your heart and is, as we have said, a universe unto itself.

When you consider the vastness of the universe that you see outside of you, you must understand that within you have access to the same vastness of a universe within you. All the Beings of Light that surround you, and all the great Beings that have ever been, all the angels and collective energies dwell within you inasmuch as they dwell outside of you. Thoth or Hermes, the original energy of the Hermetic philosophy, teaches: "As above, so below, as within, so without." We're taking a long road across the heavens to bring you your answer, just as in the old days the chariots would carry the sun upon their back from rising to setting and would make the course through the dark night until they rose again to represent the fullness of the cycles.

So, love, light, gold, god, goddess, sun, all are representing the energy that your heart wishes to express within your ministry, as you find yourself in situations where you can bring a smile, and can touch a heart. Situations where you can bring a level of comfort, where you can crack open a heart and have them laugh in spite of their tears or their sorrows or their impending death. Have them recognize the life force that is there and the continuity, for as the sun goes down in a blaze of color, so it rises in a different blaze of color from a different direction. And so, these souls are eternal, and as they leave, they will come again; and as they embrace the light within their own heart, essentially, they can be healed before they leave.

So, the music that you bring is vital for penetrating beyond the mind's limitations and the rigid structures that have been placed around it, and the armor around the heart to keep them safe. For music has a way of touching the very soul and opening those windows and doorways to a response of life force energy that is joyous and that is connected to the face of Union that we call God or Goddess or All That Is. There is, within music, the ability to carry them across the waters, to carry them into the spheres and dominions, into those vibrations and dimensions beyond the mere concerns of the physical. For they are in a place within these institutions where they have very little control and feel diminished because they are at the mercy of procedures and technology and authority. Music is a common denominator that cuts through to the very heart of love, of emotion and caring.

We know that we have answered your question. There is a connection of this one with the music of the harp and its use within the hospice and the music within the hospital. However, whatever expression works for you is a calling that is extremely elevated and highly, highly honored and regarded in all the worlds, in all the realms and within the hearts of all the angels and guides that work with you and surround you, and all of us at this time. You are feeling this Presence, are you not?

- *Very much so.*

- Do you have any further aspects of this question?

- *No, thank you very much.*

Q. (NB) *You had said earlier that when we were little, we were not afraid to follow our heart and if we didn't like anybody, we weren't afraid to say. We didn't have to pretend. As an adult, what do you recommend without hurting somebody's feelings? How do we stay in the world without judging, but yet being protective for yourself?*

A. Very good question. We were talking somewhat tongue in cheek as you understand, because, as an adult, you have been acculturated to different ways of being than the child has. And you have certain levels of responsibility towards social behavior and concern or consideration for the soul journey of another. So, there is a directive to understand that non-judgment, as you said, is the foundation for how you find the way to say "No, thank you" or a way of saying "It is time for us to part" in a manner that does not come from anger or judgment.

It is vital, as a first step, to honor yourself by setting the kinds of boundaries that are necessary, so you do not have to constantly ward off vampire energy or allow others to impose their will, their needs, or their overbearing nature upon you. Be clear what your boundaries are, and lay them out energetically, then perhaps in writing. Where it is necessary, have clearly written agreements, so that one will not come back and say "I thought we said this" or "I seem to remember that we agreed upon that," because this is not to your highest benefit, nor to anyone else's.

And it's important to surround yourself with that protective sphere of light every day and remember that it's there. Not out of fear, or separation consciousness. Consider that you do so out of the joy of being surrounded within a sphere of golden light that is filled with love and guidance and your team of angels. So, as you approach the subject, perhaps in the same way that Shungite does, by taking a negative torsion field[50] and reversing it into a positive one. You then approach the subject of "I don't like you" by saying, "Thank you very much, but at this time I do not feel drawn to going in that direction."

You find a way to use tact and compassion with those who are not necessarily able to recognize what boundaries represent. They need to somehow be told firmly that there is a "No" here. For, when it is a "Yes," you can do so in a different vibration. But when there is a "No," it needs to be firm. It needs to be backed by love and compassion and a sense of self-authority, so you are not giving yourself away. You are not allowing yourself to be anyone's doormat. You are not kowtowing to somebody else's authority, but you nod knowingly, so that they feel or think that their tirade or their lecture is being received.

It may also be advantageous, that you know how to be invisible. You know how to avoid setting somebody up for a confrontation, when you are not in a place of love, and forget to take a breath before you speak or act. Therefore, you learn to take that breath and consider what might be the best way to approach relating to somebody from the highest possible energy. First, by putting that sphere of light or column around you and then, if you are able, by encompassing them with their own sphere of light. You then allow those two to merge. This is one of the exercises of either John Henry or William Marshal51 or The Ones with No Names, and it does require of you to maintain your own field at the same time as allowing the other, so-called "other" to have their own field. You access them at the soul level first, where those two fields can merge and there is the possibility of a transcendental experience, of moving beyond dissention or separation. Does that make sense?

- *Yes, thank you so much.*

Closing Meditation

So, let's put our right hand on our hearts and our left hand on our right. Let us feel each other. Let us feel that energy of being one tree woven together as one trunk made up of many strands and that we are connecting all of our roots into the Mother Earth, into that beautiful space of connection with all life that Pan represents. We honor and send our roots down together into Mother Earth, deep into her very core, and we allow ourselves to feel this connection between each of us and Mother Earth. The connection of her roots with our roots. We allow this energy of nurturance to spiral its way up to our crown, up through this canopy of interconnectedness that we represent, even through the fields of the mind, through the fields of logistics, of logic, of thinking. It is possible to think pure and beautiful thoughts, and they will be as the fragrance of that which is given as the perfume of the canopy of the trees that weave together to form a oneness with all of life. And so, as we feel this interconnectedness with each other and with the Earth and with all life, we allow everything to settle back into the breath and into that beautiful space of stillness.

Know, that we are always there to answer your questions, that this one is always ready and willing for you to call upon him. We hope you will be able to have a support buddy to communicate with, for the joy of it; to be able to share your concerns, your feelings and your wisdom with each other. And if you feel there is a resonance, it will be a beautiful thing. If there is not a resonance, then you can move to someone else, without judgement. And so, we leave you with our blessings, with our light, our love surrounding you always, within your heart and around you. Know that you are loved. Know that you are here to fulfill your purpose and that you are here to help create structures upon this planet that will help the New Earth to manifest and blossom within your time, within your life and within your experience. For you are indeed blessed beyond measure. Aho!

Voice Five
John Henry

13th September 2020

Preamble (This message was received during journaling (automatic writing) on 9/11, the Friday morning before the Sunday session and was intended to be shared prior to the main message.)

"Belief is the greatest factor in creating reality. This is the power of the mystery school. This is the secret teaching of the ages. It is so simple. There are components in this picture that also relate to the interconnectedness of everything, of all life, of thoughts as energy to travel or transmit their energy across vast amounts of space and through great eons of time. So, healing can be miraculous, spontaneous, instantaneous. The mind is more than the brain or the individual thinking process. It is the container for consciousness. The unlimited potentiality that is held in the acorn to become a mighty oak is a great mystery. Within the quantum reality, a thought has wings, and not only can fly and travel, but can heal or harm. On the so-called other end of the journey, a thought can be accepted or rejected and can either be effective or ineffective. A thought sent with intention has great power but, as with hypnosis, there is a need to access the internal process of belief to affect results. This is also the power of words spoken to the cells. The biology is also a container for the beliefs because it has been programmed and operates beneath the level of the conscious awareness. This is why affirmation said in a state of Alpha or Theta, in a meditative state, has the accumulative effect on the entire being to shift the old restrictive patterns held in the biology or in the person's mind from negative to positive., Shungite, if held or in one's presence, is constantly working to transform negative energy into positive.

These principles are powerful factors in the efficacy of HeartThread® to create new patterns and realities by replacing the old inner consciousness structures with new and more beneficial ones. This little lecture or presentation is given to you to share. It is the gist of our teachings and the way in which John Henry's love has guided you and been at your side behind and before you, guiding you through all the steps you have experienced over the last many years of your life"

Let's go into the heart space together. Let's put our right hand on our heart and our left hand on our right. Let's begin to feel that connection with each other as we allow the stillness to pour in through our crown, feel our feet connect with Mother Earth and feel that column of light connecting us from Heaven to Earth and Earth to Heaven, our hearts in the very center. With every breath, we allow ourselves to become stiller. With every out breath we allow everything to dissolve in that place of stillness, as we feel Mother Earth beneath us, and experience our groundedness, the sense of being rooted in Mother Earth. It allows us to settle in our body. It allows us to feel that we are not just a mind or thought or an emotion, but that we are grounded in the very form that we have been given and chosen for this journey, for the experience of this lifetime. We also are able to connect through this column of light to that space of Source above us, within us, that connection with the spark of Divine Fire that animated this body and allowed our consciousness to become part of the form and the collective that we each are.

We also are connecting with all the angels and guides that are surrounding us and watching over us, and with our brothers and sisters in the cosmic and galactic worlds. They surround this planet and watch over us with great love and great tenderness. All the Realms of Light are present with us as we connect our hearts together through these beautiful threads of gold. We are weaving a fabric that reaches out from our very centers to connect with all our loved ones, our friends, our neighbors, those we have held in our hearts, whether they be still living or not. We are sending this vibration of weave out into All Space and All Time, across this planet, into all worlds and all universes. It brings blessing and amplifies this light that we are, through a column of light. The column expands to become a sphere of protection around us all, so that only the highest and purest of vibrations are allowed to be in this space together with us.

It is such a joy and pleasure to be with you. Many of you already know me as John Henry, the one who brought HeartThread® through, through the one Flo Aeveia. It has always been my intention and delight to assist you to find a way to have ease and grace in your life. We teach that which we call self-authority. We teach it, especially in these times, where you are challenged by the authorities that are bombarding you with lies and deception. In order for you to be able to make sense of this bombardment, it becomes crucial for you to understand that, at the very core of what we have said in our little preamble, your belief system creates your reality. It is necessary to tear apart all of your assumptions, all the assumptions that come from your ancestors, parenting, colleagues, and your education. All these patterns are right now in great need of scrutiny, assessment, and perhaps many of them are ready to be overthrown. As you shift your beliefs and pay attention to the words you use which reflect those beliefs, and to the thoughts and feelings you have, you begin to create for yourself a life that begins with a new slate, with a brand new, fresh page or journal in which to write your story instead of the old story.

The old story can go on a shelf somewhere, in case you need to reference it one day when you write your biography or some fascinating novel that needs to draw on some of those incidents that you thought were so important. But you have decided now you are ready and willing to let go of it. It is interesting to see how, on national and global and cultural levels, many of the assumptions that have been regarded as 'the Truth' are actually extremely erroneous and have been fabricated. They have been orchestrated as a means of formulating identities that are in no way based on fact or truth, and in fact, were deliberately engineered somewhat recently in your history or herstory.

The very nature of the way in which you think of your divinity, of that energy that we call "God," as having a male aspect, has been programmed into you by thousands of years of conditioning. "Goddesses" were re-defined as 'consorts,' wives or daughters of these male deities, and were almost always relegated to a subsidiary role, a supporting role for the male energy. As we have said before, if you consider what was written in the beginning of the Old Testament, that "man" was created (not woman, but man) in the image of God, the truth is that "God" was created in the image of "man," (not woman!). In fact, the Goddess was revered for thousands upon thousands of years as the creator of life and the supreme deity. Women had the dominant role in society. They were the originators of writing, administration, culture, justice, agriculture and the management of money, and oversaw many of the foundations of civilization.

It is important to recognize this, because we are going to be working with the energy of heart. It is important, as much as you can, to continually assess, examine, explore and question every single assumption you have. The world today, even as its many structures, foundations and systems are disintegrating, is based upon a narrative that has been accepted by almost every single one of you as 'Reality,' whereas, in fact, it is a distortion. So, in the very imagining of what a New Earth might look like, it becomes quite a challenge to do so outside of the box of all the constructs, scaffolding and infrastructures that you are so conversant with.

You go to the bank to deposit your money, you use your credit cards, and you have various kinds of exchanges that have replaced the old barter systems. You have structures of how to do everything. Even this very technology that we are using to communicate with you, was never even in existence until recently. The concept that one could walk down the street with your hands in your pocket and a funny little thing in your ear, and be having a conversation with somebody 1,000 miles away had not even appeared in the consciousness perhaps 50 years ago or even less. It is important to realize how things could change at the drop of a hat and how important it is for you to consider everything, to examine it and look at it with a fine-tooth comb. Look at it under the microscope and see what is of value for the new energy of cooperation, non-judgment and non-separation, and what needs to be cast aside and relegated to the scrap pile as no longer relevant and certainly as not sustainable. For nothing that is unsustainable will be able to continue into a New Earth experience.

We have talked about the freewill experiment. We have shared the fact that it is coming to an end now with this epoch and is being replaced by the "free heart experience." Because your collective, your civilization and much of its "history" or "herstory" has been associated with the energy of the mind, with thinking, with ideas, constructs and technologies. Even the ancient technologies of building structures with sound and movement and with the force of the energy of magic, your financial system, structures for the delivery of food substances and all these sorts of things, all these systems are based on the performance of the mind, of thought. They access what you might call the magic structure of the universe, the sacred geometry, and the way in which everything is interconnected, but through a linear perspective. You see through the linear perspective of your scientific nature and vision, a perspective that affects your ways of thinking, writing, reading, or communicating, and it affects how you see everything. You see with a linear perception of time and space.

However, juxtaposed with that, is the 'New Science' that is a Quantum reality, in which it is possible to be in more than one place at the same time (certainly if you are an atom or molecule) and to be able to connect with a vibration or consciousness that is thousands of miles away through an instantaneous thought or feeling. It is now important and vital that the energy of the future be based upon a shift in consciousness that revolves around the heart and the field of the quantum understanding, the quantum consciousness that is the purview, the domain of the heart. This is because within the heart is access to all knowledge, and all wisdom, even to the Akashic Records[52] where every single thought, every single fall of a sparrow that has ever happened throughout time and space is recorded and stored. It is accessible through the heart, and in many ways this is the promise of the future, that, as you live more and more from your heart, you have instant access to truth. You experience it viscerally, in your body, in your heart and in your emotions. It is the etheric sense of connectedness that is the domain of the heart. For the language of the heart is the language of connection, in fact, of interconnection.

The holograph is a representational way of seeing everything, through a 3-dimensional perspective, of visualizing or understanding this interconnection of all things. So too, is the world of fractals[53]. These images and ways of seeing reality are not part of your normal experience. This is especially so when you live within the linear framework of having to get somewhere on time, and you feel you have to rush. Whereas, when you take that breath and recognize you will be there in the perfect moment, you shift your consciousness into a different kind of reality that is aligned much more with the heart. You become more and more conversant with the ways in which the heart operates within your consciousness and within the interconnectedness. Thus, when you have a feeling that Auntie May is about to call you, and there she is on your screen, these kinds of things become second nature to your life, and you begin to live your life with the ease and grace we were talking of. You understand that miracle, magic, abundance, a sense of ease, peace and stillness can always be there for you in every moment no matter what is going on.

Accessing the heart is the way to go to that space. It is right there within your very center. All it requires is to put your right hand on your heart and your left hand on your right. As you take a deep breath, you shift the location of your consciousness from the head, from the mind, to the heart, and that breath shifts everything. You can let go of that burden that is sitting on your shoulders that you have carried ever since you were a little pipsqueak. Ever since it was laid upon you, that you were responsible for your parents and all their trials and tribulations, and you had to carry it throughout your life. What a burden to place upon your children! Or for your ancestors to require of you to perform rituals of things that are not to the benefit of anyone because it has been told that they must do so! There are many, many aspects of your reality that are going to come up for scrutiny, because, at this time especially, the challenges that arise, be they family or financial or health or relationship, are going to present to you the demons that you are now getting ready to meet face to face as the Spiritual Warrior. You are the Warriors of the Heart, not the "worriers" of concern.

In fact, we have stated this, and we will write this out for you at another time* (See below, after closing meditation) but once upon a time it was shared by me that the greatest thing I would like you to eliminate from your belief systems and from your thought process, is worry, the energy of concern. If there's anything that we could say it is important to eliminate, it is worry. It is placing your energy on areas that you do not wish to experience, which is another way of saying worry or fear. If your energy is focused on the things you do not want to have in your life, you are creating them through that focus. It is important to let go of that kind of energy and replace it with only benevolence, with only positive thinking. This can be done through the process of affirmation, of being in a state of meditation, in Alpha or Theta brain rhythms. When you are in a state of heightened receptivity, you say to yourself aloud statements of what you do want, framed positively, and do not refer to anything you do not want, not even to negate them.

This can also be done through HeartThread®, where you are replacing the old stories, patterns and negative imprints with new, alternative thinking that supports benevolence and nurturing and is conducive to your thriving. It is important to understand the nature of the ways in which you constantly are programming yourself. It is said that there are something like, perhaps, 60,000 thoughts that run through a person's mind in a day and that something like 90 or more percent are negative. The programming to think negatively has been imprinted in you through generations and generations of indoctrination, throughout all of your lifetimes.

It is also so with this life. Most of these imprints are imbued into your system from a very early age. Even before you came out into the world, with your first breath, you were experiencing the thought forms and the emotions of your mother when you were in the womb, and from your father and your siblings and others around you. These negative beliefs were also imprinted into the consciousness structure you inherited later on, when you began to access consciousness in a more aware way. For the first 7 years, almost every single belief that you have, was programmed into you as a sponge that had no ability to discern. Your critical thinking only began to develop after your 7th year.

In some ways, it seems like you are almost fighting a losing battle; but because you are Warriors of Spirit, because you are the Ambassadors of the Heart, you have agreed, whether through your contracts or through your presence here, you have agreed to carry the light within the surrounding darkness. You have agreed to fight your demons within you and, where possible, without. You are, and you have agreed to become, a one who carries the sword of truth and is willing to use it as a Warrior of the Heart in a loving and compassionate and non-judgmental way.

The foundation of almost every single negative thought is separation consciousness, polarity thinking. It is a projection of a 'me-versus-them,' 'us-vsthem' mentality. It's the judgment of an 'other'. The work you are here to do is the letting go of these ways of seeing things, through the eyes of duality, of separation. It requires recognizing that oneness may be a truth for you in your mind, but it has not percolated its way into your sub-conscious awareness. It is necessary to reprogram your sub-conscious mind, so you move beyond the perception of reality as based on separation. Once you transcend the dualistic ways of seeing and thinking, you recognize that beneath the apparent conscious surface, everything is interconnected.

The understandings that are derived from Quantum physics have utilized scalar[54] waves and Tesla type inventions to create technologies which can achieve the most remarkable results. Many of these technologies have been with you for eons, for many years. However, from the earliest days of the 20s and 50s of this century, or the previous one, they were used in secret, not for the benefit of the people. Brilliant inventors were eliminated and their discoveries usurped. In many cases, evidence of these inventions was destroyed because it posed a threat to the financial interests of those in power who control the resources and technologies. Much of this is available to you today because it has become commercialized, feeding the bottom line, the mighty dollar or yen, or whatever.

We would like to focus on what it requires of you to live with your heart open. What does it take to live and move into the heart from the head? Essentially, all the words are nice, and they're all nice admonishments, and they're all great ideas. But if they remain in the mind, in the head, they do not shift your reality. So, it is important to recognize that the shift of focus, of location, is a major first step of going to the heart by putting your hands, whether it is actual or in your imagination, upon your heart. By shifting your focus and attention to your heart, you immediately invoke a space of connection with the energy of your higher self and the wisdom that dwells within your heart. There is an innate connection between all humans that we call the

HeartThread®, and when you go into the heart, you have that ability to connect with others. You also can do it through the connection with the Soul Seed just below your heart, in that space where the ribs come together, there behind the xyphoid process. When you go into the heart, you can communicate with the soul of somebody with whom you are having difficulty.

The best way to access the heart is to focus there with a deep breath. Please join me now in taking a deep breath, in......., and out.......... You will immediately notice that the whole system relaxes. Somehow, a little bit of that stress, of that weight on the shoulders, tension, relaxes. There's an influx of stillness. There is also an experience of your diaphragm moving outwards and back in, of your chest rising, a sensation of your physical body, so that, through the focus on the breath, you are connected with your physical form. When you combine this with connecting to Mother Earth, through your feet or seat, you are becoming fully present.

In order to be in the heart, you must be in your body because the heart is the main monitor of all the processes of your body. Your heart has more connecting points and has control of more hormones and more neural pathways within your system than the brain does. The heart and the brain, however, function together as partners with the body. Together with the emotions, the mind and the soul, these aspects are actually one interconnected whole. So when you access that quantum field of your heart, whether it be through the breath, a shift in focus, or perhaps through a mantra, there is a connection made with the divine aspect of who you are, with your spirit or essence. A mantra is a repetitive use of word, phrase or image that immediately takes you to your heart. It will be your special alignment, depending on your culture or spiritual upbringing, that creates that stilling of the mind and connection with a higher resonance. You can use a chant or an image of a deity or a sacred word, aloud or in your mind, but it serves to bring you back to the breath, and thereby, the heart.

There are many ways for you to focus on going into the heart. One beautiful way is to think of something in your memory that brought you great joy and a great sense of warmth within, where your heart felt open, soft and vulnerable. Perhaps you felt a golden glow around an experience or person, an exchange or communication, or a great love for them. When you think of this, your heart opens. Your mind goes into a kind of neutral space of connecting with the beautiful gold we share with you at the beginning, which we pour into your crown and surround you with. This is a reflection of the energy, blessing and love of the many guides and Holy Beings that surround you (and are surrounding us right now). We are part of your presence. We dwell within your heart. You have become used to externalizing everything and putting it outside of yourself, whereas, in fact, everything is within, and the heart energy is an energy of 'within.' So, as you take that breath, as you say that mantra, your mind goes quiet and the heart opens and then, perhaps, you can let go of some of the armor or the walls you have placed around yourself to keep you safe.

The mask you feel you must wear to be safe from somebody else out there, cannot keep you safe. It is in the heart that your safety lies, for within the heart is your connection to God/Goddess, the Divine, to Spirit. This is the space of that golden energy of internal connection with your higher self. Your higher self does not judge your so-called 'lower self,' for the self that you regard as your personality is your servant. That being that you think you are, is there in order to keep you safe. It really has your best interest at heart, and when you corral it into service for your highest intentions, it is a great asset. So, love yourself, all aspects of yourself, because this is the transformation from thinking of yourself as unworthy or un-beautiful, or whatever it is that you judge yourself to be.

None of these perceptions are the truth of who you are. All the guilt and shame that has been placed upon you, is an imposition upon you. It is as if they stamped you with these imprints, and you allowed them to penetrate into yourself and accepted them as yours. But that innocent, pure child does not have to accept them and is able, now, to let go of them. You are ready to release the past, the story, the pain, the betrayals, all the judgments of peers, and of everybody else; because you were too this or too that, or you came from the wrong religion or the wrong side of the tracks, or you are male or female, or you are whatever. You allow it all to go up in a balloon to the far horizon and disappear. And you consider from your heart, "Who is it that I can forgive now because they acted from their woundedness, because what they did to me, they did through contract with me in the Swing Between Worlds? And they played their part admirably, just as I play mine in other peoples' lives, just as I agreed to trigger you, and you agreed to trigger me or to abuse me;" or whatever it may be. These stories are not part of the New Earth, and it is necessary in your examination of all your illusions, of all your concepts and assumptions, it is necessary to let go of everything in order to be fully present in the heart.

Those of you who are HeartThread® practitioners, it is time to take up that staff again and use it, whether it be for yourself or your friends and family or others. It is why we are insisting you communicate with each other now so that you can share, so that you can tell people what you're feeling or what your breakthrough was. So do a HeartThread® exchange session with someone, just to let go of some of that extra layer of stress that you have accumulated through the craziness of everything around you. For the energy of the heart and HeartThread®, or similar modality, is what is needed now to be Ambassadors of the Heart. We are asking you to join us as the Army of the Heart.

Know that I, John Henry am always with you. My job is to help you find that space within your heart to become free; to have ease and grace, beauty, love and abundance in every moment of your life that never ends. This is my mission. This is why I will be with you wherever it is that you call upon me. And I will share with you. I will feed you. I will answer you and I will certainly be there when you are in a

HeartThread® session with someone to give you the words to say as you empty out and become a vessel for healing for others, as well as for yourself. This one is a good resource, for HeartThread® is his passion, and it is our intention to revive and expand this practice on a much larger scale.

One more thing. We would like to urge you, and we use that word knowingly, we would like to urge you, when you take that breath, to consider letting go of urgency, that sense of rush, that feeling of pressure, that you have to comply. That you have to face a deadline, and if you, for some reason, miss it, the whole world will end and somebody will not like you. The very need for approval, the very sense of having to rush to get somewhere, all these things. There is of course a way to deal with them so that you are always on time and do not leave things to the last minute. And things come up. It is understood. However, it is the energy of constant rushing and constant urgency and the constant sense of obligation, of performance. It controls your thinking. You get the idea. When you take that breath, when in the midst of this rising of your shoulders and the tension and the stress and "Oh my God, what's going to happen to me if I don't arrive at…, or I don't get the job done, or I don't pay the piper?" That deep breath will allow you to relax and move back into what we have called 'the quantum flow of the heart's way of being' instead of the mind and the conditioning.

Know how much we love you, how much we as a group are there with you. We are supporting you. We're cheering you on, we are not ever judging you. We are loving you so much. You have us always at your beck and call. We are surrounding you with protection, love and guidance. Call on us. We are not outside of you. And I especially, John Henry, I want to thank you for this connection, this commitment that you have made to be a part of this group and part of the willingness to examine everything and to begin to consider what the structures you bring forth into the world might be, and how you may collaborate and cooperate with others in expanding these structures. A friend of this one shared that there might be 15 or 50 different groups around the world all striving to end hunger, all separated. Why don't they all come together and be so much more effective? So, we would like you to consider this. It is important that you share some of the benevolent things going on in your world.

Another friend of this one, the Israeli who is a major activist, has talked about those on the front lines waving their banners and fighting for freedom and justice. The heart is the frontline. You must support those who are doing what you cannot do, whether it be through your prayers or through your dollars or through intentions, or just through a word of congratulations or a word of thankfulness for those who are working behind the scenes and in front of the scenes to change the world, because you have this opportunity now. So, we will leave you with this sense of a bigger picture and also of that little picture, of that place of your own heart which is really the access to the greatest picture of all, the picture of Love; of being Light and embodying it.

You, embodying Love and Light. And you understand and know. You do not need definitions for what this is, because your heart knows the Truth. We love you. Aho!

The Energy of Rush

The energy of rush and urgency, the accompanying energy of worry, the energy of fear and all the great threats to peace that keep people stuck outside of their hearts, prevent them from receiving the grace and blessings of their guidance and angelic helpers. So, it is within a sense of overwhelm, that it is important to bring the focus back to a deep breath, the sensations of the body, the vertical connection with Mother Earth as grounding, and the Heavens above as a source of inspiration, and then the heart in the center, in the within. When you open your ceremonies and invoke the four directions, you always add the above and the below and then the within. This is a healing practice, for it allows you to have a sense of place in the universe. The focus on the hands upon the heart creates a shift of location from the head to the heart. In this manner you are able to release doubt and judgment and the mind chatter that is so incessant.

It is reported that a human thinks, perhaps 60,000 thoughts a day and most of them, perhaps 90% plus are negative. We do not have the exact figures, but it is so important to watch, to monitor and change the patterns of thoughts, the words you use and the belief systems. Everything we teach, and all the realizations we direct towards those on the path to higher consciousness, are encapsulated in this recognition. Recognize the need to become aware of your thoughts, your body and the energy of fear, worry and urgency that accompany your day, and then take that breath. For the breath is your connection to Source. It is that place where you are connected to life in the physical world. As you take a breath, you become focused on the movement of your lungs, your diaphragm, the chest, and there is an ability to reset the program, just like that, because you can. We leave you today with this realization.

John Henry Q&A

Q. (MS) *Very interesting that John Henry spoke of letting go, taking a breath. You re-read a passage just now about that. It's sort of a question for John Henry, why does this message keep coming through? For me, it's a very important message personally. I was born into a metal year, which is represented by lung and large intestine for those who don't know that specific aspect, so, both my month and my year are metal. We are currently in a metal season, (autumn is considered metal or lung) and we are in a metal year (it happens to be the metal rat year), so all this metal keeps coming through in my life. And I have had lung issues in my life, asthma; I've had some pneumonia when I was younger. So, this is really a very prevalent message for me to really look at this lung, breathing, letting go, because the large intestine is part of the letting go. Lung and large intestine are connected, one is breathing in, one is letting go, and so I'm trying to get the deeper message. It's getting hit over my head in so many ways. I'm trying to really go in and figure out what the answer is, and maybe your assertion just now that we're trying to reset the program by just connecting to the heart, maybe that's part of the answer, but I wonder if there was anything more that you could add or John Henry can add to this.*

A. Thank you. So, while you were talking, we would like to know if you have issues with skin?

- *I do, yeah. That's also related to lung.*

- Exactly, so it feels like what is underlying much of your experience is that it is true that the message of going into the heart is being bombarded at you. It feels that underneath of everything there is a deep sense of grief, of pain, of loss. Perhaps much of it is a replication in this life of patterns that have been part of your previous, past or parallel lives that you are now clearing out for yourself, but also for your ancestors, your family, and your lineage, and much of it is associated with a deep sense of grief. It is very difficult in this culture for a male to completely allow grief to come to the surface. It feels like this is, in some ways, your work and you probably, as we feel already, are in the midst of becoming or have been a leader and a supporter for men on their journey to be in a place where it is safe to be vulnerable, to express fear, to express grief, and especially, to express anger. We are not as conversant as you are with the five elements of the Chinese system, but the energy of anger has a very strong association with the hardness of metal. In fact, it is used and has been used over the eons as the tool for violence, harm, and war, and so it has created deep suffering and great grief in the world. So it is now being asked to be rectified, to be changed and at some deep level, to be forgiven.

Again, we would remind you of the contracts that each one makes before and when they incarnate, to become a figure, to work with your soul direction, to heal karma[55], but also to become a counterpoint, or a trigger for others and to allow others to trigger you in order to bring up what needs to be resolved, forgiven, and healed. For it is now the time, and it is already accomplished, the very awareness that you are, as John Henry says, as I say, "you can do it, because you can, just like that." It requires a shift in perspective, in consciousness, to recognize that all these symptoms, and all these directions are there for you to move through this particular threshold because you are ready. And by the going into your heart and taking that breath and allowing your lungs to fill with that golden light of God's Love and Essence, allowing us to be around you and within you; allowing every cell to be transformed, just like that, in the moment, taking time out of the equation. As the saying goes, "I am Light and Light I shall remain. There is nothing but Light, and there is no Time."

The quantum field exists outside of time and space. And it is your prerogative, as a spiritual warrior who knows how to command, to issue a directive from your intention, to release any pattern that is associated with old grief, and the layers of rage. The anger sits on top of the grief, often. You will be able to shift all of this, just like that. Perhaps you need to yell and scream and find a punch bag or whatever it is, to access the pain, or perhaps, it is right there at the tip of your heart, at the tip of that heart's tongue. You are now ready to clear out ancestral pain, as well as your own personal pain, and in many ways, this is the expression of heart, lung, and breath energy, of moving beyond figuring out. Because figuring out can go on forever, and it is an activity of the mind that is not in alignment with the heart. So, when you focus on the heart and allow, especially the receptivity of the soft feminine aspect of yourself, you will be able, and you are ready, to let go of all these symptoms. Instead, as you move through this year of metal, you will begin to focus on other directions that will be so much more peaceful and supportive to you. It is just a phase. Allow it to be just a phase that is part of an old story, very old, and you are now in charge of releasing it. Does that make sense?

- *Totally, yes, you are right, right on. I mean, it's something I felt, especially regarding ancestral grief. I also have a Jewish upbringing, you know, so I think there is something related to that as well.*

-Then you carry a good dose of guilt and shame. Welcome to the tribe. Yes, we are clearing, we are all together clearing these ancestral patterns, and it's vital work. And it can all be done in the silence of the heart, in the silence of your home. Thank you so much for that question.

- *Thank you.*

Q. (MSG) Oh my gosh, I related so much to what MS was asking and the response. I have had similar patterns in my life and so that was very helpful. Thank you. I feel like I've worked through a lot of the lung and large intestine, and now the skin is what it is. I also have heavy metals in my body, mercury and lead that I'm trying to unload, but I do feel the ancestral piece very strongly. Anyhow, I just wanted to name that, but my question is: Early on in the sharing, John Henry talked about clearing out all the old stories of your life and having a clean slate, telling your new story and putting those old ones away somewhere. And I went, "Oh dear, I'm in the process of writing a memoir. Okay, but I do believe that how I'm writing it, is from the perspective of later in life, seeing the meaningful events and what the lessons were and what beautiful thread was woven through my life to unfold my purpose," and so, I hope I am telling the new story. This is a similar guidance to what I got from the Kogi shaman and I just want to be careful with that, that I don't end up dragging in old things in the wrong way, you know, as I write this, because it's a lot of energy to go and focus, to go into writing a memoir, so any guidance that you or John Henry have around this will be helpful.

A. Yes, thank you for your affirmation, and your comments in relation to your sharing. We are encouraging you all to share with each other, to connect with each other and communicate, so you have the ability to exchange your personal stories with even just one person. Just so you can have a witness. And so, in writing your story and your memoirs, it is important to recognize that you are not dredging up the past in order to angst about it, but you are indeed looking back at those places that want to be released, acknowledged and recognized. You are then able to distance yourself from them so they no longer have power. So, when we refer to putting your story on the shelf in order to write your memoirs, in many ways, this is the purpose of being able to let go of the story. Put it on a shelf instead of burn it, because it has a value for yourself, for your ancestors. It is a therapeutic device to write your story, and it is important that you write, all of you, write what comes up for you. Write, draw, dance, paint, sing about what is being brought forward for you as an expression of healing, as an expression of a shift of consciousness, because there is always going to be someone who could benefit from it.

The process of putting things on paper is a very powerful way to release it, because the very writing of it takes it out of the realm of mythology, and creates a new myth. It's taking your own personal her-story and converting it into a myth that's just a story, that belongs to a past, to an ancestry, to a way of seeing the universe in a way that the mind needed in order to make sense of it. But it no longer has reality in terms of how you live in the present and in the world of today, and how you move forward. So, there is a great learning experience from writing your memoirs. Have we addressed all aspects of your question?

- I think so. I believe I'm writing it from that place of meaningfulness to help others see that what they go through, the trials and tribulations, actually, have beauty within

them and truth if you're able to listen from that place. So, yeah, it's a sorting process and to show it from the place of "there's meaning," even if, when at the moment we might not see it in our life, it takes the future to look back and reflect and see that we've been guided and helped, and synchronicities have been happening that now makes sense.

- Beautiful, beautiful, yes. We wish to affirm what you are saying and also, we want to bring in the aspect of water. You are so drawn to water, and that is an expression of the heart and the lungs, the way in which water flows, the way in which it has movement. But it is also the source of life. It is the carrier of consciousness. We also want to accentuate the fact that you are hosting in a room at a convergence; you are asking people to share their stories, to share stories of water, and fire, and other elements. There is a similar process, a catharsis in the telling and sharing of a story, and connecting it to the elements and the field of the heart, to sadness, the past, and the ancestors. Storytelling around the campfires impressed and impressioned the young ones, when they heard them, and the tribes and the family. This is what created the mythologies, the religions, and gave rise to the practices, rituals, and ceremonies. So, your work is very important in all the aspects of it for yourself personally, but also for the collective and also as a path. Storytelling, writing, and the expression of the emotions. As they get healed, it becomes a way of healing the ancestral patterns and creating a movement towards structures for the New Earth. Does that make sense?

- *Very much. Thanks, thank you so much. Yes, it's helpful, very helpful to see it that way. Thank you.*

Q. (CR) Discuss how we can help to change our ancestors on the other side in this life, the stories are not inert.

A. It is important, when you go into meditation and do your practice, that you connect in with the heart, fill yourself with light, and send it to others. Open your chakras as was recommended, or do whatever practice brings you into the heart. They can be at a great distance in time or space, or within the evolution of souls, in the past, the ancestral realms. It can be to the kingdoms of the Earth or wherever; hold them in light for healing, for release; offer it as a direction for those who are lost or in darkness to be able to find an avenue towards the Light. This is a practice that you can easily do within and from your own heart. It is also something you can do for yourself as you look at your own patterns, when stuff comes up for you. You can ask whether it is part of an ancestral pattern and whether these ancestors are willing to come forward and be healed or be redirected into the Light. Because they have the ability to choose to move to the Light if they feel they are trapped or locked up within some darkness, and maybe they have not been able to see that avenue.

You can also call upon the presence of your angelic helpers, both yours and theirs. You can also, during a HeartThread® session, call in the ancestors to witness, or to become a part of the healing process, both for themselves and for the client. So, there are many ways to work with this. If you have the ability as a shamanic practitioner to cut ties, this is another way to deal with the letting go of old oaths, old agreements and promises. You can ask, request, or demand that whatever oath, promise or curse there might be, be annulled. You have the power, through your own heart and connection with Source, to break that tie, to release any agreements and to no longer have any obligation to fulfill something that was agreed upon within the ignorance of a past life, where you did not have access to the whole picture or the whole consciousness.

So, this would be our first level of answer for your question. If it is not something you feel comfortable with in your own practice, we would recommend that you look for someone who has the ability to help you sever that tie. Do what you can. Smudge and release any connection with any of these beings, light candles in your home. Go into each room and direct the candle towards each wall and say, "I command that any energies that are of the darkness or of the past that no longer have light or love as their intention, that they be gone, that they no longer return to this space," and you clear all the space within your home, and you can do so also within your own heart. You take on the power of your own command, and you use the light and the power of your guides, and your angels, and your guardians to support you in clearing away any adherence of old hooks from the past and from ancestral patterns. You can get help from others, or you can attempt to do this on your own. Feel in your heart how much you are able to achieve and how much you need to get the support of another who has perhaps more practice and more experience within this field. Does that make sense?

Q. (LS) You spoke about letting go of this sense of urgency and when you were speaking, I felt like that was directly for me, because I have lived most of my life with this sense of urgency and needing to figure everything out and get the right answer and know where I'm going with any situations that I will be OK. And it dawned on me that the one symptom I struggle with in my body with my digestive tract is urgency and having to run to the bathroom all day long, and that was an interesting reflection from my mind, reflecting through my body and I never quite put that together before; this whole sense of urgency, of "I have to do it now, have to figure it all out now. It's going to be too late. If you don't do it now, you won't ever get to it". And then I remember you mentioning that to be in the heart, we must be in our body. I've been striving a lot to be more in the heart, but I just still have a hard time feeling connected to my body, so I was hoping you could speak a little bit about that for me.

A. Thank you. Much of the sense of urgency comes from childhood; needing to be nice, needing to comply with the expectations of authority figures around you, or somebody whose approval you need. So allowing yourself to let go of any kind of urgency, whether it comes from within (which is actually internalized oppression from childhood) or from without, is a way of experiencing your self-authority. It's recognizing that you are not incumbent towards anyone, no matter how much you love them, or you would like to see them happy. You are always the source of your own happiness, your own truth and priorities. You are connected to your own inner source. The more you go into the heart using the breath, the more you will discover your connection with your body, because the process of separating them out becomes a process of believing that they are separate. Understand that no part of you is really disconnected. It's all connected.

So, as you contemplate and go into that space of inquiry around the urgency and the need for your body to have some communication with you through this process, you start to uncover hints. We would also have you consider connecting with (MS) because of his practice and ability to tune in to these elements related to the Oriental Medicine he practices. Perhaps he could also give you some kind of guidance and perhaps there can be an exchange, because, as you have expressed before, you two are healers, and this is a way in which you can all support each other by sharing your gifts with one another.

Remember that we shared with you the statement that you can do it "because you can", "just like that," letting go. So it is something you might need to do as part of your practice, reinforcing the ability to tune in and to be able to let go, just like that, within the wording that you give to yourself. Perhaps use an affirmation and constantly reinforce it in whatever way you can. "I am letting go of any disconnect between my mind, my heart, and my body," for instance, and you say this in a state of Alpha or Theta, in meditation, and you constantly reinforce it. Then pay attention and recognize that something is shifting. The breath and the letting go of the sense of urgency, of needing to please somebody; all begins to grow within you as an expression of the letting go and of feeling your body. You have used your body as a sounding board, as a litmus test to know whether you're OK or not or how you might figure out what's going on for you. The letting go of the figuring out and the movement into the heart through the breath, is the direction we recommend for you. Is that making sense?

- It makes sense; my brain wants to figure it out. Yes, it makes sense.

- So good, you laugh at your brain, because all your brain is, is a collection of neurons, it is the mind that is what we call that container of consciousness, and you have within it the ability to figure it all out, and the ability to let go of figuring it all out. You can vacillate, you can go between the heart and the mind. In that process, you are exercising access to the heart more and more. Imagine flipping. Remember we talked of location? Imagine flipping from head to heart and focusing on a different response and see what comes. Play with it, have fun with it, draw it. Instead of feeling oppressed by this challenge, find ways to turn it into your power, into your dragon. Empower yourself, love yourself. Also note, it is an interesting thing that this one and I, John Henry, often have very special communications and insights that show up when he goes to the bathroom, because, as we said before, he goes into neutral. Intuitions and guidance and inspiration will pop in when the mind is in neutral, so you have access to lots of opportunities to have this available new insight. Play with it. Have fun and laugh a lot. Thank you.

Q. (NB) *My question is about my longing to follow my purpose, what I was born for in this lifetime. I went on a spiritual path, but I seem to go back to the corporate world. However, even in the corporate world I do embed it with spiritual principles and I know it's much needed there. Yet at the same time, I want to be in my full expression without hiding it but fully expressing it. If I can get any guidance on that, I would be so grateful.*

A. Yes, we are seeing you create your own structures for pursuing your purpose within the corporate world; not necessarily in the way you are doing currently, but in a way that allows you to be more of a freelancer who has experience working with those who are in their heads. They operate from a corporate, disciplinary way of seeing things, bottom line being number one, people being unimportant. These are the things that the corporate world holds as priority, so here you come, turning it on its head through your offerings and being able to supply brand-new perspectives that allow the bottom line to actually manifest at a much higher level, so it becomes a win/win. Cooperation and formulating structures that are based on cooperative ownership, cooperative leadership and consensus become the models for the New Earth. They get incorporated into the corporate structures that you work with. And if you are not able to use these kinds of approaches with the organizations you are now in, then you migrate, maybe gradually, but you migrate away from them to the ones that you yourself generate. Or perhaps you do it in partnership with others, or in a different form. But you express your purpose in a way that is meaningful for you. Given that you already have access to this world, it is important that many of these corporations including the big ones, in fact, begin to shift their focus from what is unsustainable and non-beneficial to what is beneficial for the whole. Does that, in a very succinct way, answer your question?

- *Yes, thank you, Raphael.*

Closing Meditation

Let us go back to our heart by placing our right hand on our heart and our left hand on our right and again feeling the deep sense of that inspiration, the breathing in of stillness; feeling the filling of the lungs with light, with the golden energy of connection. Sitting, each one, in our own hearts first, allowing them to expand into a lightness of being, allowing ourselves to feel that ground beneath us, of being connected down into that which is gravity. Then we rise up to Heaven with that lightness of being, connecting with the guidance of the spiritual realms and then feeding that space of the heart in our center. Then let's send out this beautiful weave of connection, of threads of hearts to all of those here and those connected with all of us, in all realms, in all worlds, so that we are like a gyroscope that is aligned above and below, and is spinning its beautiful radiation of gold light into the universe. As we do so, we are bringing benevolence, love and light to all beings, especially sending it to those who are still trapped in the ignorance and darkness of not knowing that they are Light and that they are connected to the whole. And so we will allow you to take those breaths and let go of anything that you are still holding onto, of any urgency, or feeling any obligation to anything but your own heart. Know that we are always with you, to guide you and to answer your questions. And it will be in the stillness of your own heart, that still small voice will arise to be able to hear our answers. We love you. Blessings and peace.

JH (2008) "If I could tell you anything that I learned in the years since I've been making this transition, it's 'don't waste a second of your time thinking about something you don't want. Do not waste your energy worrying. Do not waste your energy feeling responsible or judging anything else or anybody else. It is a complete waste of your energy field. It's why you eat so much, it's why you talk so much, it's why you go around in circles; 'cause you're misusing the energy of your God given stream.'" Transmission through Flo Aeveia Magdalena during a HeartThread® practitioner training in El Rito.

Voice Six
Ashtara

20th September 2020

Preamble: Message from Journal (Saturday 19th September)

"Wherever there is a distortion based on judgement or comparison or woundedness, feelings blind the people to the only truth that matters. And so, whatever shows up begging for resolution becomes the place to shine the light within and redirect it from the exterior situation or relationship. "Where am I failing to have love and compassion?" Looking at what prevents us from being open-hearted is the Great Work. For, if it reveals how our wounds are affecting our feelings and our behavior and attitudes, then we can release the attachments and allow the light to expand out and let go of the story.

There are so many stories, there is so much of Heaven and Earth that is available to straighten the pathway and produce a common thread and a common goal that supports the blossoming instead of the withering. It all boils down to what prevents each one from love of self, and that includes the personality, and allows release of attachment to judgement, even of the "ego", even if the ego is the enemy. For who is the enemy, if not the mirror? What is the enemy for, if not to bring back home the projection, so it can be examined and its power over you to be diffused in the great Light and Love of God's Radiance?"

==

Let's take a few moments to go into that sweet, deep breath. Put our right hand on our heart and our left on our right, so we settle, and we ground; we notice that there is a column of light around each one of us, filled with the most beautiful, golden light, and it is connecting us down to the very center of Mother Earth. Let us connect with her through our gratitude and our love, feeling the beauty of the Great Mother who takes good care of us and loves us and nurtures us and supplies us with every nutrient we need to sustain our bodies and minds and our hearts. And so, when the spark of Divine Fire from above pours down this column into our hearts and into our bodies, it can animate all these beautiful energies of Mother Earth so that we have this opportunity to have this body, this vessel, this vehicle for the expression of that Divine Fire that we are. And as we give thanks to Father Sky above, to that source of all connection with Spirit, with the divine energies of the higher beings that watch over us, that love us and that are surrounding us now with their love, their light, their blessings and their peace, we are beginning to feel the weave of the threads of our hearts reaching out. They are creating a beautiful fabric of the interconnectedness, the connection between each individual's heart and soul and threads of heart with the greater whole of All That Is. We are connected with the ones we love and care about, the pets and creatures, our neighbors and friends. We reach out across our cities, our states and this continent, reaching towards the other continents and oceans, spreading this beautiful web of golden connectedness around the planet; out into all Space and Time, all galaxies, all worlds and universes, connecting us to that One Heart. And as we do this, we surround ourselves with a beautiful golden sphere of light that keeps us protected and safe and that allows only the highest vibrations into this space of connection and communication. Any energies or ancestors that wish to be present must come in love, in service, in light, for the highest good of the Whole, for healing, or to witness and to bless.

So, you can rest your hands and settle into that place of being connected. Begin to feel the energy of Ashtara,[56] this beautiful connection of this divine feminine energy. Feel this presence that is as beautiful as you can imagine, dressed in white, tall, and looking down within each one of us, blessing us with the energy of receptivity, of understanding that whatever gender we associate ourselves with, that we cannot divide ourselves even into male and female. Essentially, we are both aspects in a united framework of Oneness. It requires this unified field within to be able to accept and connect with the unified field without. So that when we judge anyone on the basis of their gender, their form, or education, we see people as separate. We see them as not beautiful or not handsome, not as mobile, not as whatever. These are all the places where we divide, where we judge. In order for us to be free, in order for the New Earth to come into being, it is vital that we continually de-structure these paradigms, structures, environments and belief systems that limit, that judge and that compare.

It is the path of the Spiritual Warrior to find a way to recognize each one as both masculine and feminine, to realize the connectivity that we have to a much broader spectrum of existence beyond the confines of Mother Earth and this planet. We actually have been for eons of time, not an isolated planet within an isolated system, but a part of an intergalactic family. Many of the great beings that you honor, project towards or pray to, and honor as avatars and Holy Beings, also inhabit other star systems, planets and galaxies. The Universe is infinite. It is made up of numerous worlds and systems which provide the ability for life to have a place and for intelligence to have expression. All serve the greatest or greater plan of this Divine Intelligence that created everything. For everything is everything. That which you call Divinity, that which you see as the Great Being, is self-created All That Is.

We talk this time about the divine feminine and the aspects of the divine masculine of humans participating in this duality, that is actually a unity and our connection to the star systems. I represent this particular one's feminine aspect. I also represent the connectivity of the Earth beings, your human systems and the Galactic

Federation and the Ones who watch over you, the Ones who are in some ways the closest to you because they are monitoring you. They are sending their love, their guidance and their protection to ensure that you will transit to the New Earth in a beautiful, peaceful and graceful manner. Because so it has been ordained by Creator. This is part of a giant flow of Time, of eons, of Kalpas,[57] all coming to a point of fruition. It may seem to many that we are at some kind of dead end moving towards some cataclysm. As lightworkers and as representatives of the Beings of Light and of the field of the heart, it is your job to understand, to know and to trust that this is only a blip in time and is part of a much bigger picture. You have allies who are from fields of Light of such a magnitude and power that the miniscule energies of these dark forces have absolutely no way of controlling the amounts of light that is being showered upon you for your transformation.

So, it is vital for you to understand and to recognize that the aspect of the Divine as the Feminine, your particular feminine aspect, is the most powerful when it is in a receptive mode, when it allows the mind to settle, to go quiet, and to release its need to hold on out of fear. This allows you to receive downpourings of love and light and the amazing golden mantle, this golden energy that is so healing, that infiltrates every cell of the body when you allow it to. The four elements that are taught by The Ones with No Names are Truth, Light, Order and Union. The essential connection of the energy of Truth is allowance. Old Chinese, who will speak with you next week, has defined love as "the unconditional acceptance of the reality of another," so the concept of allowance allows you to take that breath when you are faced with any situation that feels stressful, or has a sense of urgency. When you do not know how to pace yourself, how to be in that moment of trust, able to give to Goddess, give up to God whatever it is that is troubling you, take the breath.

This is a very simple procedure. You just give it to God, just like that. The one, John Henry, who was with you last week, he loves to say "just like that" and "because you can." This is part of the vocabulary of a new way of thinking and seeing, in which ease and grace become the norm for you. Abundance and prosperity and the solution and the resolution of all issues becomes apparent as you let go of the sense of urgency and the sense of some kind of doom. You let go of catastrophic energies, of some form of fear and imposition. As John Henry stated very clearly, do not waste one moment of your energy worrying about something or putting your energy into something you do not want. Do not give it any energy whatsoever. Focus instead on what it is that you do want, your heart's desire.

You can go into that safe feminine place within you which everyone has, and allow and recognize that you have this beautiful chalice right there in your heart, in the cave of your heart, as Herman Rednick teaches. It is that space of divine, human and angelic receptivity, where you do not have to be in control, where you can put everything; everything you want and everything you don't want. It is like putting it into a bottomless pit. It goes in, and it disappears and the things that are no longer relevant, sustainable, needed or useful, they dissipate, they go down into the black hole and are no longer seen again. And those things that are waiting to be manifested through the divine power of your imaging, of your desiring from your heart, your projects, your visions, of how to create new structures and new containers, they go to the places they need to go. They go to your angelic helpers who know exactly what to do because they have access to the vast fields of interconnectedness that makes everything possible. So, "What me worry?" Why worry when you can let go? This is part of the path of the Spiritual Warrior.

We like simple. If it ain't simple, you don't want it! If it's not clear, you don't want it. If it doesn't bring you joy, if it doesn't bring you a sense of ease, it is not for you. You will find a way if you hold out for the ease and the grace and the assistance of your golden beings, the angels that are all around you, right now, and with you each moment, surrounding you with their love, their guidance and their support. It is supporting you to hold that space of emptiness when necessary, to tune into your intuition and to take that breath and say "Oh, I almost went down this rabbit hole, but it's not the place for me right now." As you let go, you put everything in the chalice. And the masculine aspect, when it needs to act, has clear directions from your feminine side, for really it has always been the power of the feminine that has been the real controlling energy of what moves forward for the benefit of humanity and of all creatures. The male figure in front, thinks it holds the reins and that it is at the helm. It's a bit of an illusion. It's really the one "in the skirts" who knows what's up and who knows how to direct, especially the family energy. They know how to take that breath and let the guy rave on, and when he's done, "This is what we're going to do," and usually he will concur.

So, we are suggesting just a small shift in how you perceive things, because this is part of the ongoing work: examining constantly the thoughts, the feelings, the conditioning, the imprints, the projections, the assumptions and the belief systems that have been inculcated forever. It is the time to examine and to discard that which will not help to create the structures of the New Earth. It is necessary to come together, whether it be the circles of women or men, younger and older or mixed circles. It is a cooperative endeavor; to work towards that which is sustainable and which is new, where the old did not work and does not work any longer.

It does not have to be a painful transition. It does not have to be a struggle. The very practice of letting go of the story, whether it's a story of a people, a religion or culture, a family, an ancestral or an individual pattern, it is up for grabs these days. It can be a connection to old oaths and vows that you made in other lifetimes. Everything is up for grabs, everything is available, is asking to be reconfigured. The structures we are talking about, are essentially containers. What is the new container for the ending of hunger? What does it look like? What does it feel like? Who is part of this container? "How can I express my passion for this desire to end hunger or to end abuse? To end the horrific misuse of children, of slavery?" All the ills of society that you all ride upon in the advancement of your technologies, in order to maintain a particular lifestyle that you have come to accept as the normal, are not viable or sustainable. That kind of 'normal' is now being dismantled in order that some new energy can infiltrate and allow that dismantling to happen with as much ease and grace as possible. You are the Bringers of the Dawn, all of you who are the leaders, the teachers, the links, the bridges between your generation and the younger generation and the even younger generation, the little beings who are being born, and the 3-, the 4- and 5- and 6-year-olds: These amazing beings, they are filled with so much light.

It is such a tragedy to see them hiding behind these masks. May it be so and soon, that they can shine their faces, that the radiance from their eyes and their smiles can be felt and shared. That you can go back to hugging, and tenderness, and connection with strangers, with the underprivileged, with those who have a hard time just because they were born into a situation where they have become the working slaves of the system. It is necessary to examine everything, perhaps even to be political. That is up to you to follow your heart, not some sense of obligation, or some sense of 'you should, or you must, or if you don't do this you are not being true to whatever.' Everything is up for grabs! Everything is up for examination, and each time you have an "Aha" moment, a recognition, it is extremely valuable to write it, share it, draw it, and dance it. You create some form that can be shared. You create some way of expressing this unfolding that is happening to your soul and your being that you can share with others, and then perhaps they can learn from you. So, you create beauty, and you allow the beauty to spread and touch hearts, and touch souls, and you'll find ways to create circles and share your gifts, share the wisdom that emerges from that expression.

It is becoming more and more obvious that what we have been presenting as the 12 is a valuable resource for others, so it is being transcribed and will become available with the anonymous questions and answers and perhaps some of your sharings, your drawings, your poems. It will become a resource because of what it represents, even though the threads of our teachings are really the rock-bottom truths that are being taught everywhere to those who are awakening. There is a way of seeing things through different eyes, through 12 different perspectives that are so far apart, seemingly, that it allows everyone to have an "Aha" moment, to have a moment of just taking that breath and thinking "What did I just say that does not make sense regarding the New World that is a very old paradigm? That was ageism, or sexism, that was some other '-ism' that I just expressed or shared a joke about, that does not represent great respect for my brother or my sister, because of their sexual orientation or the color of their skin, or their cultural background or religion."

And so, you begin to become more and more aware. You can carry a banner, or not, you can go marching on the streets or not, you could send your Facebooks, or your Instagrams and your whatevers to share with others. And maybe it will fall upon deaf ears, like the seeds that are broadcast[58]. Many will fall on rocks, but some will take hold in the earth, and as you nurture and you water and feed and fertilize them, they will grow and become the fruits of the New Earth. You are the gardeners. You are the cultivators of the hearts. You are the feminine and the masculine come together in Divine Union within your own heart, within your own way of expressing this union, within the way of peace, the way of no-harm, the way of stillness. And you always have that sword by your side. It is not just the male warrior and soldier who carries the sword. We don't use guns with the truth. The feminine energy, the great feminine warriors and great pharaohs of old who were feminine energies, queens, and the Amazons - there have been many fierce warriors of both feminine and masculine aspects who have carried the sword of truth.

The right place for it, mostly, is to sit in the scabbard as you hold your peace and your silence in the face of babble, in the face of nonsense, when it is not appropriate to interrupt it, in a way that cannot be heard or accepted. Yet when it is necessary and when you do have that sense from within that you are being called upon to cut the c-r-a-p, then you do so. You do so with power. You do so with that sense of inner knowing, that inner strength and inner power. And you can because you have walked your path, you have walked your talk; you are now a model for the recognition of how this truth needs to be lived. And this is what you teach by example.

All of you are here, because you are ready, because you have been preparing for a long time, and what you are preparing for, very simply put, is forgiveness. It is your greatest challenge to be in that space of non-judgment where you recognize the woundedness (as was written at the beginning of this session) that it is woundedness that determines for many people their emotional responses and how they have treated you or treat another. And when you come to that place of non-judgement and compassion, you recognize that it is the woundedness speaking. It does not affect you any longer. You come to that place where you can forgive, whether it be all the harm that was done to you, or that is done in the greater society to others, or to those who cannot speak for themselves, whatever.

You recognize that there is a need for forgiveness that can reach back towards the ancestors, the ancestral patterns that are still running rife in the world. And for your own forgiveness, for your own so-called mistakes, your own so-called failures, knowing that there is no such thing any longer; that there is no good or bad or right or wrong. That which you call "good" is that which you feel you like, "Oh that was a good movie." "What made it good?" "Oh, I liked it." There is no real criterion for what is good or not good, except that which is harmful to life, or supportive of life. We do not relate from a stance of good or bad, right or wrong. It immediately implies that somebody has to cringe in guilt or shame because they have done something that requires punishment, or that they are somehow at fault and cannot ever be forgiven.

The whole concept of sin, of "original sin" is a contrivance, a great, grand illusion. There is no sin. There is only the heart, there is only the truth of Union and there's only love. Where it is absent, it needs to be found. It needs to be conjured up through the magic and miracle of ease, grace and, trust and the connection to your guidance, inner wisdom and to the truth that you know through your intuition. So, we are giving you a little pep talk. We are wanting to encourage you to recognize that it is possible to live with ease and grace and forgiveness no matter what the apparent cause or situation or the apparent illusion that is being touted as truth.

It is very important for you to think for yourself, to examine, to explore, to Google, shmoogle the answers to the questions you have in your heart and see what alternatives there are to the standard mass media answers to those questions. It is vital for you to think outside the box, and to educate your children to value love, connection, and forgiveness, and to recognize the importance of how they use words. The importance of their belief systems. Does it stand? Does it make sense in the creation of a cooperative world of love and harmony and peace and a world in which everybody has enough and has a roof over their head, and has a loving family or a loving community that cares for them. These are the foundations for the New Earth and you are here to help establish them, from your heart.

So, we want to remind you of the importance of forgiveness. It is in many ways the key. We talked about the Ego as the enemy in this little reading that we did in the beginning. Do not disparage any aspect of yourself, your physicality, your ego system, your personality system, your consciousness, your unconsciousness, or your subconsciousness. The mind, the heart, the body, the Spirit, the soul, all are one unit, masculine/feminine. It is a convenience only that you separate them in order for your mind to be able to talk and analyze and share about them. The more you begin to see everything from a perspective of wholeness, and to release the judgments, you begin to recognize the truth, that love is the unconditional acceptance of another's reality. So, we will take a moment to pause, to have an eye-to-eye gaze and see if we are all on the same page and see whether we need to go forward or begin with our questions.

Comments/ Discussion

Q. (MS) Would you talk more about forgiveness? I was always taught, or been recently taught, that when you forgive somebody, you are putting yourself on a pedestal. So, when someone does something wrong to you, let's say, and you felt wronged, and they come to you, and they say "Hey I did something wrong to you, will you forgive me?" and you go "Yes, I forgive you," you are putting yourself higher than they are. You never have that direct relationship. Now if that person comes to you and says "I'm sorry for what I've done. I take responsibility," and you feel their true remorse in what they did, then you can continue to have a relationship going forward, but if you are forgiving them, you are being like God, you are actually putting yourself higher, and you never can have that equal relationship again. Does anybody want a comment on that?

(MSG) I understand that people can elevate themselves. I think more of the forgiveness, it just needs to happen in my heart, like letting go of what I'm carrying of resentment or blame for myself is the most important part. This is the part that I feel. It's what's in my heart and my body that I let go of. That's the key. Maybe Ashtara has more to say about this.

Ashtara - What you are both saying is absolutely true. Again, let me emphasize the principles of examination, which is exactly what you have done within the context of the standard approach to forgiveness. There is also an institutionalized approach, which we have with the upcoming Jewish New Year and Day of Atonement. In this context, there is a need to ask forgiveness from God and also from your fellow human for something you have done. Many of the concepts or the belief systems, assumptions, and associations around this subject do need to be dismantled. You're right about the lack of equality present when you put yourself on a pedestal and hold yourself responsible for the forgiveness towards a brother or a sister. When someone says, "Hey, I just did something. I feel really lousy. I want to take responsibility, would you forgive me?" of course you're going to embrace them and say "Thank you, I appreciate that. I love you" and there's a reconnection. You can also say, if you want to, "Don't worry about it because there's no right or wrong, what you did, you did in the moment out of where you were at, and I do not wish to be judging you. So, yes, I totally forgive you, and it's not necessary because we are brother and sister, or we're sister and sister or brother and brother."

There are distinctions with pedestals and who has the right to forgive, and you know it is true, that whenever we separate from anyone else and if ever we put somebody on a pedestal, or even ourselves, we are out of alignment with our own truth, and our congruence with Heaven and Earth, with the truth of what we aspire to be. And it is true that forgiveness must begin with oneself, because every judgment is based upon how we see ourselves. So we believe, we understand that what you are saying is very valid, and very important, but it also goes back to that original requirement to examine everything, which you have done, and we are so grateful that you did bring this up, because it is true that whenever there is a separation consciousness involved, separative thinking, it needs to be dismantled and examined and harmonized with Truth. Thank you.

Q. (SL) One of the things I'm finding most troublesome these days in this whole fiasco that we're in the middle of, is that most of my friends are kind of like a lot of the people that I see in the supermarket. They think that since they have a mask on and since we're supposed to keep social distancing that there is some kind of prohibition against communication, and I'm just kind of being shut out by several people that I thought were friends. I find that the most troublesome thing that's going on for me right now, besides my shingles.

Ashtara - We recommend bringing everything home to within. We do understand that there are emotional responses to the stimuli from the outside and so it is vital for each one to examine where they stand emotionally with themselves. And referring to that original little piece that we read, what is your enemy, your mirror asking you to look at? Where is there a need for more love; because any other space you go to will not produce the eventual results of what you want for yourself and the New Earth, for all humanity and all creatures. So, it is important to always bring home the external situations and ask yourself, "What is it that I am being asked to bring more love to? What is it that I am being asked to find more compassion for? Where is it that I'm asked to forgive because of the distress of someone 'outside' of myself, and what is it I can do to shift that reactivity in me that will allow me to live with ease and grace, with composure and in equanimity?"

Because, the Spiritual Warrior has vowed at some deep heart, Swing-Between-Worlds type level, to maintain that space of equanimity, no matter what is going on outside. This is the essence of the warrior. When you face mortal combat, at some level you do not care whether you live or die because you know you are immortal, you are eternal, infinite. You do not care at some level, as long as you faced your enemy with honor, as long as you allow yourself to stand in your own truth, in your own power. It requires us to ask about everything, whether it is the shingles or it be the irritation, or it be the relinquishing of relationships that are no longer harmonious because of whatever. It is requiring a relinquishment of the judgements. It is a very, very hard path to walk. We are honoring you all with the deepest love and respect; that whether you like it or not, whether you even agree or not, you have signed up to be Spiritual Warriors for the Truth, for your heart, for Love, for us. We cannot do it for you, we can only do it with you, we can only help you when you ask, and when you listen.

We want you to thrive, we want you to have the deepest and most beautiful levels of communication and contact and love and sharing and joy and dance and music and celebration, wherever and however you can do it, as you come forth from your heart wishing to express this in a way that has balance. Because, if you go overboard, you cannot be in balance and maintain the balance. In the Thoth tarot deck,[59] the Magus, the great Magician, or Mercury, is standing upon the very point of the sword holding balance and juggling all the aspects like balls. He, too, is a representative of a 'he' and a 'she' combination. The divine feminine with the divine masculine. We do not like those terms because they are separative. There is no 'divine masculine', 'divine feminine.' There is only Oneness. There is only 'god/goddess' bundled up into a oneness experience. There is a human masculine and a human feminine, emotional masculine and an emotional feminine and they all work and weave together.

This is why I'm here with you today as Ashtara, as this dude's "divine feminine" aspect. I remind him constantly to soften, to receive, allow, let go. And I connect you all with the Galactic, with the huge vastness of All That Is, of this amazing brother/sisterhood that you have, that you're part of, that is watching over you, that are in their ships, our ships. That is how we met. We are making sure that no one presses the wrong button ever again, that there is no longer any devastation or nuclear disaster on your planet. And these energies, these pipsqueaks in the darkness, they are losing their power rapidly, losing control. As you feel the beauty of that golden light, you are beginning to feel more at peace, within your power and are able and more comfortable about taking that breath in the midst of the chaos, in the midst of the dilemmas and the conflicts and the personalities, taking that breath and recognizing "This too shall pass. If I am clear, if I move with love, all will be well. There's no need to panic. I have guides, I have angels. I take good care of my body, my mind, my soul, my heart, and this is my path."

Thank you all for your dedication, for being here, continuing with this work. We are all saying the same thing.

Ashtara Q&A

So, we will continue with your questions. We are all one "mush," like the butterfly, the cocoon. The caterpillar at some point becomes one mush and then the butterfly emerges through that teeny, teeny little hole that they have to struggle their way out of, and if somebody helps and breaks open the hole, they can't fly.

Q. (NB) You mentioned relinquishment of relationships. When you are relinquishing a relationship, or it is being relinquished, with or without your consent, there's that "judgment piece." How do you manage it? Do you just accept it as part of the plan and just let go because you are relinquishing the pain, the judgment, the separation to be back in that Unity Consciousness? Can you tell us more about that please?

A. There are many levels and aspects to this answer. Just as I am his feminine aspect, but in essence we're all one, just as there are so many levels and dimensions and ways of seeing things, so too relationships are there for the purpose of being a mirror, for the purpose of fulfilling contracts, for the purpose of standing as an actor in your life in order to trigger you and be triggered. It's all, as they say, grist for the mill, and, a lot of relationship stuff is about clarity. "Why am I in this relationship? What's in it for me? What's in it for them? What is the nature of our communication, of our love, of our connection, of our caring? Are we here because of the kids, or if we break up what will happen to the kids?" - the old stories; or if it's "Oh, you know, a friend is always talking about us behind our backs, but they're part of our scene." There are so many factors. It will always come back to your going into your heart and looking at the question, "Where can I love more? Perhaps my loving me more means that I can let go of this relationship. Trying to fix it never works. That takes me out of my center and there are times when we're done. The karmic connection has played itself until it's worn out, and it's time to just say 'I love you, goodbye.'" It's, we're going to use the word "judge," it's for you to judge for yourself what is the appropriate response for you, not judge in the way of condemning another, but in the way of deciding, of ascertaining for yourself where you are at on your soul journey.

When this one quit smoking pot a number of years ago, a whole slew of people started dropping out of his life and he was so grateful because his life went to a whole new vibration, with his channeling, with his connection to his clarity. And so, when you make a shift in your consciousness, it affects your relationships with others. It's appropriate sometimes, and sometimes you do not even need to do anything, they just fall by the wayside of their own accord. Sometimes you have to say "You know, I considered what you said or that place where we never really had a clear written agreement, and I decided I'm not interested anymore." Or whatever.

You have to use your own assessment of what is right for you, within your own self authority. John Henry's self-authority business is powerful. If you do not have self-authority, you cannot stand in your power and say "No!" You cannot demarcate boundaries, you cannot have clear agreements, you cannot forgive, you cannot love. It is the foundation of not giving away your power, of not feeling obligated to somebody or some other institution to continue to drag yourself to work every day to pay the mortgage, because it's not working for you. Relationship is your connection to everything around you. It is vital for you to find your own clarity within your own self-authority and to assess how much you can come from a place of love and non-judgement. It does not mean you do not make painful decisions and that there's no such thing as "tough love." There are those who have difficulty with their children and children difficulty with their parents and siblings, and it's all part of the 'grist for the mill' relationships. You say "Oh no, where's my beloved. I want a relationship. I've been alone for so long" and then you look around and you see how many relationships are on the drawing table or at the abattoir, waiting to be slaughtered because they're not working. So, you have to reconsider everything. "Maybe I don't want this anymore" Is there such a thing as this ideal, romanticized relationship whether it be friendship or partnership or cooperative between organizations and members and the whole caboodle? Everything is open to examination and needs to be available for transformation.

So, you examine everything with the same clarity, keeping that sword of truth in your scabbard and when you need to draw it and say "Okay, I'm clear. I have to cut this tie, and I can do it in the most loving way possible, and if it is with somebody I don't like, I can choose to do it with a jibe or a smart-ass comment, but why should I go there? Why don't I just say "I love you, thank you." Do Ho'oponopono.[60] "I'm sorry, please forgive me, I love you, thank you," and be done with it. And this is the path Old Chinese, Chung Fu is recommending. Look it up if you do not know it, the Ho'oponopono, and recite it to yourself about everything, everyone that you have an issue with, and see what changes. It's about forgiving, because you are going to that place where it's coming from you. It's not about them any longer. Peace.

Q. (KM) Can you recommend how to forgive? Are there techniques or practices?

A. We have just recommended the Ho'oponopono. It is a Hawaiian practice, very powerful. The fact that Chung Fu highly recommends it and has recommended it to many, says a lot. I would recommend that when one considers forgiveness, one has to look first of all within the heart and say "How can I come to peace about this situation, where I am being asked to forgive? I am being asked by my higher self, my angels, my commitment to the path of truth and love and service. What is it that I have to do in the face of the most worstest, horriblest, childhood abuse, you can ever imagine? Where can I find the strength, the power and the support to get to that place within my heart that I can forgive, that I can get rid of, that I can let go of all the blame, the shame, the judgments, that I placed upon myself as a result of something that I had no control over in my childhood?" We are going to the worst-case scenario because, if one can forgive in those kinds of circumstances, then the little stuff is easy, peasey.

For most of you, this is the journey. This is where you graduate, your last life. This is where you go into the realms of Light and merge back with your Infinite Soul and the connection with Divinity. And you want to have cleaned up everything so you go there with a satisfied mind. You go there knowing you did your best. You tried, whatever that means. You worked at it. You worked on loving yourself, not judging yourself or anyone. You recognized that place of your own elevated consciousness that is connected to Love, the Love of God/Goddess and Christ energy. You did everything you could to love, to let go, to recognize the woundedness that's behind it all, and the generations of ancestral patterns of abuse, violence, servitude and bowing down to evil authority. You are taking it on, and you'll get as far as you get, and in the way of doing it, you find a little more love for yourself and for others. You find a little more peace in your heart about yourself and your past. You get to be drawn to a way of being that is in service and that gives you deep satisfaction, and you can use the power of what you have achieved to help others get to the same place.

There are so many avenues that open up just through the energy of your intention to forgive and to deal with whatever you need to, to get there. We are coming to you from the highest levels of divine wisdom and guidance. There may be more and more Christs and Marys; they will all say the same things because they are all coming from that level of God's Love. There's nothing higher and there's Goddesses' love and Christ's love. It's all the same energy of Divine Love that we have shared with you and that we bring you as a vibration that you feel when you're in our presence. We're with you all the time. We are inspiring you to experience that love as part of who you are, so it's no longer external. We want you to internalize it. You start from within to look at what's out there, outside, and you begin to see everything through the eyes of your own divinity. When you go outside, you see all these gods and goddesses and angels and avatars and brotherhoods, and you notice "Oh, I'm always looking at them as if they're outside of me. What if I saw them inside? What if I am them, and they speak through my higher consciousness, through my higher self? What if they are me and I am an aspect of them? What if they are an aspect of me?"

Just as I am an aspect of this one and yet, I don't have a shape or form in this world, and I'm an idea, and I'm also not an idea, I'm a reality. There are so many levels, dimensions and ways of seeing everything, and so we are recommending and hopefully inspiring you to see everything from that highest into higher and higher dimensionality, higher and higher understandings in the quantum field of interconnectedness, where you begin to see yourselves as an intergalactic partner in the evolution of Consciousness throughout all Creation. For you are not separate. Your little 'one step for humanity' becomes the Great Step for all of life.

You are a representative of God's love, of Christ and Mary's love, on this Earth, inhabiting a body, inhabiting a mind and an emotional body, working towards your own evolution as an individuated soul that contributes to the greater aspect of the Whole. If you recognize that, if you realize it, if you hold that as your truth, we will be right there at your side, and we are, and this is what we are recommending for you. Go for the highest level of quality that you can. Live truth, union, light, justice, purity, innocence and forgiveness. Live truth, union; Live light. Be everything that you can possibly be. They won't accept you for the Marines, but we will accept you in the Army of the Heart. Thank you. Peace

Q. (CR) A couple of sentences that we were intermingled with the lesson today, were talking about the presence of the Ancient Ones and the Guides and our angels as beings that are with us and the Galactic Council, and they are part of helping mankind during this shift and I think it's interesting to note all the different avatars and intelligent ones that are on this planet that are connected to Spirit are saying pretty much the same message and I kind of wanted to just get at a briefing from the 'other side' as to how they see this shaking down and this beautiful energy that we're all co-creating together that doesn't get talked about. We see all the bad news especially in America. I just like to see if they could speak about it from their side again and I just kind of want to relish in the light a little bit, I guess.

A. Thank you. Thank you. We would like to recommend that you eliminate from your vocabulary the word "mankind." You understand why. Again, it is part of how we constantly redefine our wording and belief systems because much of your stories have been coming through a particular avenue of seeing everything from the male perspective. And as Ashtara, in some ways I'm pushing the other side just a hair more. All the beings, without exception, are viewing everything from the perspective of only light. Perhaps they are wearing space suits in a ship, or they are Angelic Beings orbs of light that are so bright and powerful that you cannot look at them. John Henry has recently been a 'once human angel' and is now in the realms of assistance. Every single energy that is guiding the planet and the consciousness of humanity/hu-womanity, on this planet, comes from the place of love. There is a marginal difference between love and light. In a way, love can be understood as Creator's gift of free will to humans. She then looks down upon them as children who deserve to be loved and supported. Light, is vibration, the carrier of the vibration of love, of acceptance, of wanting only the best for everyone and everything. So, we see everything from the broader bird's-eye perspective of the long-term, because the long-term in your linear perspective has been a very, very, very long time long-term. Kalpas, thousands upon thousands of years of precessions of equinoxes and cycles that are the in-breath and the out-breath of God.

There was a time when the Divine (we're going to use that term), when the feminine reigned supreme and the male was under their thumb, and we had thousands upon thousands of years when 'God was a woman,[61] so to speak. So, we have had cycles of Golden Ages, we have cycles of planets, of earths that have been and gone and come and morphed and have had civilizations upon them. You have ruins upon the Earth and Mars that reveal that there have been civilizations that lived and thrived there. We have been through cycles upon cycles, solar systems and suns that have come and gone. As we said, you are infinite, immortal, eternal and universal.

So, in this context, we see it all, we know where it's going. You have been given free will, and you are in the process of upscaling, of rebooting your systems from the Free Will Experiment to the Free Heart Experience. There will be a time when the very concept of war: "What's that, what is violence? How can somebody oppress another? How can you do these things that you are telling me were part of that ancient history/herstory of 100 years ago?" What does the evolution of humanity, of humankind look like, when it's seen as the progression of Time towards the current Golden Age to which you are moving? Is there a difference between this one and the other ones? Is it because they are so far back in time that they almost don't exist? Won't there be a time in the 'great future' when the in-breath of God will once again be bringing back the darkness and the violence and the horrors of cycles that have become a necessity, somehow. Perhaps the next Human species will have to go through lessons, because that's the only way they know how to evolve their souls towards greater Light? These are questions which can bother the mind, but in many ways are irrelevant to your current situation.

Look at it from the perspectives of it being a blip in time, of "this too shall pass," there is a silver lining to every cloud and everything works for good. Do whatever you can, like the Shungite, to take a negative spin and reverse it to a positive spin. Find the gold at the end of the rainbow, find the beauty, find that bright eye behind the mask, and have your conversation and if you need to stand apart 6 feet, so what? Where there is love, there is a future and there is light and there is beauty and there is heart and that's all you want to concentrate on. So, we see you through the eyes of Love. We cannot see you any other way. There is no place in our consciousness for judgment, there is no such thing as the judgment of souls in the dark fields of Hell or Hades or Amenti.[62] There is no sin or punishment. It is all a creation of humans in order to control, and we are not into that. We do not support that. We are helping you to come to a place where you are far beyond that, and we will have you take everything with a giant pinch of salt. And it is healthy salt. It is sea salt, organic salt, but it is salt nevertheless. And it is not accepting what you are told or what the whole world might believe.

Did you know that in Israel, every single person is under lock-down? If you are caught in the street, it is a 400 shekel fine. You can go to jail if you do it. The people around the world are taking this far more seriously and with much greater deprivation, and suffering than you have. When you go to the store, you can buy all the nice things at Trader Joe's and get your organic food. And who knows when it might end and what you might have to do to grow your own food or support your own developing community of your neighbors, so think positively, think globally, think locally, think communally and think cooperatively.

And think "love." Examine everything as we do, 'under the microscope, under the magnifying glass of Love' and as much as you can, emulate us, talk to us, ask us. We will go to the ends of the Earth to help you, bring to you what you need. It's our job to support you. You are not alone in your isolated perspectives as a separated entity, as a human that has become a separate entity, that sees itself as apart from the Whole. Part of our 'job' is to support you to have that which your heart desires for the emergence of your own alignment with spirit and soul, beauty and love, and blossoming. Remember the blossoming versus the withering, that comment in the beginning? We are here to help you thrive and blossom, and this is our gift for you. This is why you are going through what you're going through, why you are listening to us, because it is your intention to blossom. Why suffer? It is true there are many that suffer because they were born into a situation that they are not able to shift, and perhaps it's their karmic connection; but out of your compassion, perhaps you can help them with a few dollars or with your support system that sends helpers, or perhaps you are called to do what you feel to do. There is no judgment. Everyone must follow their heart and that will be a good answer for every question. Thank you.

Q. (MSG) I have been getting pieces from everyone's answers. Ashtara said "Do not disparage any aspect of yourself" and I was like "Okay, that's about self-criticism, self-judgment, and you know it's not like I've not been working on this my whole life." It just came up again, something I think I'm doing really well with letting go of some of that, and then I was in this venue on Zoom all week, with all the other speakers and presenters, and I was having a wonderful time and there was so much richness, and just toward the very end, in some circles we came together to harvest what happened in our different rooms. I noticed that part of me doing the comparing thing and going 'Oh, everybody else is so much more articulate or has something more important to say' and that little part comes up, and I want to "just like that" let that one go because I feel it gets in the way of me living my purpose. I'm here, I made a commitment to be here, to be of service, and it comes up in my memoir writing group and other situations where people praised my writing or say how much they love it or it touches them, and I want to enjoy it like they are, instead of always thinking "It's not the way I would like it to be, it's not good enough." I don't know if anyone else can relate to it. Yeah, so I'm just like so ready to let that go and be free to just be who I am and offer my gift however it's measured. I want to not care about that anymore.

A. Thank you very much. As we talked about the enemy, the mirrors, commitment, the sword of truth, it's all there. It is your choice and decision to say "just like that" and let go of the story, "Every time I notice myself comparing, I can also remind myself that everybody here is doing the same thing." Everyone is comparing themselves to people they have put on pedestals, who don't want to be on pedestals, who also carry all the judgement that the whole human race carries, because of the conditioning, because of the ancestral patterns that have been instilled into you for control. That sweet little girl that you were has not gone anywhere. Embrace her, see through our eyes, see yourself as beautiful. Use affirmations, Ho'Oponopono, use HeartThread®. It is one of the most powerful tools you have to shift these patterns.

Create a new story. Let go of the old story; it's not real, it's just popping up in the mind to remind you to get rid of it. Constantly change the story to the one you want, not the one you don't want. Again, you have said all these teachings are the same; they're all based on a foundation of self-love, because you are a reflection of Divinity. You are an expression of God's Love in action, or Goddess's Love. Sometimes it gets very tiring to be politically correct around male/female and all the other stuff! There is no need when we shift our whole way of seeing and thinking to a holistic perspective. See yourself from that same point of view: "I am, and if I'm not, I will be, whole, right now or tomorrow or in an hour or as soon as I have said my affirmation, I will be whole." You know, be creative, use your writing, take the Mickey out of yourself, "judge" yourself with humor, so it's no longer judgment. Watch movies, comedies and laugh yourself silly.

Everyone is so serious on this 'spiritual path'. You are all these warriors carrying swords, fighting dark knights with heavy armor, the Lords of the Ring fighting the wraiths, and it's true at one level, but it has become so tedious, so heavy, so serious. If there's no joy or laughter in your story, you don't want it anymore. When you're looking at yourself and you are comparing yourself to that other one, perhaps their makeup is a bit better and they've gone to the beauty salon, and they look sharp because they're glamorous and... Cut that c-r-a-p. It doesn't serve you to compare yourself. No one can do what you do. No one can be or write what you write. Read it with new eyes, with fresh eyes. Look at everything with our eyes, or with your friends' eyes. You did a tremendous job holding down the fort for all those people, all those rooms with all the wisdom and you were the host. You did an incredible job. Pat yourself on the back. Allow yourself to be congratulated. You deserve it.

There's no such thing as 'don't deserve.' You earned every single compliment, and when someone says "You did a great job," you say "Thank you" and you let it in. That's the way of the feminine. Let it in. You have to receive as much as you give. If all the time you're running around helping and fixing everybody and being the great speaker on the pedestal, you've lost something precious. You have to receive, you have to be open to have lots of money, lots of success, lots of compliments, lots of friends who love you and support you and want to be with you. If you are sitting in an ivory tower, all perfect, you're going to be a lonely dude, and you don't want that. You want to have joy in your life. Let *that* be your focus.

You have the tools. We have given you many of them. You can let go, just like that, because you can, because you are a divine aspect of God. Because God is within you and you are a Goddess; you're a priestess of the highest order. You have had many, many lives in which you have been that, in which you helped tremendous numbers of people, in which you have been on pedestals and on thrones. It's all part of the Whole, and you are here now to bring about a New Earth. And if you don't love yourself, you're gonna be wasting a lot of your time and energy. Peace.

- Comment (NB) It was such a beautiful question, so just know one of the things that came up was "We don't hear. Nobody else hears us the way we hear ourselves and nobody else sees us the way we see ourselves." So, thank you.

Ashtara: Beautiful reflection. You know, if you look at yourselves now and you compare yourselves to a few weeks ago, a mere 5 or so weeks ago, you can actually feel and see how much progress you have made in your own soul's growth, and how much more, in spite of everything and all those voices, you do love yourself more and you have achieved great strides towards being those creators of those containers in the world. The world has been waiting for you to bring together your circles of friends, your beloveds, your compadres, whether they be the other women or the other men or the young people or whatever it is. You are closer and closer to your goal. Your goal is a part of who you are. There was more writing this morning about the journey and the destination; they become the same. When your journey is filled and your destination is filled with the same vibration of you living in the moment in your fullness, there's no longer any distinction. You're not waiting for some future date to be who you are. You can smell the roses. You can enjoy the journey because you're walking a beautiful path along the stream, wherever it is. And it doesn't matter that when you get there, you're going to turn around and come back or that you will be on that pedestal for somebody else. See everything through new eyes, see everything through that reflection that NB just shared with MSG as to how you do not see yourself as others see you, and how we judge. And we are going to include this guy here; how everyone judges themselves on what they think they look like in other people's eyes.

You have spent your whole lifetime trying to please others, trying to be what they wanted you to be. You can let go of all of those bricks from your shoulders right now, with a deep breath and a big sigh and you can even repeat in the 'John Henry fashion' of HeartThread®, "I let go of everything I have been carrying, all the responsibility and all the weight for everybody and anybody. I am letting it all dissolve away and letting my shoulders get softer and my back get softer. I allow everything to get warmer. I melt into my own heart's love for myself. I embrace my vulnerability, my sensitivity, my tenderness. I accept who I am without any judgment whatsoever. There is nothing wrong with me. There cannot be anything wrong with me and there never was. I deserve to have everything on a continual basis without interruption. I deserve to have love. I deserve to have abundance, healthy food, an alive and healthy body. I deserve to have friends and companions and co-creators and cooperation. I deserve to have all the support in the world I ever wanted and I accept and allow it to be so. And so it is, right now. This is so because it can be; because I say so, because I can."

There is your HeartThread® in action. You can say it to yourself. Use HeartThread® wherever you can. Look at this one's website.

- Comment (MS): If you really want to take it to another level there's a song that I'd recommend everybody listen to. You can find it on YouTube. It's by an artist; her name is Alice Merton and it's called "Why So Serious" and it is a really beautiful pop song that'll just make you smile and laugh and anytime you're getting into yourself and your spiritual work and all of what you're trying to accomplish becomes so hard, you listen to that song and you'll just melt away and laugh.

Raphael: Thank you for that gift, a perfect way to end our serious aspect of this gathering. So next week will be Old Chinese, also known as Chung Fu.

Closing Meditation

So, let us begin our final little closing meditation. Let's go back in and put our hands on our heart and feel that beautiful Mother Earth beneath us, feeling our love for her and her love for us, the tenderness of that connection with being human at this time. Allowing ourselves to be human, to have everything, whether it be the trials and tribulations and emotions or whether it be, the elevated triumphs. To know that Mother Earth is always there, to know that the sun above us has been there every single day and always rises and sets each day, as we give our thanks for that Great Light that is shed upon us of all the angelic downpourings of love and light and golden bright energy. Such, such amazing support systems above, below, within, and all around us, and these threads of our hearts that weave out to connect one with the other. We send them around the world, around the Universe, to brighten the lives of those who cannot see, who cannot hear and dwell in darkness, that they may awaken, and they may find that they too are light. That they too are here to express the love of God and Goddess, that they too are here to help one another to see the other side of the coin, a silver lining. They, too, are able to feel within their heart that 'this too shall pass' and that there is a higher purpose to every single thing that impinges upon our consciousness. That we are Light, and Light we shall remain; that we are eternal, immortal, infinite, universal souls and beings and that our job here is to love, beginning with ourselves, and that we can, just like that!

And so it is, thank you.

Voice Seven
Old Chinese

27th September 2020

Preamble: Message from Raphael's Sunday morning journal for the group:

"It is important to see yourself through new eyes, the eyes of the New Earth coming into manifestation through the soul expansion and growth that is now part and parcel of the journey towards wholeness. As each one grapples with the issues of their lives, as each one seeks balance and fulfillment, wholeness, and the reason for their presence on the Earth at this time, it is important to consider and evaluate where you stand now and what you have come to recognize, understand and realize as a part and aspect of the newness. For it has been emphasized how important it is to let go of the story; your individual story and the herstory and history of what you have come to believe as truth, as the nature of the realities and norms and behaviors that are connected with and associated with the belief systems that have been imprinted and inculcated into you as reflections of the old paradigms that are now screaming to be replaced.

So, you have come to this time in your life where you are experiencing a new level of trust, of expansion and of evolution. There is a new confidence building in your cells, in your selves, that is now becoming the new sense of what it is possible for you to achieve and be. It is a new phase, a new threshold that is being presented for you to merely step through, to embrace and to feel in your heart. Because nothing that is not sustainable can last. Ease and grace, self-love and the recognition of your beauty must now replace guilt and shame. The sense of being undeserving and needing to please others, must go. You are the expression of God's Love, the Divine Essence of All That Is in the fullest sense of the idea, of these words.

You cannot allow your mind to constantly diminish your sense of worth, your self-authority and your intuition. You are the authority of your life. There is no higher, no other truth than the one inside your heart, and your constant practice needs to be to unleash the full realization of your power as a sovereign soul and the expression of your soul's purpose. It is the time for pleasure, for satisfaction of mind and heart, for love and beauty, ease and grace, for prosperity, reconciliation and forgiveness.

We are asking you to abandon your grudges, your judgments and your entanglements. Where you cannot forgive or reconcile, walk away, release, say goodbye. You tried. You did your best and now it is all in the hands of the Goddess, in the soft hands of your divine inner wisdom, receptivity and allowance to recognize that the Karma is finished, the struggle is over, the storybook is closed and you are ready for a new life. No more stories, only the adventure of the New Earth. Move now beyond fear. Surround yourself with the mantle of gold of the divine connection that protects you and keeps you out of and beyond fear and allows you to trust the guidance and wisdom of the Angels and Holy Ones that surround you, guide you and are ever at your service. There is no right nor wrong, only your deep knowing of which path to take for yourself, what to believe and what beliefs to drop. You are always guided. As you release the power and attention you have given to the negative voices in your mind, you create space in your cells, in your body and in your emotional field to have everything your heart desires to be made manifest, without effort, without fear and without worry or angst. Know that we are loving you, that we are at your side and that we work on your behalf, because we can, to bring you the fruition and blossoming that you so desire. We love you. You are precious. We are One."

As we feel the golden light surrounding us now, let us begin to feel the threads of our hearts reaching out to weave together a fabric of heart connection that grows bigger and bigger as we include within it all the hearts on this call and in this group; those that cannot be here today, our loved ones, friends and neighbors, those that have passed on or are no longer present with us, those we love so far away. And as we send this fabric, stretching its way out further and further afield, it allows us to connect a bigger and bigger fabric, weaving the threads of the hearts of all those within our cities, our states, our countries; reaching out across the continent, across the oceans, all the way across the entire planet; weaving a beautiful tapestry made up of every single heart of every human, of every creature on this planet. All life is woven in this beautiful heart-essence that spreads its way across and around the planet, reaching into other worlds, other universes, and into all Time and Space. And so, we welcome you here to this place. We welcome you today to the voice of Old Chinese. Old Chinese has been with us for thousands of years, as guide, as Angel, as one who brings great wisdom. We invite him to bring his words of truth, of peace, of love and of special guidance for this time.

Blessings and peace to you all. May the Living Spirit that is in all life come forward and fill your whole being with light, with love, with peace and with harmony, so that you recognize that you truly are one within yourself, within your whole being and that you are one with all life, with all of existence. You are one with the Great Being that has created you, that is you, and that has manifested through you at this time through your particular vehicle. Your vehicle represents the Living Spirit in your own personal and particular way. Because what you offer is unique, no one else can bring that special gift, that special presence and that special light to this planet at this time. No one else, but you.

And so we welcome you here to this space as you begin to understand the messages of the 12, the 12 very different aspects of who you are. This is the wisdom that is designing the New Earth for this time, that is encouraging you to uncover those aspects of self that no longer serve you, those aspects you thought you were. Now you allow them to dissolve away, allowing the stories to fall by the wayside, allowing yourself to embrace a new experience of yourself as a divine essence. Your essence is manifesting in power, in self-authority, manifesting as the Spiritual Warrior, and more so than that even, entices you to consider that you are the sage. In spite of having been a warrior, you are also one who has attained a level of wisdom, of grace, of ease and of a sensibility of knowing your own inner power as inviolate, so that the wisdom that begins to sparkle itself up towards your awareness as your intuition, your inner guidance, becomes paramount. It is no longer in question and you no longer doubt that you are this sage, this wise one.

You are the goddess, the priestess, the god or the priest. You are the one who knows who you are, and it is in this unfolding at this time that you move forward to realize those callings that you have had glimpses of, that you have had glimmerings of within your consciousness. You allow them to grow, to become more prominent in your psyche, in your field and you begin to understand that you are ready; that you have been battling your demons. And you may even continue to do so, continue to face those questions that we have been asking you to look at for all this time. We are asking you to come to a place of understanding. What is your truth? What is your purpose? What can you rely upon? What is your anchor? How do you connect to Mother Earth, to feel grounded in the very substance of physicality while at the same time be an aspect of divinity manifesting through a personality? You are both manifesting as a being of light as well as a being of flesh and blood with emotions, with a history or herstory, with a past, with karma and many lives and with a sense of completing all of those challenges, all of those aspects of what you have been facing.

For we have come to the turning point. We have come to that place in the center of our 12 messages. We have been engaged now, we have completed the first six, just as for the equinox. We have completed the six months of the first half of the year, of the turning of the Earth, the turning around the sun. We have begun now the seventh, that lucky number, with the ancient one, Old Chinese, who has a particular flavor, you might say, that is different from the other aspects, the other ways of seeing, the other perspectives. There have been others who channel this one, Old Chinese, that I am now for you, and each one comes with a different flavor, through a different vehicle, through a different time period. And yet, it is the path of the Spiritual Warrior that I mostly wish you to embrace as an aspect of what I represent.

I also bring to you a flavor, you might say, of the Tao, of that energy that comes from the Eastern wisdoms, that comes with the understandings of the Yin Yang, of the changing, but there always being a consistent seed within the changing that remains a constant. For it is change that is the constant element in the nature of your experience. There is also a element of being able to go into that place of the NoThing, the Tao, that which cannot be named, that which cannot be understood through the mind and through the old ways of seeing. It is important that you understand that that space of the NoThing is also the infinite potential. It is like the black hole at the very center of your galaxy that is the source of All That Is within this galaxy, within your universe, within your understanding of the great cycles of shift and time, of movement and of stillness. It is that place, that space of the Tao which gives birth to the 10,000 things, but it is not one of them, and yet it encompasses all of them. So too, you may consider your name for God or Goddess to also encompass All That Is, the concept of divine inclusiveness, an intelligence that goes beyond anything that can be imagined and yet dwells in its fullness as a seed within your very heart. And as you imagine, or contemplate, or feel this energy of No Space and No Time and NoThing, it becomes important for you to understand and to recognize that it is a place that exists without and outside the box, outside of the normal ways in which you have been accustomed and conditioned to see things. You have been forced to see the world through this lens so it has become your reality.

This is a good time within the perspective of All That Is and these messages from the 12 to consider the 12 as many varied twelves. You can consider us to be aspects of the Zodiac, the tribes, the planets, the months, the different seasons and experiences of time moving through the precession of the equinoxes. You can see us as one way of dividing up the indivisible so that your mind has a way to grasp it and to perhaps identify, to specify and even to stereotype different ways of being, different characteristics of types of people, of structures of your physiognomy or biology and your physiology. These are ways of seeing people as tall or thin, and all sorts of different ways of characterizing them, represented by the 12. And so, as part of considering these different aspects, viewpoints, ways of seeing, different paradigms, we are, in a way, at a place where it is important to recapitulate some of the teachings that we have shared with you. When you go away from this screen and you try to encapsulate what has been presented for you as lessons, as truths, as important understandings, we wish to go back slightly to remind you of the importance of some of the principles we have enumerated.

First is the importance of breath, of taking a deep breath as perhaps the most important thing you could remember or practice beyond anything else, because when you take that breath you are reconnecting with your heart. You are reconnecting with the Earth beneath you, that place of groundedness, like the tree rooted in Mother Earth and that column of light that rises up through your very heart, up to the Heavens, to that spiritual domain that connects you to the above and to the guidance of the Holy Beings and the realms of the Angels. So you are always focusing on the heart through the breath to extricate yourself from the constant babble that goes on within the mind of all humans. For having a mind is part of the package of being human.

And so, judgment becomes one of the other features of this understanding of how to consider some of the principles. For whenever we take that breath, we allow ourselves to release the judgments. We allow ourselves (taking a deep breath)….. to let go, to let go of the angst and the worry, to let go of the fear; for the fear is only a projection of that energy of worry, that mind babble that constantly is going around in your head telling you that there is something wrong. For judgment implies separation and so the great principle of Union we are asking you to embody, represents a space of not separating. It is one of not judging, of understanding that each one carries with them, baggage, their own personal set of challenges. Their woundedness shapes their viewpoint. They become the agents of the conditioning and imprints of their childhoods, of their parenting, their peers, education systems and ancestral patterns.

Perhaps at this time, on this Day of Atonement, it is also a good time to remember the idea of forgiveness, the idea of recognizing that without judging another you are more competent and able to forgive them, because you understand, you have compassion, because you know what it's like to be under the thumb of authority figures that are not in alignment with your own wisdom and truth. And yet you have taken these on. You have taken upon you the burdens. You have taken upon you the feeling of responsibility to be what somebody else wanted you to be, to become the doctor, the lawyer, whatever, on behalf of your father, your mother; to become the perfect housewife for some male figure or the perfect provider and husband for some female figure; to imagine that you can find this perfect one who will be the absolute, perfect complement for you, and will take care of you so you do not have to take responsibility for yourself.

There are many aspects to the guidance we have brought forward, and so, many of these things we have just shared are important for you to re-consider. We have asked you to examine your beliefs, to examine the use of words, because they are representative of your belief systems. We have asked you to look deeply into your hearts to find that which for you represents your calling, represents the direction of your heart's desire. We have also urged you to consider that this is a time for ease and grace, for your flowering. It is a time for you to understand that you do not have to struggle. You do not have to suffer. And you do not have to accept the old vows and oaths, the old guarantees that you gave in other lifetimes to your ancestors that you would do something that is no longer in harmony with where you are at and what is your truth today.

We have asked you to embody the light, to surround yourself with light, to fill your whole being with that golden light of Creator, and that you create around yourself and your beloved ones the protection of this light; that each day you have a practice where you ground and you connect with Mother Earth and Father Sky. You set around you the four points of light, as a pillar, as a chamber, so that you establish within yourself, within your being, this sphere of light that you can expand to provide support and guidance and protection for others. You direct this light out into the world to bless those who suffer, to give some comfort to those who have lost their loved ones. Bear in mind, however, that you are immortal, you are eternal, infinite and universal beings, and you will meet again. There is great blessing in the leaving, just as there is in the arriving. We remind you to smell the flowers, for your journey is the destination. It is, in and of itself, a space of joy, of experiencing the fullness in the moment. Do not let the idea of one day arriving at some destination, take over from the full experience of being present in the moment in your body, through the breath.

We always come back to the breath. We come back also to the understanding that time is not, that linear time is different from cyclical time and that there is a quantum reality to the experience of being in your heart that transcends linear time, that transcends the ability of your mind to figure out what is going on and what is needed. We also wish to remind you that within your heart you have access to that little one within you; that little child, that innocence that still is alive and kicking within your inner heart, within the womb of Creation that you are also, that innocence and that purity. We ask you to remember to once in a while bring that child into your heart, to your bosom. Embrace that one. Remind them that all is well. They made it this far. They are loved and all the lies they were told were never true. They are beautiful, they deserve, there is no need to struggle and suffer and their heart's desire can manifest with ease and grace. They can live in great abundance and prosperity and they will find a way to fulfil their mission and their purpose on this planet. They have come, now, to this moment in time, so-called time, where they are facing the future, where they can let go of doubt, let go of all this, all the stories, all the put downs, all the judgments, all the senses of not belonging, all that stuff. It is time to let it all go. You cannot carry it with you into the New Earth.

Old Chinese invites you to take a moment, to take a breath. To feel your heart again, to feel your body, to feel the Earth beneath you, perhaps to take a sip of water, to take a moment to connect to the others who are here with us, perhaps to open your eyes and to see yourself through our eyes.

It is also very important to understand that you are not alone. Not only are you surrounded by a team of angels and guides. Not only are you able to communicate within and without, but you are also able to connect to your inner wisdom from all time, from all space, from all lifetimes, through the Akashic Records. It is also important to understand that those who are in your life and those who are sharing this course with you and the other courses are also co-creating the New Earth that Mother Earth is calling for now. You are joined by those who follow the programs of the one Flo Aeveia Magdalena, and Sally Pullinger in Glastonbury, who also brings the wisdom of Chung Fu. They are facing their own challenges, their own insights and their own missions. They, too, are part of the bigger picture, of a greater whole and are creating the structures, the new containers for life on this planet. We have encouraged you to consider how you can support those who have already begun their missions or those beings that you are in communication with or aware of through your news, your networks and social media.

It is important for you to give that little piece of light, that little extra that is more than you need for yourself, to give it, share it, and send it out to support others working to empower structures for the new world. There are people developing ways to feed the hungry, to grow food in their neighborhoods, to provide water and services for those who do not have it, perhaps provide some relief for the financial burdens of those who are on the edge. It is important for you to expand your view, to expand your heart in a field of compassion, to recognize and be grateful for that which you have, grateful that you do not suffer in the same way as others do. Be grateful, that you have been able to receive a little bit of an expanded consciousness, and you recognize that all is not what it seems. You understand that what you are being told and what is being touted as the truth is merely one more story. If it does not resonate with your heart, with what you have been learning, uncovering, or has been shared with you, understand that not everyone has access to this greater wisdom, to these greater truths, and so it is necessary to have compassion and patience.

It is important to notice and give up the energy of hurry, rush and urgency. For you do not always understand divine timing, the importance of arriving exactly when you arrive and not be subject to somebody else's agenda. Do not give your power away to anybody else's requirement of you or obligation of you. Instead, do everything with a sense of calm, peace and equanimity, and broadcast that space of inner peace to those who need it the most.

One of the highlights of what we teach, is for you to communicate with the energies of Mother Earth, of Nature, of the spiritual elementals, those that are responsible for the creation of the beauty of the flowers, the waters, the air, the soil. These creatures, the little ones within and on the earth, produce the soil that nourishes, the compost. They are the worms, the flies, the bees, essential for all of life. The songs of the birds bring joy to your hearts and surround you always. Understand that you are connected to this greater whole and that it does not and cannot abandon you. In the expansion of your connection with all the other humans that are working towards creating the New Earth, realize there are elementals and spiritual beings, devas, gnomes, elves, all the great beings of the mythologies that are real. They, too, have a place within the great picture, and you can call upon them to be your allies, to assist you. They can be a totem, and you can also have a special animal be your guardian totem animal, your spirit guide. They will assist you to do ceremonies, to create rituals that enhance and send out vibrations from your ceremonies that bless Nature, the earth, the waters and the air. Do ceremony to free them of the pollution and to remind them of that vibration of purity, their true essence, as clean soil, air and water for the health and well-being of all life.

Remember to have healthy diets. Remember to do exercise and move your bodies, especially at this time. Remember that you are connected to the tree elements, to the beings that have their roots within Mother Earth and that nourish each other and the whole system of life on this planet through their connection with the mycelia and the root systems and through the crowns, the canopies of the trees that send out vibrations and aromas and the fine ephemeral energies of vapors that are interconnected throughout the planet. We remind you too of the importance of being custodians of Mother Earth, of being good stewards, of not wasting, whether it be water or paper, the pulp of the trees, of recycling and of being sparse of your overuse of technologies and of products that are draining your very planet of its life force.

We have many things that we have brought to your attention over these past six weeks. We hope you are cognizant of how much you are evolving and have grown within this time, whether it be from our teachings or from the other courses in which you have been participating that have offered spiritual teachings and lessons. It is important that you see yourselves in the mirror as beautiful, as deserving, as honoring, and worthy. That you see yourselves as sovereign beings who have the right to have everything, to have love in your life, to have peace, and that you are your own best guide and authority. We will take a break and then address your questions.

Old Chinese Q&A

Q. *(CR) Could you speak to forgiveness and the Day of Atonement.*

A. It is an important subject to address. This evening begins the Day of Atonement for the Jewish people. It has been one of our important teachings and practices to examine all the words that we use and their association with our belief systems and concepts. The root for the word 'atonement' is "at-one-ment." It is important because we have emphasized both forgiveness and oneness. The Day of Atonement marks a time in the Jewish calendar and practice, of reckoning, shall we say, in which people are asked to examine in their hearts, souls and in their minds "Who have I perhaps offended?" or "What have I done that has harmed another?"

There is also the aspect of "What is it that I have done in the face of God that has not been in good harmony, or in good alignment with my conscience?" Jews are required to ask forgiveness of their friends and neighbors, and those they may have offended or in some way harmed. That is the personal aspect of forgiveness; and then the other is between you and God, between you and Source, Creator. What is it you have done that you must reassess and consider how it can now be different? It is one thing to obey the words of the law, but it is another to obey the spirit of the law. There was a teaching that came from the Christ about honoring the spirit that is behind the law. The first commandment is to love each one as one would want to be loved. Or to honor and love others as you would love yourself. And that's why it is so important to love yourself, and then, to transfer that same kind of non-judgmental love upon an 'other', whoever they may be. We have emphasized the need to recognize how much baggage each one carries, and therefore the need for compassion, no matter the story, ours or theirs.

The subject of forgiveness is very important. It is no coincidence that Chung Fu, through the one Sally Pullinger, the same essential energy as Old Chinese, has been stressing the use of the Ho'Oponopono, in the *Rainbow Warriors of the Light* a course that they are conducting concurrently. So, this is in fact the same week in which people are examining forgiveness and the use of Ho'Oponopono to send light and healing to those that they hold dear and are in need of healing. This is simply to say "I am sorry. Please forgive me. I love you. Thank you," and to do this from the heart. You come from a place where it is not about saying sorry because you are wrong, but it is about a recognition of respect; respect for another, for the 'other' and the recognition that, in essence, you are all one. And there is a need to honor and respect each other with compassion. Each one has to face their own demons, and we wish to encourage and support them to move beyond those limitations that have been imposed upon them. Understand also that to be healed through forgiveness or sending light and healing, still requires a shift in consciousness. As we send healing to someone, essentially we're not just praying to some external force to heal someone of an ailment, but we are asking All That Is to support that one to understand and to move beyond the emotional and the physical mindset and belief system that needs to be shifted in order for a permanent healing to take place.

So, in essence, we are looking at forgiveness from many perspectives, one of which is the Jewish observance of Yom Kippur. It is also a day of fasting, a way of honoring the body, through ceasing to be mindless about food intake and the way in which one feeds one's body. There are so many aspects to your question, or at least to your observation, and we are very grateful for the opportunity that I can bring this forward to you, especially as your Old Chinese sage is very much stressing the need for forgiveness, and the Ho'Oponopono, for its true essence as a spiritual practice. We also like to weave together the threads of all the spiritual traditions, whether it be the teaching of the 2020 Action Course of Flo Magdalena or it be the teachings that are being done through Sally, or through this particular course that you are attending, The New Earth Council. They are all interwoven and work together. So too, the Jewish practice of forgiveness. You are all connected and all these practices are the practice of becoming whole and recognizing and honoring the One that is the All. So, thank you for bringing that forward.

Q. (MS) As somebody who's a student of ancient Traditional Chinese Medicine, who does Qi Gong and works with 5 Elements theory, my question is related to The New Earth. With the dissolution of older structures, including the paternalistic dominance as seen in Chinese culture, is the role of TCM diminishing or can modern practitioners move the path forward? My second question is: I get a sense we can use Traditional Chinese Medicine as an aspect to enhance the body on the journey towards soul ascension, but by itself may not achieve that end. Is this statement correct?

A. The answer to the first question is "No." We will deal with one question at a time. The concepts and understandings of the 5 elements, correspondences, relationship to body/mind/spirit, and the Taoist principles are valid no matter whether they have been brought forth through a hierarchical, male-dominated structure or not. The principles of harmony, the principles that have been brought to this planet through the Eastern cultures go very deep and are very powerful as a way to understand wholeness. The healing of the body, of the body/mind/spirit connection is viewed through a holistic perspective. So too, the teachings of Feng Shui[63] and of placement. Also, important are the elements of ritual and coming together in ceremony, having an altar and other spiritual practices. All these focuses are not just important but they are vital, because the energy of the Taoist understandings, as well as the practices of the Confucian perspective that came later, concerning the social principles of how to live in society, with honor and respects for all beings.

We understand that there is a need within the creation of new structures to dismantle the hierarchical aspects, as well as those aspects that developed from the Confucian teachings that focused on support of the powers-that-be. So, there are features of the patriarchal Chinese patterns that need to be readjusted in order for it to be valuable for the current time. However, it is also important even within the de-structuring of this current society that social respecting, not social distancing, needs to be upheld even with the changing of the old guard to a new guard. Understanding and honoring another, no matter what color of skin, no matter what belief system, culture or age or gender, is foundational. The new guard is now being replaced by an even brighter one with the young ones that are coming forth. It is always important to continue to examine what has value and what no longer has value from a perspective of equality, harmony, peace, and understanding the need for compassion. Does that make sense, and does that answer your first question?

- *Yes.*

- Thank you. So, would you repeat the second question, please.

- *Can Traditional Chinese Medicine enhance the body on the journey for soul ascension as a single energy or do we need to use it as a tool and not a way to achieve the end?*

- What do you think?

- *I feel it's a tool to help the body so that we can get towards that ascension phase. I don't know that it by itself will get you to ascension.*

- OK, so let us consider that any way in which one divides things will not achieve wholeness. Dissection is good for coming to a partial understanding, perhaps, of the parts of the body without consideration of the soul journey and of the element of wholeness within. So, for instance, there is the family constellation or the social structure, how one aspect is affected by the whole. There is the greater aspect of how one fits into a social system or a family system or a holistic system that does not see the body as separate from the soul and the spirit and the journey and the emotions. So, it is important that one understands that you can use various aspects of practice like Qi Gong or the acupuncture system and other holistic healing practices, but that still somewhat addresses only parts. And the parts, when they're added together do not make the whole. There is always an element of a transcendental nature that is more than a compound, the element of wholeness.

The aspect of the journey towards ascension is really not about going anywhere, but about being. You're all very busy trying to ascend, but what really you are seeking is to raise your vibration. It's another way of saying the same thing. When you see it as a way of enhancing your soul or your heart's quality, which incorporates and includes everything else, then there's less of an urgency, there's less of a need to put something outside of yourself or create a target or destination. It is very interesting, because the reading that we recorded before the beginning of our session essentially talked about destination and the recognition of the journey itself; remembering to enjoy, to have and find the beauty and humor and to smell the flowers. So, it is important that the practices are valued or understood within the context of the whole being, not seen as isolated. Does that make sense? Thank you for your question.

Q. (CR) *Along the same lines, I keep getting readings talking about how it's my body that's doing the work. It's my body that's connected and it's in your heart. Transcending doesn't necessarily mean that your body has to be present. I guess, in a sense, we put too much emphasis on this body and not connecting to the integral nature that we are, that already exists within us. I think that's very relevant just to realize what is already here in our body allowing a natural transformation?*

A. Thank you. So, again, we would like to stress wholeness. The body is your vehicle. It is your medium of expression. You are the Living Spirit that is in all life. You are a special expression of this, and your body is your temple. In every single cell there is memory. The complete Akashic record is accessible within each cell. It is also accessible outside of each cell, in the mind, in the emotional body and in the ethers beyond the confines of your physical form. Everything is interconnected. The heart, as we have said many times, is a quantum experience. It is connected to a quantum field that is beyond the ways of separation, beyond the ways of linear thinking, beyond the ways of logic.

It is also important to recognize that the body, the mind, the emotional body, the connection that you have with society, with your history or herstory, with your ancestors, with your lives; it is all part of All That Is. Everything is the Living Spirit that is in all life. This is why we address each session, beginning and ending with a blessing. We could say the All That Is, we could say God or Goddess. We could use many different terms to designate the wholeness aspect, and yet within the understanding and respecting of wholeness is the understanding and respecting of every single element, of every mineral and its value, of every atom, of every thought, of every feeling, of every connection and relationship. For everything is a reflection of everything. You exist within a holographic universe. When you bless one aspect, you're blessing the whole. When you direct anger out into the universe, it adds to the accumulation of that kind of energy that is already being enhanced by others.

So, it is important to understand and monitor your vibrations through your thoughts, your feelings, your expression, your words and language, your belief system essentially. This is again part of the reason why we have been stressing for you to examine your illusions, because each time you notice that you are engaging in a conversation of a negative vibration with yourself or with another, there is that opportunity to take that breath and shift the perspective immediately, to bring forth "Where is the silver lining to this situation? What is the truth that I'm not seeing? How can I bring love into this equation? Where is it that I am not seeing the wholeness of this? What is the bigger picture? What is it and how is it that I can contribute to the Divine Plan that is unfolding?"

So, it is important, and we thank you for the question, to always consider what is the bigger picture, knowing that "I am an eternal, infinite, immortal and universal being. I am a soul, a spirit that is here for a brief moment in time. How can I use that understanding for the highest good for what you call ascension, to bless instead of curse? How can I break the ties of cursings from the old ancestral patterns that are no longer beneficial to the evolution of life on this planet?" So, there are many ways to take this question, this answer, and make it your own. And remember, when you take that breath, within that breath you have access to all of that wisdom. Blessings and peace.

Q. (NB) So, with the vibration and the Holy Beings of Spirit, it's so easy to be in that world, that sometimes it's difficult to be in this world that we're in, and the mind takes off like into a dreamland, if you will, or, when you go to sleep, or I should say when I go to sleep...(I love going to sleep because it's the dream world, or it's a different world) How do I step into this world fully being here and not getting distracted, with the vibration of the spirit? How do I make that happen with the moment-to-moment practice?

A. Through the breath. The breath is your connection with your body and then the body remembers to ground. It remembers it is part of a greater whole made up of physicality. The body is made up of elements, of atom and molecule, of carbon, of calcium and magnesium. It is connected through all the energies of air and water, the exchange of the moisture from your breath with other moistures of other breaths within the atmosphere. As you connect with any aspect, as you connect with that dream state, you can have a little piece of your mind that is monitoring "How about my body?" Maybe you touch your Shungite, or you think of your mantra, or you remember "Oh yes, he said this or he said that." You remember constantly.

It is like making a pudding. You add your ingredients and you put them on the stove and as they warm up, every once in a while, you stir the pot and you mix them in and you remember "Oh, I need a little more spice, I need a little salt," and you add them in and you come back to the wholeness of the pudding. But it is the joy of mixing everything together that will eventually give you that sweetness of going into your dream state knowing that you have created a beautiful pudding and that that was the last thing you tasted before you went into that altered state. In fact, as you concentrate on letting go of the mind into sleep, you can feel the warmth, the joy, the deliciousness of that pudding, for the whole of you is then present, and so each time, you notice.

Because you are a Spiritual Warrior. We began by saying that you're graduating from even being a warrior to being a sage. And so, you take that personally. You recognize that you know the answer to your own question and you understand that wholeness is everything, and that it is beautiful to go into an altered state and that is fine. And perhaps you need your timer to remind you that you left the oven on and you have to go and make sure that the pudding is not burning. You have to be able to hold it all in the palm of your hand like you're juggling a number of different balls and each one is as important as the other. Does that make sense?

- That's beautifully explained, thank you.

Q. *(NB) It's true that breath, the vibration and the beautiful analogy that you created with the pudding; Is that the path to healing and fully being? Does that help you heal ailments as well?*

A. What do you think?

- Yes.

- You know the truth. Everything is everything, OK? When we separate, we are no longer in wholeness; we are no longer in the field of Union. The Ones talk about Light, Order, Union and Truth. So, there are four. When we created the Pillar in the very beginning, we wove these four elements, like the trunk of a tree from the four roots. They wove into a spiral that became the trunk and then the crown with the leaves and then the blossoms. These four elements form a wholeness that, when they come together, they vibrate in a clockwise spiral motion that we called the Christ Consciousness grid. So, each blessing, each positive thought, each experience of light, of being light or sending light, goes out into the universe and affects reality, enhances reality and creates a greater and higher aspect of reality. So, everything you do affects everything else. When you send prayers for healing, and you do it from a space of love from your heart, it can be rejected on the other end, or it can be accepted. It can be an active acceptance or rejection or it can be an inactive one. Because, you do not have the right to override someone's free will. Everything, as we said, is part of a wholeness and it is important to understand that you have free will, and that you can use free will for the highest good or you can misuse your free will for the lowest 'good.' It is your choice. As you talk of ascension, the path to raising your vibration is awareness, is focus, is placing your attention wherever it needs to be. When we place our right hand on our heart and our left on our right, we are placing our attention upon a location. That location is on the body. It is an internal location within the heart. It is a location within the mind and the consciousness of an intention; and so, it is where you focus your attention that the energy will go. These are New Age concepts that have become blasé. They still have validity, however. So, as you understand and you know yourself, the truth is "Everything is connected." And "Yes" is the answer.

Q. (SL) *I would like to have an answer from Old Chinese. I have always been able to figure out stuff. All my life I have prided myself on my intellect and I have come to learn that intellect is not necessarily an advantage when trying to ascend and many other things. I am wondering if there will be something that will replace the intellect in 5D.*

A. That is a beautiful question. It is also a reflection on how far you have come in these six weeks, in your recognition, in your understanding and in your growth. Because, it is true that you cannot figure it all out. And yet, it is also true that the mind is beautiful. There are so many beautiful things that have come forth from the mind. The poetry of Rumi or of whomever. That beautiful energy of art and creativity cannot function without the mind, without the mind's ability to control your hands, to play the music and to write the music that comes through the heart and then requires practice, that patience and that ability of the mind, of the neurons to fire in particular ways that create pathways that allow the expression of the beauty.

It is the trying that we are "trying" to get you to abandon. It is 'trying' that says "I can't," not "I can." It is trying to get to ascension that keeps you stuck where you are, because ascension is a natural process that happens without trying. It is allowing. The energy behind truth, as was explained in the beginning with the creation of the column, of that tree. The energy of Truth is allowing, because as you allow something to be what it is, it is the truth of Love. You notice Love is not one of those four energies. Love is, as we have said, and as I have defined it, the unconditional acceptance of another's reality or of anything's reality. When you accept unconditionally, you allow them or it to be what it is. You essentially become a Taoist. You go into the NoThing, you allow and accept that what is, is what is. It is part of its nature to be what it is. It is part of somebody's energy to be annoying. They have no control over the fact that they annoy you, and yet, when you allow them to be annoying, and you let go of the need to change them, you allow and accept and then you love, because love is not being nice or liking.

It requires you to shift the pattern of figuring out to accomplish, shall we say, a higher figuring out. Because, as you get these truths, as you grow spiritually, you have a higher understanding that is not as limited. It is not within the box any longer. It does not partition and divide up things that don't need to be divided up. Pigeon-holing is very useful for putting your mail into. It is useful for managing your computers and software and files, and yet, when one looks at the whole picture it becomes a limited way of operating; So, you use other ways of operating that allow your mind to be, we don't quite want to say 'your servant,' but we use the mind to serve the higher purpose of the heart and the wholeness.

So, we think you already understand this, because your question reflects a higher level of understanding than six weeks ago, and it is the letting go that allows the heart to become the more dominant aspect of the wholeness until it is just one of the aspects that is part of the wholeness and does not need to dominate any longer. Because, you're essentially moving towards a balance between the masculine and feminine aspects, between the male-dominated and the female-dominated ways of seeing. This is also why we have attempted to always represent the masculine and feminine energies through having that representation be part of the Twelve energies, even if there are somewhat more male mythological beings, shall we say, or male historical figures, we are still always holding that space for the equality of both and they can be found within the wholeness. Peace

Q. (MSG) I have a question about the role of dreams right now in the process we're all in. I've been a very strong dreamer my whole life. I've had prophetic dreams and learned lessons in dreams and diagnosed myself and other people. But now my dreams are so different. I feel like I'm living other lifetimes, like last night I was hours and hours, it felt like, in India, and I've never been to India, actually. It was so real. I was interacting with people......I was so delighted. It was full-on-light, and it just seems like my life, and so I'm curious what the shift is that I'm experiencing and what Old Chinese has to say about how this is supporting us in this process of ascension now.

A. A beautiful question, yes. We could probably spend hours answering this. Dreams are important, very important. Dreams are, in many ways, aspects of your multidimensionality. They are aspects of many different streams that are asking to be expressed and experienced and integrated, because you are not just one aspect of who you think you are. There are many "you"s that exist, that coexist simultaneously. You're aware of this on a mental level, an intellectual level, and yet, what is happening is that certain aspects of the greater "you" are being integrated into this experience of greater wholeness, so that you have much more availability as the "you" that you think you are, or that you experience yourself to be. You have much greater access to a whole field of resource, of depth and of guidance and inspiration than you have had in the past. Your consciousness has expanded to allow more and more light, peace, joy, enjoyment and pleasure. It has brought more letting go to fill your being and to open you to, shall we say, a deeper level of bliss, and greater expansiveness of consciousness. So the ability to monitor, to write down, and be familiar with the dream world is important because it is a part of you, but also because your questions, searchings, confusions or conflicts within your totality, are also being resolved within the framework of your dreams.

Dreams are so real. The people that you meet, the encounters that you have with them, they are not experiences that you can put your finger on from this life. They belong to much greater field of who you are as a totality. You are also interconnected with all other souls, each of you. So, there is a much bigger picture than the mind can comprehend, and yet your mind itself is expanding. Because more and more neurons are firing within the brain, creating more neural pathways. This affects the twelve strands of your DNA so that you have more and more of them operating as you evolve. You become more in tune with the many aspects of your being. And you might say there are twelve. You could look at this as another way of partitioning reality.

It is not important how many aspects, rays or facets there are, or how to understand each ray, division or fragments within the structures of other wisdom teachings. It is important that you relish and enjoy your dreaming and that it feeds you. Allow it to grow within you self-love and a recognition that your toolbox has accumulated a few extra tools. You have within a fuller arsenal of benevolent 'weapons', shall we say, that will allow you to enhance your purpose and to create new ways and new structures, because you are no longer within the old box and you are expanding your whole field of experience.

So, it is a good thing. It is a special and beautiful thing, and the more you are cognizant, the more you practice remembering and writing down the dreams, they will start to filter into your poems, into your sharings with others, into your healing work and into your mission to become a teacher and to gather around you circles. It will expand your ability to answer people's questions and be a guide and a leader and a model for them, because there is a greater richness of soul that comes from the field of dreaming. Does that answer your question?

Your Word, and Closing Meditation

It is important, in fact, one of the principles that Old Chinese regards as vital, that you honor your word and that you keep it. When you make a promise, you fulfil it, and if for some reason you are not able to, you take responsibility, perhaps apologize. You do not diminish yourself, but you apologize because you did not come through and you will be more aware next time. It is OK to recognize and honor it and let it go, especially as we have been considering forgiveness.

Let's go back into that special space as we put our right hand on our hearts and our left hand on our right and feel that beautiful, golden space that we have shared together. We understand ourselves as more, far, far more than we think. We recognize that we are connected through the threads of our hearts and through this golden blossoming that is occurring within each one and collectively. And it reaches beyond this group to other groups, and to all those upon this planet who are working ceaselessly and tirelessly for the benefit of the Whole and for the great healing of Mother Earth's people and creatures. We are sending our blessings all around this planet and beyond it to those beings who suffer, that they may find relief, that they may find some comfort, joy and peace. That they find ease and grace, and abundance. That they have their basic needs taken care of, food, health, shelter, companionship, friendship, connection, and love.

And so, as we are in the inner space of our own hearts, we expand this field, to encompass all of life. We send out the vibration of love, of acceptance, of at-one-ment, forgiveness, beauty and harmony, so that each one may find peace in their heart. We ask that the Living Spirit that is in all life come forward and bring the deepest sense of inner wisdom, great pleasure, and the recognition that there is no longer a need to suffer, to struggle. You are always surrounded by guides, by angels, by the healing energies of those who watch over you, your galactic brothers and sisters, Mother Earth and all of her minions, the great Devic Kingdoms that watch over you. The Living Spirit is all-encompassing and you are an expression of that Living Spirit that expresses through love, through light, and that is who you are. Blessings and Peace to you all.

Voice Eight
The Druid

4th October 2020

Let's put our right hand on our hearts and our left on our right, taking that deep breath, feeling that downpouring of beautiful golden light filling us with stillness, with peace, all the way down now through this column, from above, down through our whole bodies, through our feet and into the very core of Mother Earth. This column of light allows us to get centered and at the same time to be completely relaxed and empty, filled only with stillness, with a sense of peace, with ease. Let go of any thoughts, feelings, any sounds or distractions. Totally here, feeling our bodies with every breath, feeling Mother Earth, our guides, Father Sky, feeling the beauty of this time of the year, the changing of colors, the magnificence of the sounds of the birds and the fruits of the trees, fruits of the gardens. It's a beautiful time of blossoming and a time for each one's heart to open wider, to blossom, to feel grace pouring down and through and around us, surrounding us with a beautiful sphere of golden white light that creates a sphere of protection, keeping us safe. It is filled with this beautiful light, so that only the highest vibrations may be present with us.

Any ancestors or beings or energies that wish to join us must come in light, in love, in peace, in service, to witness, to bless or for healing. Only the highest vibrations are welcome here. As we rest our hands, let us invite The Druid to join us, to bring wisdom and guidance; to speak on behalf of the Council now.

Indeed, we always speak with one voice, even though we have many different personalities. Each one brings their special flavor, special message from their special time period of your evolution, of your cosmology, of your mythology. There is, you might call it, a shroud of mystery that surrounds the energy of "Druid." It evokes the energy of Ireland and the British Isles, the standing stones, the worship of the tree people, the oaks, the beautiful energies of that special tree, the yew tree, the sacred circles and the mystical labyrinths. The labyrinths have been transported to the monasteries and cathedrals of the Christian era and yet still preserve that energy of deep, deep connection with Mother Earth, with her cycles, with her changes. These many associations reflect the movements of the planets, of the moon, of the sun, of celebrating and coming together in ceremony and ritual to honor our alignments with other beings, creatures, star systems, and planetary alignments that are part and parcel of the energies of Mother Earth and beyond. They are situated on Ley lines,[64] at sacred sites that contain extra power and extra juice for the journey, that empower us through ritual and the observation of social gatherings. Together in sacred ceremony and sacred respecting and honoring of all life, of male and female, of child and elder, of the circles.

The spirals and the circles have been part, for eons of time, of the feeling of movement, of the feeling of connection with all life. The clockwise spiral motion of the Christ Consciousness goes out and sends the vibration of love, of healing from the heart as part of our practice now. Let this be your practice too, as you go into your silent, sacred space within the heart and establish your column. In essence, the circles that you gather around you, create this vortex of energy that calls in and then sends out the vibrations of healing and transforms the vibrations of negativity, converting them into positive energies. These then project out into the universes the energy of light and love, the energy of your divinity. They send a reminder that each one is a child of the divine, a child of the Goddess especially, as we honor Mother Earth above all, but not to the exclusion of all the gods and goddesses wherever they may be honored.

For all aspects of divinity are one, just as all aspects of life are one, just as all the molecules and atoms are great reflections on a small scale of all the cosmic motions of the heavenly bodies. This is the energetic of the sacred geometry and the forces that hold everything in place with such precision, such amazing intelligence of Creator. You cannot comprehend it with the mind and yet it can be felt in the very cells of your body when you sit upon Mother Earth or lie upon her or you place your back against a tree and feel that life-giving energy, that beautiful strength upon your back that holds you in place, anchoring you in Mother Earth. And it connects you to Father Sky and you feel the vibration of an expansion, of the canopy and of the root systems that weave together throughout the entire planet, bringing you that connection with All That Is.

It is so beautiful to hear the sharing of the message of Old Chinese; for Old Chinese too represents an avenue of respect for Mother Earth that goes back to the ancient Chinese wisdom that has profound truth within the understanding of Feng Shui and the Ley lines and the power grids of Mother Earth. So too, there is this connection, this grid work across the planet that weaves us all together.

This is especially so when we come together in circles to do our practice, to share our blossoming with each other, we open our hearts to that understanding that no one is higher or lower or better or worse than another. This is so even on the journey through the stars, even on the journey through many lifetimes. These journeys into the many-faceted and multidimensional lifetimes and dimensions that you all have inhabited and inhabit are actually woven together as a beautiful fabric, just like the HeartThread® fabric that we weave, the weave of connectedness to all life. It is also why you are able to thrive at this time in the face of so much suffering and so much confusion and terror, because you have found within your heart a thread of connection to other souls who are all in the same space of working on your 'stuff.' Essentially it is about releasing your 'stuff,' releasing the layers that have kept you captive in the past. They have fashioned you into a 'good citizen.' The authorities have imposed upon you rigid structures to control you. You are shaking off these impositions at this time, whatever they may be, and however far back they go through your ancestry. Their power is waning, no matter how tight the weave of fear they are weaving at this time, to hide the terrible things they have perpetrated, and continue to do so. Their power is waning.

The illusion, the "Grand Deception" they have created is not working. It does not have enough power or clout to last, to sustain itself. As you grow in light, as you grow in the beautiful brilliance of this golden sphere of light, that each day you surround yourself with to keep you safe and protected, nothing that is not light, nor of the highest vibration can penetrate into that sphere. Everything else will bounce off of it without power to affect you as you go into your own inner authority, and exercise the trust that is developing so strongly within you now.

You may not have noticed how much you have evolved in these last six or seven weeks that we have been together. You may not have noticed how much you have shed weights from your shoulders, old patterns, or imprints of your ancestors that have not been of the highest level. Perhaps you are aware how much your heart has become willing to be softer and more vulnerable. Perhaps, how much you have appreciated the tenderness of connection, of contact, of human touch, of eye to eye, face to face communication. Have you been connecting with those with whom you have not spoken in a long time, to ask "How are you? How have you been doing? What is going on for you?" Have you been showing your caring, giving your children perhaps those extra few hugs, that extra warm cuddle so that they know how much they are loved and that nothing can touch them that is not love? Because the future is theirs. It is the way in which you teach them and model for them that becomes their way of life so they don't have to go through the same perambulations of casting away old patterns, old vows and contracts with ancestors. Your work at this time is to clear up your confusions, your spaces of conflict, perhaps to heal an old relationship where you have found enough strength to forgive.

Old Chinese, through Sally from Glastonbury, is very active in promoting the Ho'Oponopono. "I love you. I'm sorry. Please forgive me. Thank you." When these words are spoken as you envisage someone from your past or from your current life that you have a difficulty with, and you are in your heart, you begin to feel how much this simple practice can shift things. Old Chinese has been with us this week and over a very long time period. His energy is compounding now with the energy that I bring you as that hooded mystery figure that you see, as The Druid. You perceive me as one who knows the secrets of the plants, of healing, of connecting to Father Sky and Mother Earth. I conjure up the power of the heart and the beauty of music to heal, that space for you (KM) to follow with your heart's longing to express, and bring healing.

It does not matter what time frame you consider me to be from. I may be a Druid from the past, from the pre-Christian era and yet I still dwell within your heart, holding the mystery of the land, of the serpent, of the places on the hilltops, the places where the altars were built, where the people gathered for the rituals associated with masculine energies. The Druidic rituals are also found in the valleys where the fountains, the streams, the sacred springs were honored by the people and their tokens were hung upon the trees, the yew tree, the oak, the beech, the birch and the pines. All these beautiful creatures of tree energy are so connected to the practices of loving Mother Earth, and being a part of Nature as you follow her seasons.

We are weaving with you now, we who have spoken with you so far, through this one here. The Druid brings the beauty of the Bard, of song and stories. As you release your old stories, your old patterns, you can weave together a new story in song. You can express your cultures, your beauty, your inner power through artistic expression of song, dance, movement, and art. Express the feeling that wells up within you as you start to feel this expansion of your heart within this golden sphere; as you feel this rising, the presence of your angels, your guides, perhaps of your devas, or the ones you played with as a child. These faerie-folk, the elves, the gnomes, the ones of Mother Earth hide from humans because humans have not been kind to them. As your heart is empty and free and filled with love, they feel it and they come, just as the deer show up for this one or the raven comes to peck at the peanuts he casts for them.

So, your life begins to be filled with magic, with miracle, with serendipity, with knowing and trusting. Your intuition grows stronger and stronger, and keeps you safe. It keeps you whole and allows you to have more and more peace in your life. It reminds you each time there is a small worry, to take that breath: "Ahhhh, I was noticing that I was getting caught up and I can let it go, because everything works for good, everything works for my highest and best and for that of my family and those I love. Because I surround them always, even unconsciously, with my light, with my love, with my caring." And as that caring expands, it begins to encompass your tribe, your people, those who carry the light - the other lightworkers, those who have a similar hunger in their hearts for peace, for cooperation, and to live in harmony with Mother Earth. They wish to enjoy the fruits of the labor with the soil; the organic food that you find from your local people at the farmers market, the sprouts perhaps that you grow in your home or your little garden. The juicy tomatoes! Whatever it be that keeps you connected to Mother Earth, to the water, the air, the soil. Take walks in Mother Nature. Enjoy your time with the trees, with the birds. Place your little trays of water, hang your hummingbird and bird feeders to attract these ones to come to you to celebrate, to serenade you with their songs, so that you always feel that you are connected, no matter where you are, to all of life.

The music of the Bards was the way in which the news was transported, was taken from one corner of the Earth to another. The one Christ spent time in England. He was guided and led by Joseph of Arimathea, of Glastonbury. He was taken, for Joseph had tin mines within the provinces in the kingdoms of Great Britain and Ireland and he would bring the young one to learn from the Druids. Much of his teaching gathered the wisdom of the Earth, the wisdom of Nature, the wisdom of the connection with all the Zodiac, with all the teachings of the ancient ones. He knew of the rituals of the circles, the healing of the herbs, the special use of herbal preparations, the special fruits, and those aspects of the kingdoms that were beneficial for human healing. And so, he would travel to our lands and learn from us and he was one of our wise ones when he came, and as he grew older, he traveled to many places, like India. He traveled very far and wide, not only astrally, but also physically. He was conversant with the weave between Britain, Ireland and Scotland and the Western regions of Europe, the lands of the Celts, in the areas of France and Provence and of Gaul and of Spain. There was a connectivity that expanded out and that allowed Mary Magdalene and the Christ refuge after what was called the crucifixion and the resurrection. This was part of the ways in which the teachings spread across Europe.

The teachings of the Law of One have been held and kept safe within the hearts within the secret transmissions through the ages of those who kept the flame alive. The flame of love, of service, of higher service to the Whole. They have now become a host of lightworkers upon your planet who are weaving together their different ways of bringing healing and the wisdoms that are being taught. The wisdom is coming forth from them, weaving the connection with the extra-terrestrial ones, the guides from the Galactic Federation and from the Star Nations. There is a weaving of the connections with Mother Earth and the Devic Kingdoms, from the Initiate leaders of your many ancient civilizations that have carried the truth, the teachings of the Goddess, the teachings of the God, the teaching of the combination of these. There has always been a connection with light, the golden light of love, of service. This is the highest energy possible, in alignment with All That Is, serving the One Heart that weaves us all together throughout time and space, through the threads of our hearts as they reach into all time and space.

You are here at this time, preparing to be the teachers, the wisdom keepers, guides and elders, to become channels of the Light, of these messages. Channeling is not some special thing that belongs only to the few. It is part of the natural evolution of your soul as it grows, and you start to get the wisdom through your intuition, in the moment. As you allow yourself the confidence to trust in your own wisdom, your own guidance, there becomes less and less of a differentiation between your higher self and all of us, we 12 or we 144 or the 144,000, or whatever it may be. The wisdom dwells within your own heart, within your own sacred intelligence that is within each cell of your body, within each cell of your consciousness, within the ancient memory that is within your DNA, within the 12 strands that now are coming forth and expanding out.

The wisdom teachings that were written down and were distorted are now becoming clear and being rectified, being realigned with the sacred teachings of the Elders, of the ancient ones. This truth is accessible within your heart, so that what you teach the young ones, the stories, the songs, becomes part of their unfolding. Then they will remember with deep love and cherishment as they go on to become the teachers. They will remember that you sang them to sleep and told them stories and read them the story books that you were brought up with, that thread of connection to the magic of fantasy, the magic of imagination, the grandness of the adventure, of the hero and the heroine. All these things get lost within your computer world, within your Zooms and your technology, and it is recommended for you to go back to some degree to books, to reading, to pictures, to showing an image on a piece of paper instead of pixels on a screen, to reading stories and encouraging your children to write. To write their stories, their poems, to write their wisdom, and to draw, to express through art. For the little ones carry the memory of all their lifetimes. They carry the memory of the wisdom that they came here with, and you can discuss with them. "What was it like in your last life?" or "What do you think about what's going on with this one or that one?" You ask them to let their wisdom come forward. Even the youngest ones have great memories, even if they are not yet fully able to comprehend with their minds in the logical, linear ways. They have a way of expressing their truth, and there's much in them that would teach you. You are the teachers and the students of each other.

And just as with the Druids, there was much that was taught through word of mouth. The Bards were a sect, you might say, a very special aspect of Druid culture that had to study, that had to become an initiate in the secret teachings; for when they sang their songs in the castles of the rich with their harps upon their backs, traveling from one lord to another, telling the stories, singing the songs, they were the carriers of the history of the time. They brought the wisdom. They brought the news, and it was important for them to encapsulate secret teachings within the stories. And so, their training was arduous, and they were bound by a strict oath to observe secrecy, to be true to their order. They were the wise ones, and they were the ones who gathered around in the circles and led the people. The people were always led by the circles of the Elders, by the wisdom of the Sages because the accumulated wisdom of the tribe, of the village, of the group was sacred and carried only the truth and did not allow the lies to penetrate. That was why it was essential to be so vigilant and to only create imprints, conditioning to become, shall we say, good citizens of the soul. In other words, benevolent for the society in which these teachings and trainings were intended, so that people might live together in harmony, honoring and respecting each other. Also honoring boundaries, honoring 'yes' and honoring 'no,' learning the truth of who they are and what their purpose was.

Who was to be a warrior, who was to be a sage, who was to be the Bard, and who was to cultivate the soil for the people? And always there was the sacred marriage, there was the time of the fructification of Mother Earth at the Beltane, honoring the life force energies of Mother Earth and honoring the times of the going within in the winter, the sitting around the fires, sharing the stories, the wisdom, sharing the laughter and the food that had been gathered and prepared for the winter. Life was simple and yet it was fragile, for the world of Nature is a powerful world and the world of man was a very frightening world too, because not all honored the sacred trust of the heart and the recognition of equality and of harmony and peace. There were those who were hungry for power, who wielded the sword and used control, and it was necessary to learn how to navigate within this world. Perhaps to be a warrior.

You are at a time now on your planet, as we have shared before, where having the sword of truth at your side, safely tucked within the scabbard, allows you to live perhaps invisibly and yet powerfully, and yet, when necessary, to share your truth. You are learning to be the Sacred Warriors of this Path of Truth, honoring the connection of life to life, and the extended interconnection. For it will not be long before you will meet your brethren, your fellow heart brothers and sisters, children and fathers and mothers from other worlds who watch over you and love you. They are waiting for your hearts to be opened en-masse, so that they can greet you and help you to clean up those mistakes of the past, shall we call them, that have polluted your planet and harmed all life, the creatures, and the vegetation, the children of Mother Earth.

So, we will take a moment's pause, to look each other in the eyes again and see where we are at. (pause) We are on the same page, still? Thank you. So, let us go back into the space for a short time before we take our break and feel if there is anything else that we need to share with you.

What is coming forth is the recognition of what you call the continuity of life, the fact that you are immortal souls, that life is eternal and infinite. Old Chinese always addresses you with, "May the Living Spirit that is in all life come forward and bring you peace," and it is from Old Chinese that we have this blessing. We will share with you one day in greater detail the beautiful stories of the Old Sage and the Forrest. Old Chinese is like an Eastern version of the Western Druid. He brought forth the teachings of the Old Sage by the Lake of Li who taught the young emperor-to-be everything that he needed to become a wise leader of his empire when the time came. And the young one would approach the forest and drink from the running waters by cupping his hands into the water and saying, "I am eternal. I am infinite. I am universal. I am immortal."

So, when we feel the sting of loss, when we feel the loss of loved ones, it is a good time to reflect on immortality, to reflect that the soul, that spark of divine fire enters for a short time, in a very limited aspect of reality. Your human consciousness in the framework of a physical body is but a moment in the big, infinite picture. You are here, briefly, and then you are reunited. For within the fields of the heart, within the quantum understandings of reality, there is no separation, there is only connection. The love continues and is palpable, and we understand that it is being felt and honored and recognized. So too, you arrive on this planet from the Infinite, wailing sometimes, as that one Shakespeare has so eloquently written about, and then, when you leave, you return to that vastness of the Light of Union, of expansion, where you're free.

So as one grieves, it is important to bear in mind that this is but a brief moment in time that you are on this planet. Before you look around, we will be sitting at this screen again and a week will have gone by and there will be another voice and another sharing. This time we believe it will be Joan of Arc and her voices. So, know that you are woven together in this beautiful fabric of heart connection. Those of you who practice the HeartThread®, give your honoring to John Henry, call him in. Do this practice. This practice is powerful. Do it with yourself. Do the Ho'Oponopono with yourself. Then use your time in the stillness of your meditation, when you align yourself with Mother Earth and Father Sky and your heart, to do this forgiveness practice and see how it affects your life. It will impact your connections and relationships and how much blossoming there will be for you. And as you say the words in the ways of John Henry, as you reframe the old imprints, the old wording and the old belief systems into a new form that is only positive and loving, you are releasing more and more of that weight upon your shoulders. You are letting go of more of your worries and concerns and trusting more, letting go, melting into the presence of all of us around and within you. We guide you, love you, and can go to the ends of the Earth to fetch you that which your heart desires, for service and for the highest good of you and all.

So, know that we love you deeply. It is a great honoring for us to be here with you in this way. It warms our celestial hearts to feel your love for each other, your warmth and love for your loved ones and your dedication to this path of light. We support your ability to teach others, to share your own wisdom, and to honor above all your inner guidance and your intuition as you live it to the full. We bless you in the name of the trees, in the name of the rivers, the waters, the beautiful fountains and those special places where the water bubbles up from Mother Earth. Also, those places on the hilltops where you stretch your arms out to the Heavens and send out your light and your love in a clockwise spiral of the Christ Consciousness, sending this golden light to shine upon all. This is your practice now; to be a light unto the people, to shine light wherever there is darkness and to bring home the hearts of those that are lost. We love you so much. Blessings and Peace. We will take a break.

The Druid Q&A

Q. *(CZ) I was really happy to hear and feel the energy of The Druid today and I feel a deep resonance with this energy. I laugh because both sides of my ancestry here on the planet come from Eastern Europe, and yet we have a secondary identity with the Celtic. Two of my relatives are born on Saint Patrick's Day, my mother had red hair, freckles, and they named me Coleen. We grew up next to an Irish pub. My grandmother was definitely of the earth, so connected, and within the family we have people who are so connected either with their tomato plants or their birds or whatever. The resonance is very deep for me and I feel like I am living that, and it's very heartwarming to identify with this energy of The Druid. Is there anything that I can further enhance or study? I was thinking of green plant medicine, things like that, any words in that direction?*

A. Absolutely. We are so delighted to hear this from you, and when you do move and find a location that is warmer for your heart, it's important that you have a part of it that you cultivate as your special garden, that you create altars therein to honor these beings. We want to encourage you to study the plant medicine, and to expand that arena to your sisters, your circle, those that you will find, who will be drawn to gather together with you. Perhaps you can do this practice, this study in a way that is more collective for you as a support system for each of you. Honor this practice of the herbs and the green and the growing things more and more. This is a very good path.

We also see you, when the time is ripe, taking a trip to Ireland, and to the British Isles to explore and to have fun and to honor this connection even more deeply. In the books of the Ringing Cedars series[46], Anastasia, from the forests of Russia, the Siberian Taiga, the Cedars of Siberia has shared very special teachings, especially in the first and second books. The author, Vladimir Megré, who wrote the books tells of his experience with her and how she and the children that they had together live within the Taiga, with the 'wild' animals. She shares how to create a Kin's Domain, a sustainable small plot of land on which one can live, which can generate and provide all one's needs. The people of Russia have for a long time developed these 'Dachas' where they spend more and more time, grow food and supply much of the organic, healthy vegetables and fruits to the people. She tells of how she astrally visits and supports these 'Dachniks'.

Within the area of Bosnia and Russia there were many sacred circles. In Bosnia there are large pyramids where great civilizations existed that were connected to the Earth-based practices which were woven together around the planet. Megré found Dolmens within Russia, huge stones, one that leans upon the others, that are mentioned in the series. He was led to explore them. There are photographs of them in the books. He shares about his pilgrimage and mission to restore the remembrance of the Ancient Ones of that land. It can reconnect you to a much broader lineage of wisdom traditions, be they from the East or from the West.

Many of these teachings came from the West from Atlantis and from the East from Lemuria. There are also existences of past civilizations even further back, that were very deeply connected to the trees, the growing things and with the Devic Kingdoms, the Leprechauns and the Little Ones. So, we encourage you, very much, to further your studies. There are a number of books, about the wisdom of the plants and of the animals. This one has on his library shelves many books about the connection between the heart and the plants and the growing things.[65] It would be good for you to research, to read, to listen and to practice a way of expressing and cultivating your own connection with this way of being, through art, through some form of creativity as well.

You do not have to wait. You can still do some of this practice even on the land where you are, because whatever you plant will bear fruit, whether it be roses or other flowers or some growing things that will, in the coming years bring forth fruit, because you benefit the whole as you put your love into the Earth and into the seeds. In fact, the one Anastasia has given a practice for how to bless the seeds before you plant them into the earth, so that they will carry your special vibration in the food that grows from them. We are feeling that we have answered your question.

- Yes. I'm very grateful. I'm here in New Mexico now where I can combine that with the Native American relationship to the seasons and the planets and the Earth and so it's very fertile here with all those different traditions. Thank you. Yes.

Q. (NB) You had mentioned that, as we shed, as we let go of those beliefs and structures that don't serve us, we are thriving. Can you speak a little bit more to that specifically? I can see that, I can really see that thriving more as I let go. How does it relate to when all those financial structures are falling apart? We're shedding. How will we thrive in that? What is your vision for that?

A. First of all, you say you see already some of what it feels like when you shed, that you thrive more, so in essence we're asking you: Can you feel it? Feel it? That's a question for you

- Yes

- So, understand that thriving happens in the moment, in the present. It happens around all of your activities. It happens around your family structure, your business structure, mental structure and energy, your thought forms. It's how you approach, perhaps, considering a step towards the future; but it all happens, in a way, with the release of the breath, into a release, into a sigh, a way of letting go of one extra little piece of worry. So that the more you do the letting go, the more you are opening up space within your cellular structure, your memory, your DNA, your being, your cells, to embody and encapsulate more light, and then to radiate more light. So, you become lighter. The more you become lighter, the less you worry, the less you have issues and the less you fear. Because there's a certain aspect of the question that relates to the future that is attached to fear. "How will it be in the future? What if?"

So, as you release any worries, and you trust, you thrive in that very moment, and the "what if" unfolds without worry. And the fields of endeavor that you find yourself led towards, begin to take shape and begin to mold for you the new structures, and we are here to assist you to build new structures for the very civilization that is in disarray. This is going to be your own personal life structures, your inner consciousness thought form structures, but it will also manifest as cooperative ventures and structures within the world that will be based only on thriving, on cooperation, peace, love, sharing and on win/win situations. As the structures that are disintegrating disintegrate, your thriving grows and blossoms, and you begin to feel and notice that you are already practicing ways of seeing and doing and being, that are different and new. You have a deeper sense of security in your guides, in your helpers, in your own inner wisdom and in that state of peace and stillness that you're cultivating.

So, it takes you out of the future and brings you into the present, into the moment, into your body and into that ability each time to take that breath. Every time you take a breath and release even a teeny little worry, you become lighter and freer, and you open up space for the new structure to come forward. Does this make sense?

- Yes, it does and, since this is such an important aspect, the breath, and I think this question has been asked before, while it's such an important aspect, why the forgetting?

- Because! (laughs) If we were a little one asking a question and you as a parent would say "Because!" So, let's go to that simplicity. Because you are human, because you are bombarded by fear. It surrounds you. You walk out into the streets and perhaps you have forgotten, but all of a sudden you see people walking around with these funny masks on, and you think "Where am I? Am I in some movie? Did I show up in some surreal play of Sartre? What's going on?" And then you remember "Oh, yes, the vir-us! The whatever. And it's constantly bombarding your field. So, you are still in the process of needing to constantly remind yourself not to swallow the illusion, the Great Deception. For we would remind you that this whole thing was created in a lab that specializes in germ warfare – a biological weapons lab. It is part of an energy of control. It has no power over you when you are sovereign, when you are in your power, when you project only positivity, when you look after your immune system and you fill your heart with love. It cannot sustain. It is not transmitted in the ways that you have been taught. There are many lies and deceptions around this entire phenomenon; and so, the more you let go, the freer you become of the entrapment.

It requires many breaths because you are constantly being reminded of the lie, of the worry.

It has been with you for thousands of years. When the ancestors were tilling the soil as serfs, and had to provide food for the lords, it was always a struggle. Life traditionally has always been a struggle, and part of the new paradigm that we bring you is the message that it is not necessary to struggle, and that suffering is a choice. You are working diligently on releasing the old choices, and embracing the new ones. That is why it requires numerous sighs, numerous breaths and numerous interruptions of the voices in the mind. Because they have been patterned, programmed, imprinted into you through your conditioning. Does that answer the question?

- It sure does. And I saw KM's daughter feeding us with joy. That was just so adorable and so timely. Thank you.

Q. (LS) It seems to be a culmination now of everyone's answers but with the first question I had fear triggered in me, like from being grounded and feeling great to what you talked about, the fear suddenly coming up about being a herbalist and I'm actually studying Western herbalism and Native American herbalism right now. I felt very called to do that this year, to finally get into that. I've tried to move forward with it for years but always get stopped by the fear of legal ramifications, something possibly bad happening, all that age-old stuff. So, what I'm understanding though, I guess, to a deeper level now, is to just continue to breathe through that; like I'm shaking right now just thinking about moving forward with it but, you know, all this past week it has just felt so good and so enlivening and I can't wait to start more of the nutrition and herbalism that I've always been afraid to do. I get to the point of starting my business, having a few clients, and then I just completely shut it all down, because of the fear. I don't want to do that this time.

- Can I ask you to go there now?

- I'm there now.

- We are with you. So, feel all of us in your heart. Feel the fear melt away together, because you are not alone and you're not alone in this; and your body, your mind and your soul are all hungry to feel that release. And it can happen through that breath. The more you remember the feeling of that breath, of the stillness replacing the thought, the fear, the feeling, and allowing it to dissolve, even if it's just for a moment, in this moment. And if you say the Ho'Oponopono to yourself, if you forgive all your lifetimes, if you forgive all of those who ever harmed you in all those lifetimes, and you embrace, you said the "age-old." It sounded like "Angel," so we are asking you to replace the "age-old" imprints and fears with the "Angel" imprints, of that expansion of golden light within you that is indomitable.

So, the memory of this feeling that we are all sharing together, of just being light with each other and of letting go of fear, that imprint, that angelic imprint will be something you can return to, because your memory will hold it. And each time the fear comes up and the shaking, and the breath comes in, (deep breath and sigh) you let go, and you give it to Mother Earth. And then you begin again, just like that, because you can. And it becomes simple and you're empowered, because your path is a powerful path and you cannot any longer allow yourself to diminish your power; and you will not be harmed. You will not be punished. You will not be crucified or burned at the stake for honoring your power, your wisdom and your truth. You have powerful protection and you have the most incredible guidance and access.

As you develop your trust and the breath, and the release, it becomes a new habit, even if you have to do it over and over and over. It becomes softer, and easier, and lighter, and the melting becomes so beautiful that you just want to melt, 'cause there's nowhere else to go. And as you handle the herbs and you smell the burning incense and the smudge, and you feel the connection with the ancestors that practiced, that knew, that were safe, you become stronger and stronger in this connection, because Mother Earth is with you, and all the creatures and all of those beings, the devas, are there with you, strengthening your practice and drawing to you the ones that need your work. For you are creating a new structure and it is not going to be dismantled by those energies. Surround yourself each day with the power of love, with the Golden Sphere of Protection. Always, it goes with you, just as the Golden Mantle of the 2020. And you feel that energy as much as you can and let it all go into the golden light. And you can do this and you know, now, that you have all of us behind you and with you. Thank you.

- Thank you.

(MS) I don't have a question as much as a comment. I'm just sort of getting on this train with NB and LS and what the message that's being said is really connecting. You had mentioned using a deep sigh or sighing to release worry and so, sighing is a sound that I've learned that comes from the kidney energy, which is very much related to ancestral issues because the kidney is where we get our genetics from, and using the breath and the sigh, so the lung is connecting us with inspiration, taking things in and at the same time the large intestine, (I know I'm using different terms here), is letting things go, so I just, I guess the question is: Are we trying to get rid of old ancestral issues or mistakes with the deep sigh, or is it our own stuff, or, yeah, I guess that's maybe the question.

A. We love your questions because we know that you know the answer! All the above, is it not!? Right now, we could call all of our ancestors to join us. Imagine that they're like an arena of beings on some cloud sitting above us looking down and admiring and touching or whatever they're doing, and you have an array of ancestors who are here to witness, because only love and light and truth are possible in our space; so that only the ones that are ready to listen to truth, to let go of ancestral patterns that are harmful or that are limiting or judgmental are here. They will be able to hear this and let go of those, as you in your own breath and sigh, are able to let go of whatever it is in your system that wants to be let go of. Because we're moving into the New Earth, only that which is wholesome, valuable, of light, of love, of peace and cooperation is allowed to come there with us.

So, this transitory period is about letting go what does not work. And so, for those ancestors that need to hear it, there is no longer a need, a requirement, an agreement, an oath, or a contract, to suffer. It is no longer part of the equation of the New Earth and it is not necessary any longer to hold it, whether it be etherically or ancestrally or dimensionally, to hold it as a projection towards the next generations. It can be let go of with that etheric sigh. The ones who have bodies can feel that release, the ones who no longer have bodies can imbibe it etherically. Because they too are dwelling on the frontiers of the Great Light and have not allowed themselves to fully enter. So, now is a good time to release those patterns of suffering, to release the belief that suffering is necessary to grow, to gain; that it is possible to let go of suffering, there is no need to struggle any longer and there is a thriving being asked of us. The efforting required to enter the new world is not the kind of efforting of struggle and strife and trying and doing. It's the efforting of letting go. It's the creating of the inspiration moving into practice through love, through allowance, through ease and grace and abundance.

It is part of the New Earth that everyone should have what they need, with great abundance and joy. And that they can let go of the struggle; to exist even. They can let go of that old, silly idea that they have no right to exist that was imprinted into them, perhaps even in the womb. They can let go of all the 'past' lives where they did harm or were harmed. The past is over, the story is finished. These are the simple teachings that need to be embraced now to move into the new world. You are at the forefront. As you do this, it becomes part of your nature to live it with ease and grace and then others see it, and they feel it and they say "What do you do to make you feel so peaceful? How come you don't get upset? How come such and such does not bother you? How come you are not affected by Trump, or by whatever? How come you have this state of peace within you?"

This is what we want you all to have. We want you to live in equanimity without judgments and projections, without assumptions. We have asked you to steadily chip away at the meanings of words, of beliefs that had been not helpful for you over your past. We have been asking you to examine the words you use, the beliefs you have and how they impact you and to replace them with positive ones.

So whatever systems within your physiological structure are playing this game of letting go, it is necessary for you to recognize that, because everything is so interconnected, everything is happening simultaneously. The ancestors are being freed, the ones that hold those conflicted, confused places are allowing themselves to feel the truth and let go; and the ones that are not here, that are not even able to be in the light, will somehow eventually find that space from you, because you carry it and they will feel it. At the same time, your body releases some of the tension, your physiology, your biology releases some of the imbalances, your mind releases some of the worries and your shoulders release some of the weight and get warmer and softer. And everything harmonizes and the space that you go to becomes more and more familiar, and softer, more tender, and more beautiful. It becomes a place you want to be more and more; and it's not separate from your everyday place.

And this you are feeling, right now, together, with us, just as we did with LS. It's a feeling place. It's the true space of your heart. It's that chalice, that soft, feminine place that is becoming more prominent in the world now. It is not about teaching details and wisdom and practices. It's about feeling the connection you have with us, more and more. The feeling of having us be within you, not outside of you, holding that constantly within you as your truth, your practice, your teaching. And that creates the new structure for you to step into, to do the new practice that is part of what you came here for. So, we think we answered your question.

- *As Buzz Lightyear would say, "To infinity and beyond."*

- Aho! We're learning a lot from you.

Q. (CW) You said earlier about how everyone has the ability to channel and to access their wisdom. It's something I've always struggled with and it only takes someone to mention that I need to access that inner meditation or something and I get really anxious and I know that's making it really harder for me. So, I can see how all the things that you mentioned already would help with that but I thought it was worth asking it anyway to see if there's something else that I could be doing that would help me to more easily access that for myself.

. Thank you. So the first thing we would ask of you and request of you, is that you look in the mirror and see how beautiful you are, to let go of the good old British stiff upper lip aspect that has been part of your culture and acculturation, and to recognize that you are totally worthy, deserving and safe to bring through the wisdom that is so much part of you and part of that beauty. You are able, with those breaths and those moments within that space that we created with you all twice now, that you can go into the memory of what it felt like, just by either listening to this again or imagining it when the fear comes up, or the whatever comes up. Focus on that place within you of deserving, of being so honoring of who you are and of that sweetness, that innocence that you are and carry, that seems to have got a little worn away with time. We want you to embrace that again, to hold your little girl in your heart, in your arms and love her, and remind her, not only how powerful she is, and how innocent, but how deserving she is. She carries with her this lineage of truth, of wisdom that wants to express itself and she is safe now. She is surrounded by our guidance, our wisdom and our protection.

And that sigh! Each time it comes up, allow the sigh, because it's the breath, but it's actually the release of the breath, that sigh that takes with it, kind of washes away the imprint, the worry. Let go of the story. The old story is very ancient with your family lineage and your ancestry. But there is within it also that wisdom. For the fear is because of the wisdom. The fear comes because the wisdom was not honored and allowed and therefore had to be put down by the powers that be, and that also is within the memory of that lineage. And so, do the practice of forgiveness and release, the Ho'Oponopono and releasing of ancestors.

And that is something you all can do. You can call in your ancestors. If necessary, you light a candle and you do your smudging and your sage and your palo santo and you invite your ancestors and say "Hey, it's time. Let's get clear. For you and for me, and for all of us. Let's get rid of all that stuff we've been carrying and fighting over, and worrying about. Let's trust. Let's replace the fear now with the trust and let go of any need to suffer, any anguish, even the pain of loss. Let it become a place of power, a place of connection to the higher realms, to the expanded consciousness of knowing our immortality, our eternal flame, that infinite connection we have, that universal connection.

And so, just remember that you have the ability to channel. You can write, if it's easier for you to practice, you can talk into a voice recorder or your phone, or just talk and let the wisdom spout forth. You can try to write some words and let the flow, the stream of consciousness take over, because it's like the chugging, those first few turnovers of the engine before it fires and starts. As you begin with a few words, the sentences grow and all of a sudden you find that you're saying the words, and your mind is somewhat blank, and the words are coming forth. The emptying of the mind allows the words or whatever needs to be channeled. It could be music, it could be art, it could be movement. Whatever that flow is, get used to allowing it more and more, and practice. Practice being empty. Practice the sigh. Practice changing the old voices, shooing them away. Countering them with "No, I am worthy. I do not need to please anyone else but myself. I'm not here to please anyone. I am not here because I owe anybody anything. I've done my duty. I've paid my dues. I deserve to blossom now. I came here to bring my wisdom and I do it now because I can." Blessings and peace. Does that make sense?

- *Yes, very much, thank you.*

Q. (SL) I have avoided asking this. I've been taken aback by all the terror and fear around me in the world these days. I've managed to personally not suffer from that too much. I try to keep my balance. About 5 weeks ago I came down with the shingles and I have been suffering greatly for 5 weeks and I'm thinking, maybe there's something inside of me that wants me to suffer or that's making it necessary to hang on to this. Maybe I'm trying to join the rest of people in the world and I needed to suffer also. I don't know. Please, your thoughts.

A. Thank you. You are experiencing a very profound transformation. Everything you have ever been in all the many years of your life. 'Many.' We use that truth without any judgment, just a kind of assessment, shall we say (laughter). But you have been around the block a few times and you have ways that have become entrenched. And you have had much of that shaken up, first by the experience of the shaking up that has been around you with the fear and the profound resistance you have to allowing that to be part of your reality. You understand that this is a grand illusion and that it is sad and it is painful and there's a lot of suffering that has been caused by the energies that are very inconsiderate, to say the least, are cold-hearted, are cruel and you've had to carry this and you've had to look deeply into your own being. It has precipitated for you a very deep transformation.

It is not so much that it requires you to suffer. It requires you to have a 180 degree or whatever degree turn to allow yourself to assess, not just the patterns that are related to viruses and all the belief systems that are structured around them, but even to your belief in what does it take to heal. What does it take to shift out of an old pattern that has not been working and has in some ways precipitated this suffering, and move towards a more, shall we call it, enlightened state of understanding the nature of healing? What is healthy for the body and the mind and the emotions and the entire field of being human? "Where are the changes needed that would help to eliminate these manifestations of underlying patterns that can shift all this and take me to a whole other place where I no longer have the shingles and I am no longer suffering?" It is going to take your determination, your practice, to change aspects of your lifestyle that are going to support a whole new way of being on the planet for you. We would highly recommend that you call MS and chat with him, because he has a view of systems, the organ systems and the energetic and chemical systems of the body. His understanding and knowledge could give you some very helpful direction. You have others who are practicing and working with the herbal medicines and the shamanic practice. You have such an array of resources right in front of you on this screen. You have been given some guidance, the book that we shared with you, Medical Medium, that lays out the ways in which these viruses within the body that have been hiding in the organs for so long, all of a sudden, they get encouraged to come forth and begin to wreak their havoc on the system.

You are good at understanding systems, but you have been looking at the wrong avenues of approaching them. Begin to restructure your understanding of systems, kind of like a sacred geometry understanding. Look at the Oriental systems of the meridians and the organs and the elements. Look at the Native systems of understanding the correspondences between the herbs and the different organs and the different earth-based energies and elements within you. Look at the Chinese system of yin-yang, 5 elements, Feng Shui, meridians. Look at all these patterns, perhaps share time in Nature and try the Druidic ways of conversing with trees and water and asking your own guidance "Where does SL's intuition come into play? Where is it moving away from the mind, the logic, and allowing something else to bubble up within me?"

So, you are unfolding for yourself tremendous movement that is almost like earth-shattering for your whole system, for your physical and emotional and your mental system. We are taking our hats off. We're congratulating you and honoring you that you are on this journey, that you have kept it up, that you have followed through and are working so strongly with this. And it would be a very powerful way that weaves together what we have intended for you as a group: to make a phone call to somebody like MS, to LS or to CW or even CZ, who is here in Santa Fe. Have a little chat and say, "What do you think? What do you suggest, and how do you recommend that I approach this book that feels so foreign to the way I normally see things?" Or whatever it is that has triggered this huge transformation. And take those breaths and try the letting go. Try the forgiveness practice, even towards yourself. Make sure that you eliminate those voices and replace them. It is all the same practice wherever we look, wherever we ask.

These foundational practices exist in all the teachings of wisdom of all ages and all beings. If they are not there, then you should put them in there because they have been missing. It is now that we are bringing this compendium to you, and we will do our best to clarify this in writing too, as we work together to weave the stories, the teachings, the viewpoints of the 12 and produce some form that can be shared with others. Perhaps as a book, which it seems we are moving towards. The fundamental teachings of the breath, the body, above and below, the heart, the letting go of old voices, the looking in the mirror. These practices are your guidelines. They are your markers and as you notice the shifts within you, you start to recognize that within another four to five weeks you will have accomplished a tremendous amount of transformation. And you will feel, and perhaps you already feel the difference. You also, some of you, are participating concurrently in the 2020 course, perhaps you are with Chung Fu, with Old Chinese. You have other guides and other channels that are bringing forth wisdom.

They are all teaching love. They are teaching light. They are all teaching the practice of letting go of fear, of being in your body, of connecting to all the realms and to Nature. These practices are given to you, not in order to load you up with exercises, but to give you simple ways of remembering to breathe, remembering to let go, remembering to change that thought pattern, just like that, to be in the moment, to show up with your heart open. This is the simple teaching: chop wood, carry water. Let go of the old need for your ego to have some kind of glamour whenever it shows up, whatever shows up. Let it be. Have a look. Let it go. It's that simple. Does that make sense?

  - *Yes, thank you very much.*

Closing Meditation

Let us go into the heart space. Let us give thanks for each other, for Mother Earth, for Father Sky, for all the guidance and wisdom that has been with us, for all the love that we have experienced from all the beings of light that surround us, that dwell within us. Let us again feel Mother Earth beneath us, feel that space filling with stillness, knowing that we can carry that peace of mind wherever we are, calling for the blessings for the little one who joined us today, for all the little ones, that they may grow up with beauty and strength and joy and celebration, as they experience the fullness of the New Earth that is for them, as much as for us. For we all are one. We are, they say "in this" together," but, in fact, we "are" this together. We are the All That Is. We are expressions of the love of All That Is. We are the most powerful energies upon this planet when we embody love; and when we express it, even more so. May the love and the beauty that is in the spirit of all things, the Living Spirit that is in all life, accompany you on your journey, this week and beyond and until we meet again. We send you our love and our blessings and surround you. We love you. Blessings and Peace.

Voice Nine
Joan of Arc

11th October 2020

Let's take a nice breath, that beautiful, sweet breath that we're so familiar with. Let's go into our hearts, putting our right hand on our heart, our left on our right, allowing the stillness to pour down through our crown like that beautiful golden mantle spreading over us and in us. Reaching all the way into every cell as it pours down a column of light, as it filters its way down through our heart, down through our feet, all the way down. We connect with Mother Earth now, feeling our gratitude, our love and our connection; feeling the column and the energy and the light and the love rising up from our feet, from the center of Mother Earth, up towards the Heavens through our crown. It radiates down again, like water moving up and down, as if a stream of light is pouring through us, connecting with our guidance, with the ones that watch over us and love us; connecting with the 12 energies; connecting especially with Joan of Arc. Let's begin now to feel her presence as we reach out through our hearts to weave the threads of our hearts together, weave them with the threads of all of our loved ones and with all beings upon this planet, sending out that beautiful vibration of our hearts, of that golden light, to touch every single heart on this planet and beyond with love, with light, and with a sense of peace. You may rest your hands, dear ones.

It is a great delight for me to be with you today. You have known me as Joan of Arc, as the one, the young one, that one in France a long time ago. A beautiful story. A story of courage. A story of being completely true to one's inner voice; following through what you might call "the halls of hell" into battle, into conflict, into arenas that young women are not normally meant to go. And yet, everything was ordained. There was no right. There was no wrong beyond that impetus, that calling that I had to answer. And so, with you too, what is that strong impulse that drives you to create that which is your destiny upon this planet? What is it that goes beyond the judgments of age, of masculine and feminine, of gender, of rich or poor, of powerful or weak? What is it that allows you to overcome all obstacles, no matter how daunting they might be; whether they be outside you or inside of you? For there is nothing outside that does not have its corollary within your heart, within your mind, within yourselves.

As above, so below. As within, so without.

The sword of truth is a mighty blade, and it has two edges. One must be very careful in using everything, especially the sharpness of the sword of truth. One must evolve discrimination out of judgment. It is important to always remain humble, to remember that power can corrupt, that absolute power corrupts absolutely. In my time, I was surrounded by many, many people who carried great power and who exemplified corruption. They no longer had access to the truth. They no longer had access to the fields of the heart. It did not really matter, that idea of uniting France under a monarch, restoring the monarchy to a particular lineage. It was not necessarily some great high, evolved mission that I was on. However, it was the one that was before me. It was what my voices asked me to do. It was somehow determined that a young girl of under 16 should lead France to victory, should be betrayed and should be burned upon the stake. For what purpose, who is to know? Yet somehow emblazoned in the heart of all beings is a softness, a consciousness, that is inspired by something as magnificent as my story. Something. There is a deep and strong inspiration to follow the inner voices, no matter what.

How could it be that one who was not even able to write letters or read, should, from a small, humble village, find themselves at the court of the king and find the very means to achieve this, have access to information, to truth that was known to no one else but the king or the king to be, the Dauphin? How is it that voices within can be so powerful? How is it that the movement of the heart towards a goal, towards achieving some ambition that is for a higher purpose, can have so much power and can bring forth so much miracle and so much magic? It also brought forth the loyalty of seasoned soldiers and warriors who had been embittered and fought many a battle and had seen the worst of the worst. And yet, they followed me to the death. They were my faithful companions. Without them, I was nothing, and yet I gave people hope. I rallied people around a vision. It was a simple girl, a simple, unschooled villager who was able to somehow manifest a destiny for a whole nation even before there was such a thing as a nation.

Yet now, as time has moved upon the stages of your planet, and you live within a culture, within a civilization and within a story that faces, what you might consider hopeless odds in terms of turning around a situation; whether it be the depth of pollution, the great greed, or the terrible things that people do to each other (which is not that much different from my day). Whatever it is, some great impulse is needed in order to change these incomprehensible terrors, this overwhelming amount of power that has tremendous technology behind it. It has the ability to destroy so much, and is already destroying so much of the Earth's atmosphere, of her soil, the water, her trees. All of humanity suffers at the hands of this pollution, at the lack of regard for the sanctity of life and respect for human beings and the creatures.

In spite of it all, there is nothing that cannot be done when you follow your heart, and gather together with those who are loyal, who follow and are able to see the vision that you carry in your heart. Gather around you in support, those who recognize that alone it is very difficult to achieve the overthrow of all that seems so evil and so harmful. And yet, as you hold dear and hold fast to your inner vision, to your voices within you, the voices of your guardian angels; as you keep alive your heart's vision and begin to manifest it in small ways within your life, one step leads to another and before long you are not alone. You are marching as a team, as an Army of the Heart, marching forth from that place of Light, marching forth with swords of truth that remain in the scabbard, as we have discussed earlier in these sessions. The stories or the teachings or the wisdom are always the same. It is always about the sword of truth, the within and without. It is always about cutting away that which does not serve you. Stopping in your tracks when you notice that you are judging, worrying, projecting into the future your fear or concern about this or that. Stopping to catch yourself and take that breath, in, and out; to go into the heart and to be fully present in your body.

Old Chinese, in a recent session reviewed these teachings and enumerated them for ease of being able to go over them, to share them, and for the ability to let others know what it is that we have been discussing in our time together for these last nine sessions.

The sun turns around, and the Earth turns around, and the seasons come and go and change. You are now approaching the harvest. You are approaching the time when your voices must be heard and must be acted upon. You are facing the time for the harvest of everything you have worked towards over this period. How far have you come? How much have you shifted within your consciousness? How much have you been able to capture the words and belief systems, the ideas, projections and worries, and interrupt them? Replacing them with voices of love, with voices of peace, with the allowance that is the foundation of Truth. Let this allowance of love come in and replace all those endeavors of the mind that want to keep you fixed in the old visions, old concepts from your heredity, upbringing and your acculturation. How much have you been able to pay attention to your thoughts, to your feelings, your ideas, the times that have been hard, perhaps those moments of depression, those moments of thinking that you will not make it, or those moments of doubt where you do not feel you can take one more moment, one more step or one more breath?

You have come to this place to do exactly that: to take stock in each moment of what your voices have shared with you, whether they come from channeling through this one or others or whether they come from your own inner wisdom as you enter your meditation time, but it is definitely the time now to take stock. In the next three weeks you will be asked to consider what structures you are putting in place that are emanations of your own voices, of the messages that arise within you that will not be gainsaid. What is the inspiration that has told you, time after time, what you should do for your own highest good, for your own deepest enjoyment and pleasure and for your own ability to see yourselves as magnificent; to see yourselves as expressions of the divine in action, to recognize that you are here but for a brief moment and that you will return to the Great Light of Creator, to Union with All That Is before you can snap your fingers?

It is important, as we reach this time when most of our teachings have been explained, when most of our inspirations have been given to you, to take one more breath, to move forward with one more step, to gather around you your circle of allies, to reach out to one other person and share. You never know to what degree that call might just inspire somebody else to feel that relief, that sense of comfort, to have a voice, to be able to have someone to listen to, even if it is a story? The very telling of it to a willing ear can allow it to dissolve away. It seems that the overall impressions that are coming forward appear to be about the stories. What is the story?

How many times have you heard the same story from the same friend or colleague, or not so friend, who goes over and over the reasons why they cannot do something because Mercury is in retrograde, because their stars are aligned in such a way that they are helpless or hopeless; because they just don't have the juice for it? Whatever the stories, perhaps you're tired of hearing the same old stories from some of them, and perhaps, just perhaps, you are tired of listening to some of your own story. It does not require more than a simple decision to let go, to constantly let go. Every worry about the money, about the relationship, about the health can all be let go of. You are an immortal soul. You are infinite. You are universal. Immortal, eternal, infinite and universal. You are here but for a moment, and even while you are here, you are still immortal. You are still infinite and universal. You have access to a quantum field of the heart. It is right there beating within you. You can breathe rapidly, or you can breathe slowly and deeply. The choice is always yours. Every thought, you have the ability to examine. Every belief system, you can examine and let go of, if it does not work, if it does not elevate you, if it does not bring you peace. Peace of mind, peace of heart.

We have urged you to consider. Perhaps the pinnacle of all of our teachings is about forgiveness, for forgiveness is that place within you where you no longer are attached to outcome in regard to a person who is connected to your story or with regard to you being connected to their story. You have that power that you have within you to follow those voices, whether it be a Saint Catherine or a Saint Mary or a Jesus or some other guru or Angelic Being that comes to you with a voice that says "You must follow this path because it is your destiny and it will bring you great joy; and it will bring you great delight; and you will overcome all the obstacles if you are true to my voice, for I come from within you. I am the voice of your conscience, of your consciousness. I am the voice of your Higher Self." It does not matter what name is attached to it, for it comes to you through the filter of your Higher Self and it is your voice that will take you to the heights. It will take you to that state of peace, for when everything is said and done, like in the song A *Satisfied Mind*. Peace of mind, the ability to rest, rest in that peace of the heart; of knowing that you always do your best and then you let go and you allow, and the magic and the serendipity and the ease and grace and the miracle and the flow of abundance begins again.

It is never ending because the Universe does not want you to suffer. The Universe only wants the highest of thriving for you, the blossoming, the great joy in your heart. All of your angels and guides wish for you to experience absolute bliss, that expansion of soul and heart that is attuned to your connection with the divine, your understanding beyond the mind; that you are an expression of God/Goddess, of All That Is. This is a living reality in every breath, in every second. You can feel it in your whole being when you allow yourself to, when you rest in that deep breath. For that is all you have. Each moment, your beating heart and your breathing lungs are signifying that you are alive. The great gift of Heaven for you is this life and it is yours to choose how to optimize it, how to make the most of it, how to bring that joy into it, how to spread that joy and that light and that understanding that everything always works out for the highest good for everyone concerned, even beyond the appearance. For you are Spiritual Warriors. We have said this.

Just as those that were beside me riding into battle knew that this might be their last day upon the Earth, they mustered all their forces. They gathered their forces because they understood that they were moving forward for the sake of a higher purpose, of some destiny; what they called in their hearts "freedom" and that it was necessary to follow through. They did not consider killing to be the wrong or the bad or the evil. It was part of life for them in that moment, in that incarnation. They were soldiers. They did not sit in some suburb and judge that which is good and bad and right and wrong from some perspective of being a, what you call "Baby Boomer," or "Yuppie." Their lives were appropriate to the time just as yours are, just as it is still necessary for you to pursue a path of destiny that is your calling, your particular calling, and you must follow through with the voice that is within you.

If you do not have that voice, you must find it. You must go within. You must go into that breath, into that space of peace, of the NoThing. You must go into the warrior mind, into that place of inner calm and ask and wait and listen to that still, small voice before you follow it. Each one has it. No one is denied access to their intuition. You might feel it in your body. It might come as a thought in your mind or you may feel it as some emotion. It will then permeate and begin to take over the whole of you.

When it begins to show up in your heart, then you know this is your path, these are your steps. You ask "What shall I do?" Part of you knows the answer. For it is that part that leaps with joy when you consider, when you ask "Shall I do this or shall I do that. I really feel the obligation to do this or, I have this feeling that if I don't do that, I will upset somebody. What I really want to do is go have a nap or go for a hike, or read a book." When you do find what it is that you really want to do, you get the message. "Ahh, that feels so much lighter, much better than all those obligation things that I feel I have to do, whether it's for myself or somebody else." As long as you are able to follow through and do them at some point. In the moment, you know what brings you joy and that is where your heart wants to lead you.

It is important to be gentle on yourself, to stop being so serious, to stop worrying. Ahh (she takes a deep breath)……. and let it go! Each time there is a worry, you become an adept, and let it go. And as you soften, something else will take its place. You will remember to trust. You will remember that all these years you managed. That little child that is so dear within you is still here. That child managed, blossomed, became you. That child and you are inseparable. Within that innocence, that purity, that beauty in your heart is all the hope, the hope of the world, within the little child. It is the little children that will lead this world into the state of the Golden Age, of the New Earth, and it is your job to cultivate them, to encourage, to inspire them. It is your job to be true to yourself so that you can then let them know what that looks like, what that feels like. Not through words, but by example.

Just as when you get that voice, that deep inner urging to create these containers, these structures that we have talked about. It is time for you to put pen to paper or pencil to drawing pad, to write your vision, to write your structure, your container, to formulate what it is that you are moving towards, how it is that you will find out what your steps are. It will be necessary for you to call somebody, to share it. "This is what I'm coming up with. What do you think? What do you feel?" Do not wait for the last minute. Call somebody, even if it is not within this group. Just connect and share, because these ideas that are bubbling up need to be foundationed, and as you share them and as you draft them and draw them, as you begin to create your poems about them, or songs, they will become more and more real and then they will attract that energy of allies, those warriors who ride into battle with you, whether it be to the death, or to the life, whether it be for a higher purpose that through the history or herstory will be shown, perhaps to have been misinformed. It does not matter, because the movement, striving to achieve without striving; That movement toward the unfolding of your vision is what is important.

The voices did not tell me that I would be burned at the stake, that I would be betrayed; and yet even in that last moment I had done my duty. I had fulfilled my honor. I had fulfilled the promptings of my voices. You might say I went out in a blaze of glory with the cross held up high for my eyes to see as I transcended, as I ascended, as my body fell by the wayside and I entered that realm of the highest light, of the greatest union that is possible to know, as I entered the fields of Beauty, of Union. So too, each one will achieve that, not necessarily in the same way. Hopefully not. We do not wish it upon you. You have already had experiences in past lifetimes. That is enough.

You are here to create the structures for the New Earth. You are here to model them. You are here to gather them together. You are here to lay them out and create the foundations for them out of your heart's longings, out of those voices within you that cannot be denied or gainsaid, and we are not talking about those voices in the head that say "Man, you can't do that. Who do you think you are?" All those voices are not the same voices that fill your heart with inspiration, deep joy and bliss, with light, for if there is no light and no love in any endeavor, it is not for you. If you cannot find fun, enjoyment in your doing, then cease from doing, then wait for the opportunity to do that which your heart embraces with deep satisfaction. It is important not to judge. I was judged as a little girl from a village in the countryside, a country bumpkin. That was the judgment of me. And yet, they did not know what I carried, what strength was possible, what ability to follow through I had and pursued. And how I was able to inspire others through following my voices.

This is the message of Joan of Arc. There is a beautiful story and as many stories end, there was a sad ending, or so it seemed. I live on in the hearts and in the minds of many who are yet inspired by me. There is no judgment for one who rides upon the horse into battle with themselves, with your demons, with your fears, with your worries; even with your opponents, for, as we have said, they are your greatest friends. For they agreed to create with you that old story. And as you learn forgiveness, everything becomes light and filled with that golden essence of your true heart's longing held in your cells.

So, we will take a moment to pause as is our wont, and look you in the eyes again, to see if we are still riding that horse together. We have some new people. It is good to see. Welcome.

Perhaps you feel a little overwhelmed at this time, perhaps the imposition of what we call the Great Deception is heavy on your shoulders and in your heart. Perhaps looking and gazing upon little children wearing these stupid masks across their face as they walk out in nature or everybody turning aside so they do not look you in the eye in case somehow you infect or affect them. The Great Deception is intended to inculcate fear. However, you do it, face your own fear. Do not worry about others' fears. Find the strength within you to understand that fear is your greatest, we shall call it, challenge; but we are going to call it your greatest friend, because when you overcome fear, nothing can touch you.

You are here in the face of a pandemic of fear to hold the light and the truth; to hold up that cross as you burn at the stake, steadfast, trusting in that which is sacred for you. It may not be the Christ or the Christian religion that you follow. Whatever belief system you have, or religion or whatever it is that you hold dear; hold that up before your eyes as your inspiration. Find that mantra, that, when you say it, your heart softens and gladdens and you let go of the thought. However, it works for you, come back to that place of innocence, of purity, of knowing what the lie and what the truth is in your heart, no matter what you have been told, perhaps even by the great guru who told you "You must do this" or "You must do that", and your heart says "No, this does not feel right," or perhaps it is your governor who says "You must do this" or "You must do that," and your heart says "No!"

And you'll find that your heart is not alone; that there are many hearts rebelling against this imposition upon you and your freedom, of your ability to think for yourself. We would recommend that you stop watching the news. Stop reading the news. Stop counting numbers that are configured by the same ones who have created the epidemic of fear, of control. We will go deeper as we progress through the next few sessions because we understand the corruption. The Dauphin may have looked like the savior of France, but he was corrupt to the core and yet I knew what I was dealing with. I still had to follow my voices. I still had to follow through with my path as a warrior. I still had to face my fears and my doubts.

Aside from fear, your other greatest enemy and friend is your doubt, because each time you take a step forward, those words of doubt in your head will say "Do not listen to those voices. You cannot do this. You are not capable. You do not deserve. You are not wise enough to carry this truth." As you doubt and as you face your doubts, you come to the conclusion that you have nothing to lose. In fact, you have nothing to lose but your life. Life is not finishing with the moment of death. You are an immortal soul. Nothing can change that. Nothing is more powerful than your Eternal Spirit, what the one Old Chinese calls the Living Spirit that is within all life, that expression of God's Love, that power of the Light that descends upon your planet from the centers of the galaxies, that is over-lighting everything for the highest good. This movement towards your New Earth is unstoppable. You can doubt as much as you want. It will not matter. It will still come to be.

We are recommending that you trust, that you allow our guidance to be with you always, that you allow us to be those voices for you, whether it be we 12 or all the angels and guides, all the Holy Beings. Many of us have been through the pangs of fear, the terrors of the Inquisition and the fires of the stake. We are still here in the Ethers with you. We have run the course, shall we say, of all those lifetimes and are here guiding you, letting you know that you are always safe now. The worst is over, that the past is over. The power of those who have imposed this deception is weakening and weakening and weakening to the point that it is in dire collapse and you are needed to hold strong to your inner voice and to the power of your light. Hold strong to that column and that Sphere of Light that you surround yourself with and send it out into the world for inspiration. For you must become an inspiration for others. This is your greatest work. The foundation of the word "inspiration" is "in-spire," which means to "breathe in" in Latin. The foundations of your language, of your words, are profound, many of them. Be inspired, receive the divine inspiration to counter the doubt and to open up your heart to trust through the faith in your purpose and in your voices. We have said enough. Let us take a break and we will come back to answer your questions. Thank you.

Joan of Arc Q&A

Q. *(CR) Joan of Arc mentioned that the Dauphin was corrupt and yet she fought for his cause and then was betrayed. And still, she never stopped. She didn't know some of the betrayals that were to come. She also mentioned that doubt is our friend as well as our enemy. What she's inferring is kind of like: any lesson that we have to learn from, is our enemy at first, but then later becomes a friend as we resolve it. I wonder, on the other side, when you look back upon your life and you know you gave it your all and the situation didn't end up the way you thought it would, yet it doesn't undermine the fact that you and your spirit and intentions outweigh the outcome. Joan of Arc might like to say something else about that. It's a very powerful component of her story.*

A. Well, I think you put it very well, in fact very much so. You have encapsulated what you might call, the great challenge of being human. One never knows the outcome in advance, otherwise what is the point? And when you look from the perspective of the Swing Between Worlds, you decide or agree to go in there, knowing full well that you have your mission to accomplish, perhaps. So it is in the book *I Remember Union*.[66] Prior to their entry into the world of flesh and blood, Mary, the Christ and Judas understood that they were not able to see or be responsible for outcome, and yet that it was possible to follow through with that which was their calling. If you look at the whole picture of so many lives, whether they be your own soul having incarnated thousands upon thousands of times or the number of souls that have ever been on this planet as separated entities that come from many, many soul families, it is again like looking at the sand, the grains of sand upon the shore and understanding that within the infinity of everything that is, each moment, each breath, each step, each decision, each action is important, and not important at the same time. You must need to go beyond outcome, beyond the mind's decision about things and the mind's way of categorizing right and wrong within a limited context. Even the Dauphin had his moments of recognition.

To call somebody corrupt does not mean that the spark of their soul was not also playing out a destiny pattern. And who could ever imagine what the "history" of Europe would have looked like if I had not heard my voices and had not gone into battle, or I had not created that ripple in Time, to actually show up in the world with my story. And even though I personally, as a soul energy have let go of my story, it still remains to inspire, just as the movies and the book that Mark Twain[67] produced were creations of great inspiration. They could inspire a soul to great heights for what they see as a higher purpose at the time; and it is within a context. Just as we ask you to create containers, to create structures, they are essentially contexts. The context of creating the end of hunger on your planet is a mission. It's a destiny. It is an enterprise, an enterprise that you would say is always aligned with the good or with a higher purpose. And yet, perhaps, there is another perspective. Perhaps the ending of hunger would end the ability of millions of souls to clean out their karma by going through a life of starvation. Who is to judge? We're not saying this is the case. We are just merely bringing up possible perspectives.

The reason I speak to you as one of 12 voices is to give you a broader perspective for yourself on the bigger picture. So, what you say contains much truth and we are grateful that you have expressed it so well, and at the same time, when you follow your own voice as I did mine, it is not just about outcome; for you cannot stop, even if you did know the outcome. Let us say that Christ knew he would be crucified and yet he did not stop because of that from following through with his mission. And again, this may or may not just be a story, for there are deep mythologies within the consciousness of your civilizations and your religions that have great truths within them, whether or not historically they can be proven, so there is always a higher outcome. It goes beyond that which the mind is able to comprehend. What I bring is the inspiration to follow the voice. Peace.

Q. (SL) My question is about humility. It's hard to stay grounded in humility and I'm wondering if you can kind of cover what kind of focus do we need to have to stay grounded in humility. I think it should be something starting in school. It's that type of subject, but it's kinda hard to pin down, I think. I'd like your thoughts on that.

A. It is a most profound and extremely important question. You could say that, alongside of forgiveness, humility would be the great companion. For humility is one of the most elevated aspects a human being can embrace, true humility. For true humility requires a soul, a human mind, a human consciousness to go beyond all their training, everything that they are taught by society, by their ancestors, by their upbringing, by their schooling. In fact, and you are very correct, there are so many things they don't teach you at school, and if you were able to rewrite the curriculum, humility would be one of the most important aspects.

Again, we would draw your attention to the story or the mythology of the Christ, for Christ did not concern himself only to appear with those "successful" ones who are the lawyers and the doctors and the ones with the nice bank accounts, nice houses and nice cars. He associated with lepers, with the outcasts of society. He lived in humility and he did not judge. He also did not do anything for himself. Within the formulation of his mission, everything in his ministry was for service to the highest good. Service to the highest divine energies that he served, as well as to the simple people, who lived humble lives. True humility is an aspect of the soul that recognizes but does not judge themselves as worthy or not. It is not a consideration. It does not mean they do not love themselves, but rather they do not see themselves as the most important thing to satisfy. Humility requires one to be able to serve, to see oneself as the servant of the people, or a higher purpose. It would be required in a civilization that represents a higher level of consciousness as a society, that their leaders or teachers, before they come forth to teach or to lead, understand the true nature of humility. It does not mean that one does not take care of one's personal needs, but it does mean that, when the heart is the source of all action, like Mother Teresa, her selfless service to the poor came from the understanding that each one, however humble, was an expression of the Christ in form, that no one was higher than another, nor was she.

This understanding reflects the true nature of humility, of not placing yourself above someone, but also not placing yourself below someone, for it is necessary to see oneself within the essence of humility, as one who is willing to serve. It does not mean being a doormat. In fact, the greatest service can require one to have the highest aspirations and the highest intentions and highest consciousness. The one Judas, who was vilified in the religious writings and teachings of Christianity, was the greatest servant of the Christ, for he agreed to do that which he knew he would carry throughout his lifetimes as a soul, the stigma of one who would be regarded as the betrayer. And yet, in service, in humility, you might say, he agreed to take on that role out of his great love for the Christ, knowing and accepting that he would become called "the betrayer." In the same vein, the Magdalen understood and agreed to her mission, knowing she would be called the whore in the written scriptures that would follow. They followed through because these two loved the Christ as much as they loved their own lives and were in service to a higher plan.

So, again, we are asking you to always not judge, to view everything from an open-hearted, open-minded perspective. It is important that you understand that there are two sides to this blade of humility, to the coin of calling yourself humble, for one who regards oneself is humble would not go for the glamour, nor would they draw attention to this quality. It is like the healer. No true healer would call themselves a healer, for they know they are only agents of the divine or are assisting their 'patients' to heal themselves. So, again, it requires a constant reappraisal of your intention, of the purity of your heart, of the innocence of who you truly are. This is the only place of assessment for the true nature of humility. It is definitely a very profound and highly elevated goal that one would want to achieve, to exemplify humility.

Humility is also associated with forgiveness, with letting go of judgments of self or other, of allowing, of letting everything be what it is, for then you have no need to control outcome and you can rest in your own humility by trusting that when you do not wish to aggrandize yourself or live within any kind of glamour, you are serving the highest purpose for which a human being can come to this planet. You're serving from the heart without the need to be congratulated or recognized. You know within your own deepest part that you have done what you have intended, and that is reward enough. We could go on, but we believe we have touched enough on the answer to your question. Does that make sense for you?

- Yes, thank you very much. That's probably the longest answer to that question that I've ever experienced. I appreciate it.

- That means you have asked that question before?

- I have. I study humility as well as other traits that I have little of.

- It is a sign that you have plenty of!

Q. (KM) I felt like when you were talking earlier, you were speaking to me. A lot about what I've been going through this past week. Since we've been meeting together and having everyone talk every week, I haven't had much fear. I know that you and other people have talked about fear in past Sundays and I understand how a lot of the society could be experiencing fear, but I never really had it except briefly during Cov-id in the hospital. But this week, for whatever reason, I feel like I have the sense that things will start unraveling this winter. My daughter was diagnosed with type one diabetes when she was two and she's three now, so that brings a lot of fear into my life because with that disease you are reliant on a lot of technology and medication for her survival. Part of the question is not related to the fear about what's behind it, but it's about trying to dig deep, about the spiritual significance of her developing this disease, and part of it is I blame myself a little bit because it was one of my biggest fears, actually, was that someone in our family was going to develop that disease 'cause I recognize how difficult it is. So that was one question: What is the spiritual significance of her developing the disease, and then the other question is: would I be right in the sense that I should be preparing and getting ready for this time that could be quite chaotic in our civilization, or am I going overboard, and the more that I'm thinking about it, am I creating that reality or that timeline? Is it more likely that that type of timeline is going to occur because I'm thinking about it more? Does that question make sense at all?

A. Yes. Thank you for your questions. Difficult ones to answer at some level. As you understand, there are many perceptions and many levels to your question and to the answer. It is not required that your daughter carry this disease throughout her life. It is possible to heal everything and anything. It is also possible to overcome fear. You are a very powerful person and if you have created anything from an unconscious level of fear, you are also capable of removing that fear and countering it with love and with light. And with the understanding that you and your daughter are always, surrounded by a team of guides, guardians, angels, and beings who are capable of bringing to you what you need for the highest level, for your own deepest satisfaction, and for ease and grace in your life. Know too, that your whole planet and the unfolding of this "Deception" has, at its highest purpose, an evolution into the New Earth, and that it is destined for you and your children and your family to move into it. When you worry, it is required of you as a Spiritual Warrior, to let go of the fear, to take that breath, however many times you feel the fear. It requires of you the courage to ask for your guides, for your helpers to give you a feeling of relief from fear. To reinforce trust, the knowing that you are able to experience, because of your power, the deepest faith possible. For there is part of your soul that has come to teach what it is like to work within the field of all this fear and of all the scientific claptrap that is touted as truth, and maintain equanimity. That field does not allow for the strength and the highest purposes of love, for soul energy to change things, but you know better.

We have talked about the power of prayer to heal. So too, you are able to create magic in your life when you trust and believe and know. It is interesting how the money always shows up at the very last minute because somewhere inside of you, you have that faith, even if the mind continually bombards you with the old patterns of fear that have been inculcated into you as a human being over lifetimes. You have all grown up with this lineage and ancestry, and the patterns from childhood. So, it is also important for you to get as much help as you can to release many of those patterns, because they are part of your cellular memory. However, because you are a powerful, we can call you a goddess, (we understand that it will not infringe on your humility to do so) and you have this power within you to shift every single pattern. You can shift that place within you of guilt or judgment that you perhaps created something for your daughter because of this that or the other. Let go of that. These are stories, just as the story of the vir-us is a story. It is true that something was created in the biological weapons lab and it was released to the public, but the whole thing of masks and the contribution of the expanding proliferation of 5-G has been hidden and changed and modified and turned into something it is taboo to talk about. All these energies will come to their own demise.

There are benevolent forces in the world that will ensure your survival, and yet it is still necessary to make sure you have enough medication and enough batteries and enough of the technology that you need for the time being to see you through, perhaps. We do not want to say how long, but we recommend you give yourself a year of having enough supplies, good water and protection from all the technologies as much as possible. It absolutely makes sense to take precautions, to behave in a way that makes sense, to have adequate supplies and constantly battle your inner demons, so that fear does not control you.

Allow the fear to talk to you. Discuss with it what it really wants of you. We are not going to tell you why your daughter has this, because she too has a soul. She agreed to come into this planet and carry this burden as did all of your family as a way, shall we say, to enhance your ability to love more, to love in spite of, to love because of, to love with. So, there are many levels to these understandings as you peel away the layers of this onion of fear. We would highly recommend that you get a HeartThread® session. If you are a practitioner, and can do an exchange, do so. Use whatever resources are available to you to release some of the imprints from childhood and from the ancestral patterns. Use some of the practices we have shared with you during this course. Talk to your ancestors, and cut ties that affect this situation.

Your daughter is a very bright and very powerful and very advanced soul, and she made the contract with you to come in and experience this. She is really helping you to become that goddess, to become all powerful within the face of fear and judgment, to release all doubt and to release all guilt. It is not in your highest interest to give any credence to any kind of guilt or shame or blame whatsoever. Each one carries within their heart their innocence and purity, and every single other voice in the head, as we have addressed so many times, can have no power over you when you let go of it and send it away and give it all to God or Goddess. You have been trained in these practices in other lifetimes and it is your time now to take up that sword, take up that scepter, take up that crown and that chalice and fill it with love and with light. Put that sphere of Golden Light around yourself, your children, your husband and your family each day when you meditate, before you go out or watch or listen to something. Surround yourself with your sphere of protection of angels and of guides and go forth knowing that nothing will harm you or your daughter and that you will make it through this time and that, in fact, your spirit of calmness, your ability to have that equanimity in the face of fear, will help many others to feel comfort and to feel the grace that is available to you when you trust. Do we make sense so far?

- Thank you so much.

Q. *(ZS) My initial inquiry was in regard to some anxiety that I've been feeling and I feel like it most likely is a collective anxiety. I'd like any wisdom on how to transmute it. I know that as the transmission was coming through, I heard a lot, like, let it go, let it go. As far as the anxiety goes, I feel like sometimes it's unknown where it really comes from, so it might be a little tough to let go in a way. Another inquiry that came up was in regard to unconditional love and loving others as ourselves, but then remembering to love ourselves first. I have this relationship with this being that I've been intertwined with for years now, and I'm learning boundaries and I want to just unconditionally love them and be there for them; but then learning how do I put myself first, and if loving myself first means not communicating with them... How do I find that balance of unconditional love if you and I are the same and there is no separation? I'm kind of finding a little difficulty navigating that balance in these really profound times that we're living in. Does that make any sense?*

A. Absolute sense. Thank you for your questions. It is important to understand, it is very difficult perhaps, to understand what it takes to consider that you come first, even in spite of what we have shared about humility and service. It is necessary, beyond just setting a few boundaries, to recognize the importance of those boundaries, of agreements, of clarity, of understanding what it is that you are feeling in the moment and how to respond to that. We have a feeling that you might be required to give up use of any substance if you are still using; that in order to create absolute clarity, it is necessary to follow that path of the Spiritual Warrior, which means that there is nothing in between you and your heart, your soul, your body and God that could create any kind of, what we shall call, unclarity. It is very deep soul-searching that you are asking for. You are asking, in fact, "When do I cut a cord, and when do I try and fix a cord? When do I set a boundary, and when do I allow that boundary to be broken? When do I have clarity, and when do I not? Who is it that is experiencing what I'm experiencing, the anxiety for instance? How much is this the collective, and how much am I reflecting the collective? Who am I? What am I? What am I here to do?" All these questions are rolled up together. All these queries are included within the completeness of your inquiry.

It is important, beyond everything else, to come to a place of honor and value of you, beyond your conditioning, beyond all the imprints and beyond all the messages that are coming from outside of you. This includes what is coming from society and also includes what is coming from your partner or from the one you are asking about. "What is in my best interest for me now, and how can I see it clearly, and how can I move forward, no matter what the outcome is? Where do I need to cut cords? Does it go as far as my mother and my father and my connection with them and all the obligations I took upon myself to see things through certain kinds of eyes? Does it go as far as my ancestors? Does it go as far as my habits? Does it go as far as this one that I'm asking about?"

We would not tell you, I will not tell you, beyond advising you to go to that place of the voices. I represent one who follows the inner voices because they had become so strong within me that I could not deny them. You must cultivate your own ability, as a powerful woman, as one who stands within her authority, as a priestess and as a goddess of knowing your truth. What you are suggesting in your questions is that you do not know your truth, you have not gone to the kernel of who you truly are and respect it with the utmost sincerity; that you honor that innocence and purity that you truly are, and are not willing to compromise for anything, with anybody, for anything.

We are admonishing you to go deep into your heart, to honor and love yourself above all, first. This too will clarify for you what should be your priorities, where should you cut cords, how much are you allowing the external forces of chaos to impinge upon you and how much are you able and willing to face your own strength and power and allow it to be the source of your self-authority.

Closing Meditation

Let us put our right hand on our hearts and take that lovely sweet breath that we all are so familiar with now, that is filled with golden light, with so much love from our guides, our ancestors, from the Holy Beings, from Mother Earth, from each other and our threads that weave our hearts together. Let us allow it to fill our whole being. Let us allow it to expand out, weaving that tapestry to all that we love, all we care about, and to all beings, even those that dwell within the darkness; that the light and love that radiates from our hearts may allow each one to open their hearts and grow in depth, in sweetness and in vulnerability; for it is necessary to come to that place of tenderness of self-love and of recognition of this beautiful power of service and the deepest power of forgiveness and of humility. For as we embrace the whole world with our hearts, we send our light out to touch all hearts, knowing that each one is immortal, is infinite, is eternal and universal. Thank you for your presence with us. Thank you to all the guides and the angels that have been sharing with us the space, that are continually watching over us and surrounding us with their love. May the Living Spirit that is in all life fill your hearts with peace, deep, deep peace, the peace of knowing that you are always safe, knowing that you are loved and that your love is cherished in all worlds, in all dimensions. Blessings and peace.

Voice Ten
Ganesha

18th October 2020

Let us begin by putting our right hand on our heart and left hand on our right. Today is Sunday the 18th of October 2020. Today we welcome Ganesha to speak with us to share his/her wisdom. So, as we put our hands on our heart, let us connect with Mother Earth beneath us and Father Sky above us. Let's take a few deep breaths, allowing the body to become fully present, allowing our consciousness to become fully present within our bodies. Let's feel that connection with Mother Earth beneath us, and a column of light, reaching up towards Father Sky, to the Heavens; feeling our hearts right there beneath our hands, allowing that energy of stillness to pour down into us, to fill our whole being, that whole column with light, to fill our hearts with that golden glow of God's love. Allow it to expand and encompass each one in this group as we weave the threads of our hearts together, forming a beautiful fabric, a fabric of golden, heart energy that weaves its way into all of our loved ones, our friends, our neighbors, fellow city people across the nation, across this planet, spreading this beautiful golden web of light, of love and of heart energy all around Mother Earth; allowing it to touch the hearts of each soul, each heart, each human, each creature upon this planet. It fills them with a sense of hope, of comfort, of peace; with light, no matter who they are, what they believe, or what they do not believe. And as we bless each one, let us settle into that stillness, into that center, into the peace, into the heart.

So, you may rest your hands. Today I come to you as the one Ganesh or Ganesha. I am not male, I am not female, I'm not an elephant either, I am an energy. I am an energy that represents, on one level, the deep and enduring philosophies that have come from the East, from the continents of India and the energy of that area, the high mountains, the places of great poverty, and the places of great ones who have come and brought great wisdom, great teachings that have emanated originally from the lost continents and migrated their ways to the mountains and through these countries around the Indian Ocean and within, deeper into the highlands and the mountains of India, Tibet, Pakistan, and even across the Plains and across the vast expanses of Asia. For the great wisdoms of the East hold much honoring in many of the hearts of many of the people. It is a very strong connection that there is between the Vedas[68] and the teachings of the Indian continent and the Tibetan and their Buddhist teachings and practices. Many of these originate in Lemuria and Atlantis and these teachings are all based upon Oneness, the Law of One.[69]

For the only truth, as we have shared with you right at the beginning, is Oneness, or Union. All other truths are merely reflections or shadows or diminished versions of this one truth: that we are all connected through this golden energy of light through God's love; that we are all expressions of this love of the great Divine. We use the term "God," as we have said many times, because it is short and sweet and simple, and we could use the word Divine, but it doesn't quite carry the same energy, for there is within your consciousness an attitude towards that word "God." We all understand by now that we are referring to that indescribable energy of Creation, that intelligence that is the Intelligence of All That Is. This is an intelligence that could conceive and create everything that is possible and yet is inscrutable, and cannot be named and cannot be understood through the mind.

So, we bring you this energy of great devotion, a combination of great worship, and great suffering, of being able to use and also suppress the energy of the body, of the flesh, in service of the highest alignment that one can attain And so, you have a country of sadhus, of ones who practice various kinds of abstentions, flagellations, self-inflicted torture practices that we would not for you in this day and age recommend. There is a tradition, of overcoming the temptations of the flesh, even the simplistic ones, even the ones of survival, the ones of sustenance. There is this very strong desire to merge with the Divine, to become one with God, to reach states of awareness through great initiations and through great suffering on the part of the body. To align and achieve states of union, states of higher consciousness, and altered states of being, so many walk the streets as mendicants, as beggars, as sadhus, as those who sit upon nails, and those who hang from their toes, or whatever they do for whatever purpose they have in mind in order to achieve a state of freedom from the controls of the body and the body's system.

This practice has foundations that go back into the mists of time, and are encapsulated within a particular mindset, a particular religious approach, a particular rigor of practice that we are not asking you to embrace or suggesting as a way of being in the world today. For our intention is for you to live the fullness of life, to embrace the body, to honor it, to give it the best quality of food, water and exercise, nourishment and love that you can possibly instill upon it. Recognize that the body is the temple in which your soul has come to express that God nature, that divine energy of oneness and that you will not necessarily find it through the flagellations of the body, through the denial of your natural ways of experience, or of expressing the needs of the body to have its basic food and water and sleep and rest and exercise. You must be able to be at peace with your body, to not need to escape, but to fully inhabit your temple of flesh. In fact, instead of trying to merge with some divine exterior energy, I want you to focus on the within, merging your soul, your mind, your spirit with your body. Then you experience and express as a wholeness, as a oneness. This is something that we have shared with you before and want you to be completely aware of.

Ganesh or Ganesha has long been regarded as the remover of blocks, of being able to overcome that which you might regard as impossible. We call it the 'remover of obstacles,' and the obstacles that most of you at this time are experiencing are the kinds of obstacles within the mind, within the body and within the emotions. For in order to become at peace with yourself, it is necessary, for we have called you Spiritual Warriors, it is necessary to overcome the obstacles that you and that your upbringing have placed upon you. Many of those obstacles are ephemeral. They do not really exist. They only exist as thought forms, as beliefs systems. They only exist as ideas that you have accepted and allowed to become realities for you, so that sometimes you are not able to even see that they have no reality. They are essentially imprints from your conditioning that have been passed on from generation to generation and from time to time, and from ancestor to ancestor.

We have shared these things with you over the extent of this course. I would like to encourage you to reach out to me, to reach out to Ganesha, to ask me to assist you in overcoming your obstacles, for there is no reason why you should have them any longer. The water will flow around and over the obstacles within the stream or the river. You cannot stop the water nor will it restrict itself by the fact that there is a boulder in the middle of the river. For the water will, with great ease, weave its way around and over that stone, that big boulder and go around it. In fact, it may even undermine it and go beneath. It is important for you to recognize that all the practice you have been doing up to this point is to bring you to a place where you are able to identify your obstacle, to externalize it in such a way that you see it for what it is. It is no longer hiding within you in some undefined way so you are not able to describe what it means, what it stands for, and what it wants of you.

It certainly is not the intention of that Divine Intelligence that created you, that you should live in limitation, that you should live restricted by this box that you call your obstacle. It could be of physicality, of health, of emotion, or need or longing for companionship, or for the children of your heart. It could be for your life to become clear and close or to find a way of reconciling with someone that you have had a difficulty with, or an argument. Perhaps a person you feel that you cannot forgive or feel love towards. It could be your financial situation, something about the flow of money, of cash, of energy of abundance that has not been able to quite make itself available for you. Usually these are the three areas of the greatest concern: health, love (relationships) and money.

It is not necessary for you to have obstacles in your life any longer. You have the power, the power of your will, the power of your heart, and the power of your soul, to release the obstacles. Some of you have been learning about the golden nugget within the center of your Soul Seed, the connection to your intention for this life, to your blueprint, to your purpose and to your contract. You have come here to create new structures. You have come here essentially to blow apart your obstacles, to move around them or over them or through them. It is absolutely possible for you, and it is what we wish for you. So, call upon me. I will come. I will be there with you, and I will assist you. You can whisper to me, because you may feel some shame or guilt about what it is that is your great obstacle, and you can whisper it in my ear, as there is no judgment and all that is in your heart is already known. Your guides, your angels, your gods and goddesses know your heart. They love you. They have no conditions upon their love. They understand that you are human and that you are working your way towards your multidimensionality, into a space of love where everything becomes love. Everything becomes non-judgment, non-separation; everything becomes a oneness that does not distinguish and at the same time allows all individuality to have full expression without limitation.

We have talked to you about discrimination, and it is important too, because we are still harping upon the idea that you may yet have voices in your mind, in your head that diminish you, that do not allow you to see your full beauty, your full power, and your ability to love completely, to be able to forgive yourself and others. We do not bring you new messages. We have essentially traversed the whole range of teachings about oneness. It is now more that we are trying to, or we are intending, we don't try, we are pouring our love, our light, our blessings, our guidance, and our wisdom into you, so that you embody it, so that it is not external and so that you can become ready to establish those structures.

Remember the structures? Structures for the new world that will be based, in many ways, upon the dismantling of those obstacles that you have regarded as the great mountain that you have not been able to move. That great unimaginable, unpassable, hugely visible blockage within your path that you wish, "If only it could be dissolved away, then I will be able to see the green grass on the other side of that mountain." For you are God's creatures. You are the creation of the Divine Intelligence and you have within you the power of word, of command. Your willpower was not just intended for you to satisfy the needs of your body as a human being, as a flesh and blood being, as an animal, but it is an expression of your highest being as well. It requires of you to be able to give the command and know without believing, without thinking, but know from deep within you, that what you ordain shall come to pass. You may have to wait a little while with patience for it to come about in its perfect timing. For not everything happens just like that, even though it is possible. As you change the words in your mind, it is certainly possible, "just like that" to have that shift of consciousness, to have that ability, just as John Henry would say: "You can, because you can."

You can make that shift just like that, in the blink of an eye, because, as we have talked with you, your stories have become boring. They have become the record with the little thing in it that keeps it going round and round and round and saying the same old thing and never progressing towards the grand finale in the end of that record, where the arm, for those of you who can remember what the turntable looks like, the arm will rise up and go and rest back in its place and leave you alone. Your recordings are now, we shall say it, depleted of any juice. The batteries that run your stories have worn themselves out, and there is no longer any energy to sustain them, nor do you want to sustain them, because they are unsustainable. They do not feed you any longer.

Whatever it was that you had with your mother or your father, whatever the most horrific abuse you experienced could have been, it is in the past and it is my honor and pleasure, it is my task and my greatest joy and reward to assist you to let go of that obstacle, that imprint within your mind that you think is unmovable. For as you have one grain of faith, so will the mountain be moved. As you have one iota of trust, and you build that trust upon that seed that grows with nurturing, with fertilizing, with encouraging, with inspiring, so that faith and trust becomes the medium of your release of all obstacles.

And we encourage you to talk with us, to share with us, to call upon me, and say "Ganesha, I do not understand why you have come in the form of an elephant. Perhaps it is to remind me that I am living on memories and that the memories that go back to the very beginning are different memories than the one I carry in my blood, that I carry in this place that ties me up in knots, these weights upon my shoulders that I so long to release and be free of. I would prefer to have that energy of memory be cleared and a new operating system replace it. So, whatever it is that you represent for me, what I see in your beautiful great eyes is only love. Whether I see you as an Elephant God or I see the other one, Hanuman as Monkey God, I do not necessarily know how to relate to this. It is not my practice or my religion, and yet I see you coming to me with great love, with great desire to be of assistance, to help me in my blossoming. I see the pink and the gold and the softness, I see the axe that cuts through all the lies. I see that you carry these beautiful flowers and that you sit upon a throne of gold and that you are honored and worshiped and revered by many people, by many millions who reach to you and ask you for their love, their guidance to be fulfilled, for their prayers to be answered, whether it be mundane or the most sublime, for each one comes with their "baggage." And so, may the memory that has tied you up in knots become unraveled and dissolve away into the great Ganges, or the great Nile, or the Rio Grande, or whatever river it is, or a great ocean that you can dissolve all of your harm, your hurts, your wounds into, so that you can be born again, re-baptized in the waters of Love, in the water of Salvation, in the pure waters that will one day again be upon your planet, pristine, life-giving, structured, as living water should be.

We ask you to let go of your story, let go of the memories. However they may be imprinted in your mind, they can be replaced by the warmth of love, by the joyful memories, by the memories of what you are here to create in the future, for your imagining becomes reality as you imagine the future that you want for yourself, for your children, for Mother Earth, for all creatures and all life. As you imagine *this*, it becomes a reality. For it is important to hold in your mind, instead of those silly voices or those painful images and memories; it is important to hold the image upon the screen of your soul those things that you would have come to pass: the children living freely and safely, enough for everyone, green fields, pure water, fresh, clean air, the trees healthy again with plenty of moisture, reaching up to the skies, reaching down into the very roots of Mother Earth. Align your hearts with the beauty that you imagine.

As we have said, as John Henry has said, do not allow worry to enter your consciousness. Do not allow your mind to focus on that which you do not want. Instead focus on that which your heart longs for. For what you long for for yourself, you long for for everyone. What you want for everyone, you want for yourself. It is time. It is time for you. It is your time. It is time to have your heart's desire become manifest. It is your time for your command, for your fiat, for your words of power to reach to the ends of the Earth, to bring joy and light and love to those who suffer. It is time for the end of suffering. It is time that those who toil hard shall be relieved of some of their burden and be able to receive the nourishment that they have to work so hard for, with greater ease and grace. It is time to let go of the shadow of control, of living underneath that dark cloud of those who wish to make you into slaves. They shall not succeed and it is because we are with you that you will succeed in bringing the light of your heart and soul to fill this planet with that golden glow of love to reach across to the edges and surround this planet with that beautiful web that we have all created together.

I am here as one who carries the axe and the flower and the ability to remove obstacles. I am here now within your own heart, within your own mind. The long nose, the snout, the trunk of the elephant may look very uncomely on a human, however it is one of the most sensitive structures upon your planet. It is able to reach with great delicacy and pick up a peanut and place it within the mouth. It is able to feel with great sensitivity, to experience the fragrances that are beyond the smaller fragrances of human experience. It is able to experience and express the greater subtleties. The big ears that are upon the head of the elephant are able to hear at great distance to feel the rumblings of Mother Earth through the great feet. I stand as one of the most powerful energies upon your planet. I accomplish tasks that you require these heavy machines to do that plow up Mother Earth, that pollute her, and that are not sustainable, that make great noise and roarings and disturb your peace and your rest. Whereas I have been from very early times, the great helper of mankind, of humankind. I come to you now as one who wishes to help you, so that you understand that the form is an expression, even if it is different, it is an expression of many facets of creation and of benefit that have been given to humankind in order to be of assistance, to create worlds, to create structures and containers for the great benefit of all humanity, of all creatures, and of Mother Earth. The ivory that I have, even if it is designed for tearing apart various foodstuffs or to create spaces within the earth, digging to plant seeds; it is one of the most precious materials upon your planet. As you look upon my features, you will find that there are many wonderful attributes that having a head, or a structure or form of an elephant allows. I can trample upon all of your obstacles, "just like that." They are but dust. They can be dissolved away.

I invite you for one moment to feel again that breath, that space of stillness, to feel my presence behind you, supporting you, holding you, loving you. Allow that stillness to penetrate your whole being. Allow everything to melt within that pink and gold, within that light. Allow your shoulders to soften, to feel the warmth of love, of softness, of tenderness, to allow those burdens to dissolve, to fall away, to melt into the dust, into the waters. Allow yourself to be unburdened, to be free, to be pristine within the essence of who you truly are, without the encumbrances of all those imprints, of all the ideas of how you should be. Imagine you are sitting upon the great beast, directing this one, this elephant, to take you where you wish to go, like Dumbo, flying through the skies with you upon the back. Imagine this great beast, carrying you safely through the jungles and forests, carrying you over the mountains, bearing you wherever it is you need to go. Imagine the support of one such as I, of such power, and imagine the great love as you sit upon me, as you direct me to assist you in overcoming your obstacles. Let it all go, because you can, "Just like that."

We will pause for a moment, to look you in the eyes again. We would like to show you something. Can you see? (A painting of Ganesha is shown. See above). That is who I am, carrying that little axe, carrying the flower, pink and gold.

I come to you to bring you tidings of great joy. As you work towards the season of the birth, of that Being of Light that came to instill in humanity's heart the understanding of the God being within, of all being one, of the bottom line of "Love each one as you would love yourself." And love yourself, as you would choose to love each one; A time of celebrating with family and friends if it be so for you. We are bringing you that sense of peace that we wish for you to have always, now. It is vital for you to know that you have that sword by your side, that you have that ability to discern, that you have that ability to cut through the illusions, to let go of your obstacles, and to rise to the occasion to become masters, to become teachers, to become adepts. You are the ones you have been waiting for. You have come here to teach. You have come here to lead, as we have said, you have come here to create structures, new structures for a New Earth. It is imperative that you let go of every single thought, of every single obstacle that would keep you from fulfilling your destiny. For you have contracted to be here at this time, to hold that radiant space of God's love within your heart, within your soul and become the full expression of it.

That one Christ taught the divinity within, and it is your guiding light. It is that place that we wish for you to find within yourself. For it is not outside until it is within, and then you become that radiance that allows everything to be a reflection of that inner light that you are cultivating each day. As you practice your meditations, your moving, your time in Nature, your communicating with the beings, the creatures, the trees, with all of life; as you go into the stillness, the silence, into the peace more and more often; as you remember to take that breath, it becomes easier and easier for you to see yourself as Light. It becomes easier to know that your light is not just shining upon and through you, but is emanating from the very center of your being. You have come to be that light on the hill, that lighthouse. You have come to hold truth, the truth of oneness. You have come to demonstrate that possibility of forgiveness, however hard it may be. This is your work. This is your mission as Warriors of the Light, as great Warriors of Truth. It is your mission to shine the light wherever you possibly can and allow yourself to be the light.

Really, you have no choice. It is what you have chosen. You may take it on kicking and screaming, but understand that in the Swing Between Worlds it was your contract. And we know this because you are here, because you are listening, somewhere, somehow, or reading somewhere down the road, you are reading our words or hearing them and allowing them to penetrate into your deepest soul's truth.

We are feeling this Presence. We wish you to feel it too. There is this emanation that comes from the center of my heart, of this place of pink, of heart, of gold, and it is shining upon you and through you, and you are being surrounded now by your guides, those angels that love you, that wish only the best for you. For we are with you always until the end of time. You have come here to create the Peace of a Million Years of Dreaming. It is the Coming Together of the Ages. All of your lifetimes have reached this pinnacle, this point in time, in the No Time; this experience upon your planet of this great challenge, of bringing light where there is darkness, of shining your own brilliance upon everyone, through 'Being,' through 'Presence,' through that emanation, that radiance, that radiation, that comes from your own heart and soul. And so, know that we are loving you, we are with you, we are within you, and we are surrounding you. And we are placing around you a great sphere of golden light to keep you always protected, to keep you safe, and pure, and innocent, so that you can do your play in the world. Remember that joy is your greatest aspiration. We wish you joy.

Ganesha Q&A

Humility

The question that you asked, SL, about humility has remained a topic for teaching and it feels like we did not even adequately answer, because humility is one of the most important and powerful attributes of the Spiritual Warrior and of the devotee of oneness. It is, in fact, more than just the service aspect. It is also, what you might call, the opposite of pride. There is certainly not anything wrong with taking care of one's needs, but it is that ability to put the good of the whole, to put service for all of humanity and Mother Earth and all the creatures at the absolute pinnacle of priorities. Whatever practice you do, whatever service, attribute your success, the good that you do in the world, not to your own personality so much, but to that divine energy that moves through you and inspires you to do it. In a sense you become an appendage of God, you become the "right hand of God" for the world. And you do that for yourself by doing it for the world.

There is this fine line between service and being able to take pride in what you do. Recognize that everything that you do, you do as an expression of God's love. And that even the "you" is not that one that is gimme, gimme, gimme, is all needy, needy, needy and is doing everything to please somebody else or out of motives that comes from woundedness. So we wish to clarify that aspect of humility and, probably, it is quite an investigation. It is certainly worth spending time contemplating. So, thank you for that question because it does feel that it is a very important place to look within your own psyche and at the same time find that space of being able to distinguish, to determine what is ego, and what is your higher purpose when you do an action that is benevolent. Thank you.

Q. (NB) *I have sketches of you all over my house. I have you painted. You are dancing around here in my house in every room, in every room I go. I just want to know what would you like to say to me.*

A. I have brought you my colors (see photo) through this one here for your purpose. I have brought these colors because they are a reflection of who you are. It is that beautiful mixture of soft tenderness, that heart space that you carry. It reflects your devotion and service to humanity, the energy of love that you broadcast without any effort, and the gold. The gold is the nugget that was spoken about by Flo, an emanation of God's love for humanity. It is an expression of your own kernel, that seed or nugget which is your soul's expression in the world to bring benefit and to help. In fact, it is the foundation of your work in the world for creating structures. For every structure that you create will come from the golden ray. It will come from the highest energy that you are able to transmit and to allow to come through you.

It is also a way to understand that we have come to you as an energy of the 12, but I come to you as an energy of deep fondness from your own tradition, from your own lineage that goes back to the very earliest times on your planet. The creation of a practice of humans being able to attain enlightenment through the devotion, and what we have called diminishment of the flesh. This is the path of the sadhu, one who retires to the cave like Milarepa, even though he is from the Buddhist tradition. Yet there is that very strong ascetic energy. You have done this in many past lifetimes. You do not have to go through that type of experience in this life. This life is about living the abundance, living the pleasure, living the rewards of all your other lifetimes where you suffered. For all of you, this is a time of reward, of receiving, even though you all have this intense desire to give and to serve. You have many times gone overboard in giving and in serving, and so we want you to allow yourselves in this life to experience what it is like to receive, what it is like to allow, what it is like to live without the burdens, without the obstacles.

It is important that you become agents of benevolence and in order to do so, you must live that knowing of the benevolence of the universe. For what does that word mean? Benevolence only means the desire for good, wishing good for all, for all life, for all humans and all souls. For, in the deepest places of benevolence one could not even imagine harming another. This too, is what I represent and why you have me dancing on your walls, why you have inside of your heart inscribed this energy of who I am and what I bring. If you remember, Walt Disney created a fantasy (Fantasia) using the music, the Dance of the Fairies, perhaps it was. And it was danced by elephants to show that even this heaviest and most powerful of beings can be as delicate and light as gossamer. We represent, we call ourselves "we" because again, we have not distinguished between male or female. We call ourselves Ganesha, especially this pink and golden energy, to represent the soft feminine aspect of power. And so, we dance upon your walls to remind you of this combination of soft and hard, strong and weak, delicate and powerful, none of these terms having concepts of being right or wrong or good or bad, of negative or positive, but just embody this combination of opposites that allows the transcendence into that field of union. So for you, we represent this union of your own lineage and heritage as it combines with the greatest of all religions, of all practices, of all disciplines and followings for there is no distinction of the one heart, of the one mind, of the one God, the One that is the All. Thank you.

Q. (MSG) I have a little Ganesha dancing on my computer always because that's the place where I sometimes encounter obstacles. All of us suffer from the tendency to give more than we receive and I have attracted a lot of clients in my healing practice over the years who have that imbalance, perhaps of many lifetimes of renunciation, another word for that, of having sacrificed so much and also my clients who were raised Catholic have a lot of that idea and I get there's always the reflection of myself, of who I attract to work with. I have this understanding and I talk to them about it, this distorted Bodhisattva[70] vow. Which is, "OK, I know I'm enlightened but I'm gonna stay with you in the suffering." And I always say "No, you have to step in the radiant light place and show others what possible; step into the joy," but I just notice there's still this little stuck place with me where I don't give fully myself that permission. Any insight there? I've worked through many obstacles in my life but I want to do it more with joy and dance through them now. It's funny how you can help other people with things where you're still a little stuck.

A. Thank you for that question. It also does relate very much to what we spoke of at the beginning about humility, about pride. You might even call it arrogance, or a subtle form of arrogance that goes by as service, for the whole idea of being a Bodhisattva is that you would not know it. You cannot embrace the idea of being a Bodhisattva without having that motivation to find some glory, some glamour within that high ideal. And there may be this aspect within the heart that absolutely longs to be of service and that would deny oneself.

However, it is important, as warriors of the truth to even examine these ideas and to allow them to dissipate. For it is, as we have said, quite a fine line for you to strive to have everything that you want for yourself and to be okay with that. It is okay to not have guilt or shame. In the past, you would always put yourself down as soon as you begin to reach for something you want. Those voices inside are ready to rap you on the knuckles because you want something for *you*. It has been part of the indoctrination by your religions that you cannot be 'selfish', that you must be only for service of others. So, finding balance in everything is the true challenge of the master, to walk the middle path. So, to be a Bodhisattva is not for you. It is not for one who walks the Western way to start wanting to be a Bodhisattva, for it is merely glamour. It is not being true to your heart. What your heart wants is to have love, to have money, to have health, to have fun, to have childish innocence, to have peace, to have the joy of friendship, to have the experience of being in love with Nature, with water, with the air, with trees, with creatures, with another human being, to have cuddles and companionship. And friends; to have everything that your heart desires, to have ease and grace and not struggle.

You do not have to be of great service in order to deserve to have all these things. You don't have to give, give, give constantly. It is your birthright to have everything you want because, at the deepest place within you, you want it for everyone. And wanting it for everyone means that you are an expression of that benevolence of the Universe, and you can stop trying, you can stop feeling a need to give one more thing when your discerning aspect of that warrior recognizes that you need to say "No." There should be no twinge of guilt about saying "No, I want to go for a walk. I do not want to answer the phone right now or help you. When it's the right time, I will be available."

So, setting boundaries is important, as well as the recognition that you deserve to have everything you want without guilt without shame, without voices in your head that bitch at you, "Nya, nya, nya!" It is part of your job, as a Warrior of the Light, as a Spiritual Warrior, as, shall we say, a manifestation of Ganesh, that you dance in joy, in peace, in love, for the very joy of dancing. That you give only for the joy of giving and that you receive with that same joy, so that everything becomes about joy, and where it is absent, you step back and take a breath and ask yourself "Do I want to do this? Am I doing it out of duty or am I doing it out of the joy that I receive in giving, because I do not need to have anything in return?"

It is for you to contemplate. There is no hard and fast answer and yet your heart requires of you to let go of any idea of guilt or shame or obligation to please anyone but yourself. Then you truly are expressing your divine nature and all the obstacles melt away and there is only joy. It is not by chance that the last one to speak with us will be Joy, for in many ways her brightness was an expression of this joy of childhood innocence that we wish you all to re-embody in your life. Thank you.

Q. (KW) My question is about part of Ganesha that's often associated with new beginnings. What I've read is that he was born from Shiva and Parvati and Shiva was angry because Ganesh was doing what his mom had asked him to do, to guard her, and Shiva cut off his head and then had to replace it by sunset, and the only head they could find to replace it was an elephant's head. And so, it's like new beginnings. I would just like to get some more insight from you about that aspect, about new beginnings; what comes from that kind of thing, when we try to make things better and they're not necessarily what we're expecting them to be, but lots of good can come of it. Could you share some about that? Thank you.

A. We are the New Earth Council. Mythologies carry profound truths. At the same time it is possible to get caught up in the meanings that are attributed. Recognize that we, the Council, represent the idea of new beginnings and this is what we have come to you for. In fact, your very presence here, all of you, is an incitement, an invitation, an encouragement to create new beginnings in the world. This is a time of reckoning, a time in which you are being faced with the apparent ascendance of evil in the world, but, understand and know that essentially you are actually witnessing the disintegration of its hold. This allows the understanding too of new beginnings to have a stronger and more powerful meaning, and, as we have emphasized the idea of new structures, we recommend that within your own personal world, within your social life, and within your world as part of community, that you become a teacher, a leader, and be an inspiration for others. Each step that you take upon your path becomes a new beginning.

We talk much about thresholds. This is the time of the new moon. It is the time of new beginning, an ascension process, where the moon becomes bigger and bigger as it starts to move towards fullness. It is a time of new beginnings in your own personal life and an invitation to look at where there might be lack of clarity, where you might have clutter, perhaps a certain level of confusion. It is a time of allowing yourself to begin again with a brand-new slate, perhaps to attack that closet and empty it and then reorganize it and get rid of much of the clutter that has been in there that is no longer necessary. Do that also with your own mind and your own ambitions, and with your intentions for your life.

So, yes. It is definitely an important time of new beginnings. You will have a new time structure before too long. It will not be too long before you come upon the winter solstice, another time of major shifts, beginning again, for the motion of the Sun to begin its ascendancy again in the heavens and grow stronger and brighter even within the darkness. There are many ways for you to contemplate the question you have put forth because, essentially, you have brought forward an aspect of Ganesha that I did not express, and we're grateful for it.

I would recommend that you pull out pen and paper and that you write your understandings, that you create your expressions, your teachings, wisdom that can be shared and perhaps included in our book. It will be available as a teaching that those who have not been blessed to be with us in this process will be able to access and gain from. So, it is absolutely a time of new beginnings. It is the middle of a period of darkness to light. It is very much of a time of new beginnings and we honor you for the question, for what you bring forth and the wisdom which is within your heart. Thank you.

Q. (CW) It was around obligations. As you know my mom passed over recently and I had a sense the other day that in her passing she has allowed like a release of obligations on the family, like some of those contracts maybe that we had. It feels that some of that has fallen away. And even the timing of when she passed was on the Equinox on the 22ⁿᵈ of the 9ᵗʰ month of 2020 at 9 o'clock and she was 88 years old, so that balance seemed to kind of be quite significant, and I think we had the funeral, the cremation on Friday which I believe is a new moon as well, so also kind of signifying a new beginning. And my brother seems to be able to be moving on from some of his stuff as well. So, I just wondered if you had anything to say about that.

A. Yes, thank you. As you know, numbers are important. There is a profound underpinning of the energy that numbers represent and of course the number 9 is about completion. It is 3 x 3 or 3+3+3. It is the trinity that is multiplied. It is also, as you said, around the equinox time of sitting upon the fence and looking back and looking forward and deciding which direction you will go. And in fact, it is a great gift of your mother that she allows you to let go of any sense of obligation or burden. It is her gift to you out of love that she does not wish for you to feel obligation. Obviously, there is a time to take care of that which has to be done and to perhaps do some clearing and some sorting and some letting go, but essentially, she is opening up for you the doorway into the rest of your life. By leaving, she is giving you back your whole childhood, in a way. She is allowing you to begin your life with a fresh slate. She's allowing you to be totally free to express yourself in that childlike way, to remember your purity and your innocence and to be able to begin, knowing that she would not want you in any way to carry any more loads, to suffer anything for anybody else, but she wants you to thrive and blossom.

And so, as you feel her love, you understand that whatever contracts or binds there have been, whatever agreements you may have made with her or with any other ancestors, that she is, shall we say, on your side. On the 'other side' she is backing you up. She is inspiring you in your mission, in your life's work, in your unfolding as a divine expression of soul. She is backing you all the way, so we say "Go for it!" Allow all the weight to dissolve away. Allow your shoulders to lighten up from any burdens you carry, not just from her, but from any ancestors, from any of your lineages that have held struggle and suffering to be of great value. It may have served in the past as a path towards learning a greater expression of consciousness, and teaching, yet this time is about freedom. There has been a weight that has been lifted off your shoulders. It can actually be felt, so that you can feel physically lighter. You can feel that you are free, that you are now able, perhaps, to move forward in ways where before you had to hold back. And those who are part of your family will not be disappointed or feel like somehow you are betraying them if you express the fullness of the power that you carry and express the joy of living and the life that is for you to experience now.

As you do this, everyone else will find that they have more lightness of being. Perhaps there will be more permission for joking, for fun, for pulling one's leg, for letting go of this stiff upper lip that is part of your culture. You can allow yourself to enjoy more, to relax more, to feel more satisfied, and to know that your heart's desire is within reach. And what you have come here to do is also about creating these new structures. You are beginning again, beginning with a clean slate, letting go of all the stories, those that no longer serve. If there is perhaps a story that has a beautiful moral in it, perhaps it will be worth writing about. But it is definitely a time for everyone of new beginnings and of reaching for the stars, reaching to be the best you can. Thank you.

Q. (MS) *So, as a group, what is our collective greatest obstacle that you see that we need to have removed or lifted from us in order to create greater union, not just only amongst ourselves but to do our part in the world? What is our greatest issue? Once again, maybe there's some "me" in it, but it's mostly as our collective group.*

A. That is a beautiful question. You have gathered together, you that have been here for this time to see into each other's eyes. It could be with this small group, with the larger group with Flo, or those with whom you gather for sharing or to do meditation with. Look into each other's eyes and begin to see each other as friends, allowing yourself to crack open that shield, that armor that each one carries around their heart that says "I have to be cool. I cannot allow another to see my vulnerability. I cannot admit my sadness or my loneliness or my anger. It feels hard for me. It's awkward for me to open up and share my isolation or my rage about this or that. I don't feel ready." It is why we have encouraged you to pick up the phone and call someone to just chat, just for the sake of it, (we do not like the term "hell of it," so we will say "just for the joy of it.") You may find out who that other person on the end of the screen is and what you might allow yourself to share, and perhaps, as always, you will be guided to call someone who you didn't know was going to bring up some triggering for you, or perhaps will touch a tender place within you that brings up the tears or brings up the anger; and you support each other by witnessing, by just being there.

So, the greatest obstacle is this box that each one puts around themselves that has essentially created separateness, that place in which your individuality has become your armor. It is where it is hard to be human, where you are part of spiritual groups and have been for so many of your lifetimes. Part of this is that you wish to ascend, you wish to escape, you wish to go beyond the human, you wish to transcend the pain, the limitation, the sense of guilt or shame, so it is hard for you. Perhaps when you connect with your angels, your guides or with the divinity to whom you pray, you actually acknowledge what is going on in your heart, but with other humans you have this sense of needing to gather around you your shield, put around you your mantle so that only a small part of you shows.

It is also expressed on a larger scale, where everyone is walking around like a zombie with a mask. They can hide behind it. They can hold back from relating, they can become anonymous, invisible, and many of you live within this invisible shield. This one here has a very difficult time admitting to being lonely because he has always been the helper. He has always been the one to fix, to drop everything and go to the rescue. And yet it leaves him somewhat bereft, and he would not come forward and say this, but we're saying it on his behalf just to break the ice. Each one of you carries within your heart your sorrows, your wounds, your losses, your disappointments. What a joy it could be to know that you can speak freely of this with another human soul and not be judged, and be honored and respected. Whenever, at circles, at ceremonies, one comes forth and shares that which is heavy upon their heart, I have noticed how others will gather around them to give support, to give them honoring for their courage to express that which is hard upon them.

So, if there is an obstacle that needs to be removed, it is that reticence, that holding back, that feeling that you are separate, that you are different, and that somehow you always need to be the giver. For in answering these questions today, we have gone deep into that place of feeling, shall we say, responsible to please others, even to the degree of being a doormat because you cannot say "No!" Perhaps you are in a relationship with a person, or money, or health and you do not know how to draw the line. You do not know how to give up sugar or you do not know how to tell your partner "This has not been working, I need a break," or you do not know how to face your bank account and say "I must stop spending" or "It is time for me to begin to tithe, to give more so that I can receive."

We're not saying you must do anything. We are opening the field for you to examine. And for those of you who have been on this course, it has been intense each week to show up, to listen, to come forth with your questions, to hear the answers to others' questions and see where it resonates for you. So, you are asking powerful questions, all of you, because you are essentially ascending. You have transcended many of those places within your psyche and in your consciousness that, at the beginning of this course, were much more restricted and limited, and we honor you for this. We are grateful for your journey, for we all prosper. Those of us who are free of or beyond having bodies of flesh and blood, we still gain. Our souls are also evolving, even those of us who know how to give, give, give. We are also learning about receiving from the beauty of what it is to be human, learning about the power of being human, having emotions, having that which the Greeks used to call the fatal flaw, that Achilles heel.[71] It is an essential element in all tragedy, and even in comedy there is a thin line that requires the flaw to almost ruin everything, but it all works out in the end. Not so in the Greek Tragedies or Shakespeare. When you engage with the place within you that you cannot face or that is your downfall, you still can rise above, transcending and allowing yourself to experience the joy of just being human. As Shakespeare said, "Men must endure their going hence, even as their coming hither: **Ripeness is all.**"

So, this is your great obstacle. It is about wanting to be non-human, wanting to be angels. You already are angels and now it's time to be human. It's time to let go of suffering and still be human. It's time to maintain your aspirations to divinity and recognize that you already are divine. Recognize that when you are fully human, when you are fully 100% in your body, you are expressing God's intention for you. God wishes you to experience the joy of being human. Why else would 'It' have created you, if not for the greater expression and expansion of that which is divine, that which is the All That Is to experience more and more of its essence, as you, and through you. Peace.

Q. (SL) I've always felt really good about the fact that I can learn something and that whenever I advance, whenever I make inroads and learn new things, and become, in some way more spiritual, that I am helping the universe to expand. I get more excited about helping the universe to expand than helping myself to expand. Like when I run a relay race and there were several other people counting on me, I could do better than if I was just doing it for myself.

A. Well, it is a beautiful example of everything we have shared about how important it is to love yourself, how important you are to the big plan, shall we say, for if you are not happy, the world is not happy. For everything that comes into your field becomes imbued with that. It is also important to remember that you do not need to become spiritual. You already are spirit embodied in matter. It is our joy to see you become human. It is our joy to see you becoming lighter, to become filled with light, for that is more appropriate than seeking to be more spiritual. And yes, it is true. It also follows on MS's question about where the obstacles might be and how you can see yourself as an important player on the field within a team, whether it be a football or a soccer or a rugby match or it be, as you have indicated, a race where you hand the baton and you share in the glory. You share in the glamour, you share in the joy and you share in the success or the failure, but it is part of a team, of course, understanding that there is no such thing as failure, or success, as much as one loves to experience success. When one does it for the whole, then one is doing it for oneself.

It also reflects on the ideal of being humble, of living, so to speak, without the glamour, without the need to glorify self, because it's easier at some level to put all of your attention outside of you but not within you. It's like not looking at "What do I want? How can I allow myself, in spite of all those voices, to simply have what I want without the need to serve anyone, just for the joy of it?"

Closing Meditation

So let us go back into that beautiful space, that beautiful feeling, that knowing that with one breath we are entering that beautiful golden sphere that all of our guides and angels have placed around us, allowing their presence to fill our being, allowing their protection to keep us safe, allowing their love to expand out and touch all of humankind, to touch all the creatures, to touch all life, no matter what planet, no matter what star system, no matter what galaxy, no matter what little piece of earth it dwells upon. For we are all One, and we are so grateful and honored by your presence here, joining with us to celebrate the Oneness of all life. Blessings and Peace.

Voice Eleven
Guru Rinpoche

25th October 2020

OK. They wanted me to show you a few things quickly. This is the Rainbow Body from a thangka[72] that has Guru Rinpoche as the central figure. (See page 180 below) Also, a young Israeli woman who was doing her own thankas, painted this Guru Rinpoche thanka (See photo on left) on a piece of thin plywood when she was visiting my shop many years ago and I framed it. It has been on my altar for a long time.

We begin by putting our hands on our heart. There is a very strong feeling that some of what will be talked about will be "imagination." Let us breathe in as we begin to feel that alignment from Heaven to Earth, as we feel the downpouring of that golden light from above, filling our whole column with light, the column that reaches down into Mother Earth. We feel our feet grounded, ourselves connecting to Mother Earth with our gratitude and love, aligning ourselves to that central column now. We allow ourselves to feel the warmth spreading from our hearts as we weave together all the beautiful threads of our hearts, imagining, just like that Rainbow Body,[73] that we are connecting with each other, with these beautiful colors of the rainbow. Rainbow Warriors of the Light connecting with all those on this planet who are carrying the vibration of light, who are amplifying it and sending it out in order to spread this light all the way across and around the planet, so that all the creatures, all the humans that are suffering at this time may find some relief in the knowing that there are those of us, whatever our number may be, that are spreading the light, holding the light and who are true to the light.

Let's allow the stillness to fill our whole being, the peace, our inner wisdom, as we relax and melt into that beautiful expansion of consciousness, this beautiful Rainbow Body that we are cultivating. We allow it to shine into all the reaches of the Universe as we weave around the planet a web of love, light and heart energy to bless all of life, to provide protection and create a shield around all life from any harm or negativity. Let's connect with Mother Earth and send her every bit of love that we can possibly muster, knowing that it is replenished as we send it out. It fills us from below, from Mother Earth beneath us and from Father Sky above us. We are surrounded by a sphere of golden light of protection, a golden sphere that expands our consciousness and protects us, so that only the purest and highest vibrations are allowed in this space that we share. Each of us carries this sphere of golden light wherever we go from this moment on.

You might think it is unusual that one such as I, who represents an image, a mythology, an energy of great power, as founder of Tibetan Buddhism, a great magician, and a being of tremendous power and light called Guru Rinpoche, would come and speak with you through this one here. Guru Rinpoche is, in a way, the highest level of guru-ship that you can imagine. It is like being called the Holy Lama of all time. (It is good to laugh at oneself!) I am also called Padmasambhava. Why would one such as I come before you? And yet the times require that all the energies of power, beings of light, angels and archangels, Melchizedeks and all the Holy Beings that you can conjure up in your mind, are all gathering around you today. These times that you are in, require us to gather around you, teach, watch over you, and send our light, our love and our blessings to you, to Mother Earth, and to all her creatures. We send light and love to all those who are affected within the Cosmos by those things that are going on, on your planet today. There is a great battle between the forces of what you call darkness and the forces of light, the forces that wish to control you and the forces that wish you to have freedom, peace, love, cooperation and the New Earth. We are all gathered around you, individually and collectively. We come to your group and the combination of all your groups that are doing this kind of preparation for the New Earth. We are directing the most incredible levels of blessing towards the ones like you who are expanding their consciousnesses in light, opening their beings to the influx of more and more light, sending this golden energy of blessing, of love, and the highest order of truth to you.

It is important for you to hold strong, to anchor your vibration, your central column, the central meridian of your being, that energy of connection with Mother Earth, Father Sky, the Cosmos, with the energy of Source, and those overseers who are like the Ones with No Names. There are those who watch over your comings and your goings-on this planet, those who watch over you and love you and are guiding you, individually and collectively. We would like you to imagine the Rainbow Body that we have shown you. Many consider that the energy of the Rainbow Body belongs only to the highest adepts and those who can meditate in caves in freezing Tibetan winters, who have created bodies of light. You believe that they are special and that they are the select few. We wish to break down some of these assumptions and ideas and let you know that anyone can develop their Rainbow Body through the combination of practice, imagination and intention. The emanation of this Rainbow Body is an emanation of all the aspects of Light, all the colors of the rainbow that comes from your pure heart. It comes from that place of your innocence, of your free will that has turned its direction towards service, that place within you that longs to help others, that is determined to bring about a new world, a New Earth. It is for those who would do everything you possibly can to attain a state of equanimity, of peace in your own lives, so that you can become way-showers; you can become pillars of light upon the hilltops for others who are groping in the darkness. You are the lighthouses shining your light for those looking for that tiny seed, that mustard seed of light, of hope, of faith and trust. Your light illuminates theirs, so that they too can expand their light and step upon the mountaintop to shine their own light. For as you do this for yourself, you do it for the world. You do it for your family, your friends, your neighbors. You do it for those you meet on the street or in the supermarket, those who see and feel your light emanating from you, those who feel that sense of equanimity.

You do not have to be a practicing Buddhist to become a Guru Rinpoche. You do not have to be a practicing anything that has a label upon it, for that becomes a limitation. See through our eyes, and those eyes only, the eyes of unconditional love, and talk through our voices. The great ones that represent the highest energies and elements of Buddhist teaching like the Dalai Lama, whom everyone adores, he represents the religion of kindness, the religion of compassion, and he does this through his smile. He achieves this through the energy of actually being and walking his talk, being what he says. The young ones that are now reincarnating as the leaders and teachers of Buddhist practice, His Holiness the Karmapa and Kalu Rinpoche, these "young ones" have grown up with the new technologies, within this new civilization. Even though they have full recollection of their past lifetimes as Rinpoches, as previous embodiments of the Karmapa and the Kalu Rinpoche lineage, they are understanding now the need to make everything available to all hearts; that there is not one religion that is "supreme," above another. They recognize that all religions that talk of One, that talk of the Whole and that represent the All That Is, are all that will remain. We have talked about sustainability on your planet. The religions that have a particular dogma that excludes others, will not survive because they will not inspire the hearts and souls of the people. The religions that say "My way or the highway," that keep their cults separate and regard themselves as special, teaching that they are the "chosen ones" who will enjoy the exclusive benefit of some great dispensation, transfiguration or "rapture" and say that it is only for those who follow their path; these will all fall away.

It is only the love in the heart that will inspire any kind of devotion or religious practice that can survive. It is because of this too, that I have chosen to come and speak to you and have, you might say, raised my hand and said "I will be one of your voices. I have a message for you." The practice of Buddhism is very deep and provides extensive initiations for ascension, profound teachings and practices that you can do as you become an initiate and progress from one level to another. Through these practices you can generate heat, you can raise your whole body a number of feet above the earth and you can (astral) travel to distant places. You can do all these wonderful, miraculous things through our practices and our secret teachings. You do not have to be a Buddhist, however. There are many other teachings and initiations and mystery schools that offer this, but as is written in the New Testament "He thathas not love, is like a tin can rattling," (1 Corinthians 13:1, my translation). For Love is the foundation and is the only foundation that travels along the pathways of the Light, for the two are so interwoven, that where there is light, there is love. Where there is love, there is light.

When there is love in your heart, as you imagine that you are expanding your own heart's field and it is becoming a Rainbow Body, it will be doing so. As you imagine that this column of light and this sphere that are around you are becoming toroidal fields that expand out into infinity and into the Great Cosmos and energize everything within that field with a great light and great blessing; as you imagine, it becomes so. It becomes the reality. Do not disparage your imagination. Use it to create beautiful art. Use it to create those things in your life that you would like to see, beyond guilt, beyond the feeling of non-deserving that you may still have vestiges of, that perhaps still remain in your field. We have tried to help you to release them and let go of all that. Beyond these things, imagine everything your heart desires. For the New Earth is built upon your heart's desire. Because your heart's desire is not just for yourself but for the whole, as such it becomes energized. It becomes amplified and it becomes reality. It is that innocence and purity that is aligned with your intentions and your will, and is aligned with your choice to use your free will for benefit, for the highest good, that makes it all so.

It is also time for you to understand that, because you are living in such momentous times, it is time for you to find your calling, to begin to create the structures that we have been talking about. It is time because of our connection with you to write down, "This is what I am here to bring." It is similar to the course with The Ones with No Names and Flo Magdalena. It is important for you to clarify for yourself and to put down on paper that which you are here for, that which you are looking to create and how you might go about doing so. So too, to consider who there might be in your field or who on the screen you feel an affinity to work with. For as you collaborate and come together with others, your power increases and the cooperative energy begins to expand. We would like you, by the last session, to have on paper and to share with someone, what it is that you feel is your mission and how you intend to go about bringing it forth into reality. We ask you to do now; to make sure that you take time to meditate and to come up with the answers that, for you, are true and real, and come from that place of your center, of your heart, knowing that by doing this you are setting into motion all of your helpers.

There is a saying from Goethe[74] that requires of you to let go of your doubts and move towards that which is of the highest order for you; to do that which your heart longs to do. It is about commitment. It is about the power of commitment to manifest and set in motion in the Universe all the requisites of support, allies and alliances that are required to manifest that which your heart is committed to. For it is the time for commitment.

There is great threat to life on this planet through the energies of these control beings that have no idea whatsoever of the ramifications of their harm and the horrific practices that they do and how it affects all life. Even worse, they are blind to this and they are intending to do great harm to all of life. One of the aspects of this that affects each one upon the planet is your Internet system that is moving to its next level, the 5-th generation (fiv-eG). It is very pernicious and is very harmful to all life and it will not enhance any aspect of life, even if it allows you to have faster speeds, more pixels and more megabytes or gigabytes for your Zoom calls. It is harming all life. There are creatures that are falling from the skies, earthworms that are disappearing from the earth, insect populations, populations of bees that are dying in great quantities. Speed is killing you!

You are facing the 6th mass extinction upon this planet. Those who are responsible for what we have called the Great Deception, have engineered the destructive qualities of this so called vi-r-us that they have engineered in their biological warfare la-bs and have unleashed upon the population of the world. Their intent is to spread great fear and separation through this 6-foot-apart business and the use of masks, even in the most ridiculous places such as nature. All of this is combined with the technology of this fifth generation and it is designed to control and enslave the populations and impose a world of artificial intelligence to replace life. It kills. It is a biological weapon. It is not a benevolent technology and it is important to raise your voices and to find others with whom you can gather who understand the nature of this threat to Mother Earth. Seek those who are working to end this travesty, and to support them to eliminate the proliferation of worldwide 5th ge-neration technologies. Many thousands of satellites are being deployed in space and on the ocean floor. You have become addicted to and enslaved by your smartphones and are spending more and more time in front of your screens and computers instead of experiencing the natural world. Your children, who are so sensitive, are being damaged.

We have said enough on this subject. We wish to inform you that it is important for you to understand that it is vital to do some of your own research into what we are saying. When its full impact of the truth arrives at your door, it will be very shocking and very horrific. It will be necessary to accommodate slowly to the reality of knowing that these things exist and how vital your light is at this time to help to mitigate the harm, damage and the evil intent that is behind much of this control energy. We would also warn you in advance that the vac-cines that are being prepared will create within them and contain within them the technologies for tracking and for surveillance, as well as depleting your system, your immune system and that they should be avoided at all costs. Even testing is not accurate and is not beneficial to your system. It does not matter whether you are Buddhist, a Baptist, a Jain, a Jew, Christian or whatever. The energy that I bring for you is about your own highest good, health and your support systems at this time. Find ways to support each other and to become allies for all the forces that are working for the benevolence of Mother Earth, and her creatures.

It is important that you become extremely responsible about your own protection, for your vitality, and that you eat healthy food; that you eat organic and non-GMO foods, that you refrain from consuming sugar, processed foods and high-fructose corn syrup. Almost all the negative vibrational foods that are on your supermarket shelves contain these ingredients. If you look at even your "health food" supermarkets, you probably will find little nourishment and benefit in most of your packaged foods and products. You will find them laden with harmful oils, preservatives, 'natural' flavors and GMO ingredients. The highest energy food is that which you produce yourself or that you find from your neighbors and from those in your communities that are growing food and are providing them at your farmers markets and other places like that. It is important that you understand the value of refraining from the substances that can harm your bodies, that contain additives and pesticides and chemicals that are used in the manufacture of all these artificial products. Fast food is a fast way to hell, you might say, because fast, faster and fastest is a misnomer. It is actually a fast track towards disease and disintegration and it is also why your civilization has come to this place. Because speed, because rush and urgency and hurry and greater and greater bandwidths and faster speeds of Internet are all creating within your whole system an energy that is opposed to living a calm and peaceful and graceful life.

It is our highest wish for you to have the deepest satisfaction in your life, to have a sense of sufficiency, to have a satisfied mind. For nothing else can replace that. When you are at peace with yourself, then you have a way to relate to others that allows them to feel that they too can have that sense of peace.

Understand that everything begins within yourself. It begins with your commitment, and your commitment begins with your commitment to yourself. Throughout this program we have encouraged you to examine every thought, every assumption, every word and every belief system that you have carried with you. We have asked you to track it. We have asked you to replace the old, unsustainable ones with new ways of seeing. It is time for you again to remember this assignment and to take it up with a little more seriousness, because you are changing. You have changed, and now we wish you to move to the next level of consciousness. Let us say that you have been vacillating between the 3rd and the 4th dimensions with your heart set upon the 5th. It is now time to take that step into understanding that you are expanding your level of consciousness into multidimensionality. You need to keep one toe within the physical dimension, the reality of flesh and blood, where a chair is still a chair and you can bang your head upon it and it will hurt, or you can sit upon it. At another level, everything is just energy. There are atoms, swirling around within vast spaces. And the vibrational energy of an atom exists simultaneously in numerous dimensions. It is important for you to allow quantum consciousness to be a part of your life now.

What that means on a very simple level, is that you start to live with miracle and magic. You start to expect everything to go well. You start to expect to get that job, just because you can, because it is for your highest good. For if it is not for your highest good, the job will fall away. It is time for you to have ease and grace and great abundance in your life even though the voices around you are screaming and screeching and saying "We do not know where our next loaf of bread will come from," and there are many that are caught within this mindset. It does not have to be yours. There is need for great compassion and yet there is also need to understand that each one creates the reality they experience. This includes everything they hold dear to within their hearts and carry forth into reality through their belief structure. We have  asked you to replace those belief systems of limitation, of judgment and of "do not deserve, do not feel worthy;" all those things that you have inherited. Let them go and replace them with a brand-new story, with a brand-new direction, understanding that the law of attraction works. When you focus on the negative, that is what you attract. When you focus on the positive, your life becomes full of positivity. When you use and drink pure water, when you use the Shungite for your protection and for your enhancement and when you use it to create from a negative vibration, a positive one, you become like living Shungite yourself, you become a transformer of that which is negative into that which is positive. That which brings hope and comfort and joy and peace and benefit, so that those who do not have enough become empowered by your energetic Rainbow Body to believe in themselves enough to have that loaf and those fishes and allow them the power to multiply them, because they no longer are subject to those old stories of "poor me" and "I cannot" and "I'm not good enough" or "I don't deserve."

It is also important to recognize the value of creating boundaries, of creating that sphere of protection, but also of allowing yourself and your energetic field to expand to fill that sphere so that your energy system moves outside of you and is able to access the help you require, is able to accept and access the answers to your questions through your communication with these beautiful energies that are here with us. Your guides, your angels, the archangels, the avatars and Holy Beings of Light are all accessible to you from within that sphere. As you expand your light field, you also expand your protective shell, shall we call it. It is not just a one way, it is also, like with the cell, a semi-permeable membrane where the benefits and the beauty and the joy and the gold and the love can come in and the brightness of your light can go out, but negativity, because it is too large of a molecule, shall we say, cannot penetrate through that membrane.

Allow yourself too, with that which is called the "bellows breath," to breathe out your light, your blessings and your intentions to the outer reaches of the Universe, as far as your consciousness can go. You send out your vibration, and then you call in the help, the resources, the inspiration that now are directed towards you as you breathe back in, so that the bellows breath becomes an automatic extension of your Rainbow Body with each breath. For as you breathe out, you send out your vibration to the edges of your consciousness, and as you breathe in you receive from the Universe the empowerment that you need to expand more and more and more. The bellows breath becomes an amplification system. It becomes a transformer that expands your consciousness and your light out into the world, and it brings you everything your heart desires, everything you need, and it gives you access to the miracles and to the magic, to the ease and grace and abundance, and to the health and to exciting, love-filled relationships.

The three elements of money, of love and of health become filled with blossoming for you, and you are able to let go of any imprints, of any implants, through the voice of your command, through your connection with your highest selves and through your understanding of your oneness with all of life. There is interconnectivity with all life and an ability to expand your selves into this great Oneness. The cellular structure of your body, your emotional body, your mental and your spiritual bodies all to operate as a holistic synergy that's providing you the greatest benefit, the highest levels of systemic expansion and protection. Your immune system becomes stronger and stronger and the genetics become aligned with your environment of that which you are directing towards it, so that every gene is following the directives of your highest levels of consciousness. That golden light that you call in, that pours in from above and into you from all levels, becomes the way in which your consciousness attracts to you a genetic makeup that is all positive and that does not carry any vibrations from ancestral patterns that are no longer beneficial to your biology.

As you do this, you are also healing your ancestors, you are aligning with the ones of your ancestors that have been shamanic practitioners or medicine people or have been great wise ones and are there to continue to teach you and to help you. And so, you help your ancestors to separate the wheat from the chaff. Those that are still mired in negativity are given the opportunity to expand into light, and those that have been your great teachers are allowed to expand their levels of connection with you so that they become your teachers and you become your teachers' teachers, and you begin to bring to the children a new level of understanding of what is possible. You teach them how to generate the New Earth, how to create structures that are sustainable and that are pleasant, that bring joy to the heart, that bring mirth, laughter, that bring the end of this heaviness, this doom and gloom and all this seriousness.

So, everything becomes light, both in weight and in energy, in vibration. You are constantly raising your vibration in order to move into that fifth dimensionality, so that from there you can begin to scope out other dimensions. Why limit yourself to 5D? or to 5-G! You do not wish that. Allow yourself to expand at the same time as you hold that core, as you anchor your body and your consciousness in that deep connection with Mother Earth. Hold your piece of Shungite and allow it to help you to ground. Meditate each day. Go into that center of your heart and find that peace and that stillness and allow that to be your constant. Allow that to be your $E=mc^2$ (squared), whatever. Allow it to be the foundation of the vibration that you are; so that there is always peace in your heart, so that there is never an intention to harm, whether it be your own body or another's or your own emotions, your own selves or anybody's. Become free of any old patterns of negativity.

Use the affirmations in your meditative state to affirm for yourself who you truly are and your intentions for the greatest good of all, your visions for the future. Begin to dream and imagine what the world will be as your structures become foundationed in reality. Imagine what life is upon your planet with the green energy of healthful livingness for all the plant kingdoms, the free and clear running waters filled with life force, without pollution of the soil, healthy, the bees proliferating again. The bees love the Shungite. They proliferate, they swarm and create millions upon millions of bees and beehives as they imbibe the vibration of Shungite and it supports them in countering the negativity. Imagine all the creatures returning, the species that have been lost to this planet coming back to life again. Imagine that there is no need for the Dolphins and the Whales to beach themselves in order to call awareness to their plight because their navigation systems are being wreaked havoc with, the birds that are losing their way and falling from the skies; all the harm that is being done. Allow yourself to imagine the reversal of all these trends and the creation of a planet that vibrates with the energy of this Golden Light that surrounds the planet with your love.

So, I come to you, not as one representing Buddhism particularly, but as one who has carried within themselves the force of power, of being able to create magic, of being able to influence kings and kingdoms, to understand and see the truth of the Golden Path, of the middle way, of the Truth, of Light, of great wisdom. For the Buddha did not sit under the Bodhi tree thinking "I can't do it! I'm gonna fail. This is not gonna work!" He sat there, his intention pure and full. I did not go all the way to Tibet in order to create magic and play with the King and run off with his daughter or create a magic island within the center of a lake just for the sake of proving how powerful I was. It was for the intention of bringing Truth, of bringing a higher energy of Light to a practice that carried truth but had become corrupt, had become limited. There had once been great wisdom and power and energy in the indigenous systems that were in place in Tibet, those teachings that had come from the ancient continents of Lemuria, that spoke of the heart, that spoke of the green energies and the livingness of the planet. They had forgotten how to honor all life, the connection with the sources of all the creatures, the tree kingdoms and the plant kingdoms.

It is because I wish to bring for you an understanding that goes beyond even the most magnificent teachings, the most powerful practices, the most incredible initiations and mystical properties that one can develop in the metaphysical explorations of your mystery schools. There is nothing as powerful as Love. There is no energy that is more encompassing than the vibration of the heart and the connection with your soul, that Golden Nugget within that connects you to your Source, to your contract, to your agreements before you came into this life. And the way in which you connect all of your lifetimes into this one, we shall call it, "challenge" that you are now facing, is to become the Warriors of Light, the Warriors of the Rainbow Body, of the Rainbow Tribe; to establish communities on your planet that reinforce the benefit and the truth of individual worth and the collective worth at the same time.

We could continue to talk with you for a long time, but it is my intention to inspire you, not to overload you with facts and figures and exercises. Stay present in your heart and in your body. This is the foundation of all teachings, of all practice. Call in the light. Embody it. Become it. You are God's Love in human form. Express it. Find your path. Find your mission. Clarify it now. There is no more time to fiddle about, playing with different exercises and what ifs. It is time for you, as Spiritual Warriors of the Light to step forth into the world, to create benevolence wherever you can. It is time to shine your light, and it is time for you, each day, to radiate that Love of God/dess, of the Christ/Mary, of the energy of the Buddha, of Padmasambhava. Whatever you think or feel, follow your heart.

Expand it out and touch the hearts of those you love. Touch them with your hands, with your fingertips, with your kisses, with your cuddles, your hugs. Make contact. Do not be scared to touch, to communicate eye to eye, face to face directly. Encourage your children to not see separation and strangers, but to see themselves reflected in the eyes of their brothers and sisters. Like the great one in India, see each one as the Christ and offer them your help. Mother Teresa has been a great idol, shall we call her, a heroine that has shone the light of truth, no matter what stories they may have spread about her. Her devotion came from her commitment, her commitment to be the Light of God, to express Christ's love for all humanity and all life, and she devoted her entire life to the benefit of the poor and the downtrodden and those that were ostracized and separated. Allow her to inspire you, to dwell within your heart. What would Mother Teresa have done in this situation? How would the Christ have behaved? How would Guru Rinpoche respond to this situation? Allow yourselves to see through our eyes, to see through the eyes of that of the highest divinity that is available to you, for that is who you are. We love you. We will take our pause to look you in the eyes, and check the time. Let's have a 5-minute break and then we'll go into questions. You are shining!

Guru Rinpoche Q&A

Q. (SL) *I was taught as a child that imaginary things are not real and at some point in my adult life, I realized that that was a direct misrepresentation of reality, that imagination is one of the most important parts of creation and now I'm finding out that all the rest of this is really not real, so happy to come to some wisdom with that. I'm just wondering how did my parents grow up believing that imaginary things were not real? I find that astounding and there's so much wisdom from the past. How did that come about? I'm sure you have some idea.*

A. Thank you. We like your questions and your comments. It has been eons that the Earth has been dominated by energies that wished to control you for their own benefit. We do not have to go into details about all the various reptilians and extraterrestrial energies that needed the gold and the whatevers. However, what did happen is that aspects of what you became, were engineered. Your DNA was engineered. At the same time, there were many different energies that had an interest in this planet on both the positive and the negative side. This planet has been a focal point for the great battle between dark and light, the great Star Wars experience, shall we say, that has become encapsulated in movies. Actually, movies are only ways of expressing some of these realities, using imagination, but also using the understanding that memories surface from the Akashic Records about much that has gone on in the Cosmos between planets and star systems. And there has been an energy of control that has sought to possess and dominate for untold eons of time. In fact, at this moment in your history/herstory, you are facing a pivotal, transitional point from darkness to light. Not from the point of view of one needing to dominate the other. That is separation consciousness. Instead, there is a healing of the disassociation that has become entrenched in the mindset about the polarity of darkness and light, so that everything is ready to be seen now vibrationally, through union.

To answer your question; your parents inherited all their viewpoints from their parents, and their parents from their parents, as far back as you can trace the alteration or manipulation of what was going on in your civilization, over all these many years. So let's say there was a Christ person, a human being who came to this Earth and was born, whether through a real, live birth from insemination by a male, or was born from some transcendental state where Divinity imprinted the necessary DNA, and there was this miraculous birth, there was a human Christ and a human man. Whatever all these realities may have been, let's say there was one movie or story that was the truth, that was so called factual when you looked at it from a linear perspective. Five or ten years after the events, or 20 or 50, someone started to write down that story from their point of view, from their agenda, and from their desire to put a particular perspective into the consciousness of those who would read what they wrote. So, this is a way in which the story, the movie, became transformed into multiple versions, multiple novels, ingenious imaginary movies that represent a past experience. This became accepted as the truth of what happened way back in those days.

You can look at your own childhood even to access how this works. We are now referencing how it could be possible, which was one of your questions, that your parents could be so duped into letting you know that the imagination is not real, because that was the story they were given and imprinted through their education system. They merely passed it onto you and you absorbed it like a sponge in the first seven years of your life, because that's the story you were told all the time when your inner voice said "Hey, I have this imaginary friend and he's real and I talk to him and he talks to me."

So, at a whole other level, imagination is the ability to access all sorts of vibrational levels of reality that are infinite, and many of your scientists and inventors and engineers have accessed through that field of the imagination, often through dreams, the most incredible technologies that have brought great benefit to your planet, and also great harm. But the field of the imagination is absolutely the field of where creation happens. When you go to procreate, you imagine the creation of a child and it becomes a reality. Many things are set in motion. The mitosis, the division of cells begins with that impregnation and that multiplication according to sacred geometry, and so imagination sets into motion creation. It becomes the Field of Dreams. It becomes the foundation of your own creation of those structures, of those containers that will bring this planet to the reality of Heaven on Earth, what we call the New Earth. Peace.

Q. (NB) So you were talking to us about our purpose and our purpose is being the light beings and I'm just curious about, like, I've sat with it and sometimes I feel like I am on my purpose. But you could be doing anything and as long as you bring that heart presence, you are contributing in a big way and you're on purpose. Where my mind gets confused is, is there a specific thing we should be doing as a purpose and letting go of other things? Any light on that would be awesome.

A. A good question, because the answers are yes and yes. It is enough to expand your light every day as a practice. It is also time to understand that you have been children, you have been toddlers, you have been teenagers, you have been young adults, and now you are stepping into the world as fully fledged, we will call you, something greater than adults. You are now ready to put into the world, in action, your purpose from that perspective of being an adult who has grown up and knows what's up, and has access to that central power, that central column within you, that guiding light, and is not satisfied yet with just sitting and radiating light, but wishes to express their purpose in practical ways that can benefit people.

So, let us just say you get to see a smile and a thank you of gratitude from someone that your purpose has touched. You realize, however, that even though you can affect millions of people without even being aware of it, there is a different feeling in your heart and your soul when you do something that affects someone directly. So, formulating with others, gathering with others, and taking action with others sets up a whole different vibration. By structures, we are talking about establishing, organizations and doing activities. Even if you set up a stand outside your local church and you gave away lemonade or you brought some food or you brought a drawing pad and ink and pen and you gave the ability to someone to have fun. I mean, these are simple ideas that just popped into the head, but you can do any and all things out of that sense of motivation, out of that intention to bring benefit. You do not have to be a Guru Rinpoche to change the world by creating Tibetan Buddhism.

You can be an NB who talks to people and shows them her beautiful Ganeshas and says "Look, look what I did. You can do something of your own. Find your own ways of expression that satisfy and excite you." Use your imagination to know that what you do in the world will have an effect. We are asking you to become a part of a worldwide campaign to stop the proliferation of this very, very harmful technology that is going to grip your world and transform it into a desolate planet if allowed to continue. This is serious. You are facing serious stuff and we did mention that we did not want you to be serious all the time, but there is a great need for action, for support systems, even if all you did was send a check to an organization that is behind the ending of this proliferation and you sent them a thank-you letter and you say "Hey, I love what you're doing. I'm going to spread it by sending this connection, this link to others."

Do what you can within the capacity that you have to spend perhaps 5 minutes a day, whether it's sending light or sending checks or sending links or spreading the word to your children or to your knitting group. No matter what it is, do something. Become a leader. Call in your friends to have a circle, to chat. Do what feels right to you, but it is time to move beyond sitting in a cave in Tibet and practicing generating heat in your body and sending out the vibration of light and peace. Yes, there are those for whom it is perfect. The ones who came down from the mountains of the Andes, the Kogi, they did that for eons. They sent their light and their peace and they did their ceremonies, but it came time for them to get on planes and come to this crazy world of modern civilization and begin to talk and spread the word. It is time. The times have changed.

This is why I have chosen to come to you as Guru Rinpoche, because I do not want you to think in the old ways, of putting me, of putting the Dalai Lama or the Karmapa on pedestals and making them so far away that you cannot imagine doing good. This great young one, the Karmapa, wrote the most beautiful music and poetry when he was young. He did the most amazing things just out of the joy of his heart as his expression. You do not need to be some great guru or some great artist to touch somebody's life. If you do Tarot readings or you do channelings or whatever it is, that is your forte, that is your heart's love. Find a way to express it in a way that spreads the light in more ways than just sitting and doing that radiating, though we are not saying you should *not* do that. On the contrary, we encourage you to meditate and to radiate your love and your light and your blessings, to generate this Rainbow Body and send it out into the world to touch all life. And we are asking you, also, to put it grossly, get up off your butt and do something. Thank you. You will find the right avenue.

Q. (AY) I just wanted to say thank you. I'm very aware and moved by your inclusion of all these things that are for now what we can do, from the tiniest thing too, because when we think of who we are and what we bring, sometimes people think it must be huge, "I must be a guru, I must look like this or act like this" and it's so wonderful to hear all these tiniest of ideas. It's perfect for who we actually are, you know, all of those things. What I wanted to ask, something that I've often thought of, is that, you know, someone wrote a book about it, of course the sea of electricity that we're within and I'm wondering, when you're talking of these technologies, is there a way for us to be separate from them? Are we not living in them? Can we create our shields? Is there some way we can be separate from them? How do we live with them?

A. Yes, it is important that you understand that the technologies that bring you this sea of electromagnetic frequencies that you live within, have, like the coin, two sides to them. One side is benevolent and one side is not. The motivation for generating technologies that can be used by people has always been adapted to create benefit for those in control, often accompanied by ruthless methods of suppression. Many technologies were never allowed to reach you. In the New Earth, the Golden Beings of Light who come and go from your planet, the extraterrestrials, the Masters, the avatars have access to technologies that are far beyond that which you are aware of, and can assist in the transformation and cleansing of the toxic practices and rampant harm intentionally caused by the dark energies and your hidden dark governments, what is called Deep State.

It is possible that within the structures of the New Earth you can have access to this kind of technology that has only benevolent repercussions for biology. The technology exists that can convert all of your 4G/3G, all of your microwave systems, all of your smart meters, all these technologies, your cell phones can all be converted to become biologically friendly. They do not have to harm. It is important to look at the complete infrastructure that has been created just to get that smartphone to you. It involves the suffering of those who are forced to mine the heavy metals, the rare metals and minerals needed for your devices. They are under constant threat of violence, rape, and live in terror with no benefits, and minimal pay for their work, so they have become like the slaves of old. You too, have become slaves to a technology that is enforced by the power of domination, enforced by violence, to create these harmful technologies. They are used in weaponry, climate control, crowd control and death rays. All these things are part of the infrastructure that creates this dominant fear around your planet. We spoke, in answering SL about this proliferation, and the dichotomy between dark and light. These control energies have actually imprinted into your belief systems, a topsy-turvy way of seeing everything.

So, you can use the energies of Shungite in your hands, in your homes, in your offices and on your technologies. You can use them. You can spread them around by throwing nuggets of Shungite all around the world to actually weave a tighter and greater web of interconnectedness between all the grids of Shungite that are connected to the mother lode in Russia; because there is that energy of resonance, that energy of synchronization, the morphic field.[75] There is an entanglement, there is an energetic entanglement that happens between all the fields through the quantum resonance. There becomes a field that surrounds the planet and, as it grows stronger and as you support it, it becomes more and more able to counter the negative spins of all these vibrations and reverse the spin to positive. This is what the energy of Shungite does. It comes to you from outer space. It is a gift maybe 50 billion years ago from Heaven, so that now it has become available to you, because the time is ripe and it is needed. It is becoming more popular, and better known. It is just one technology that is beneficial yet absolutely natural.

However, it is also possible for you to link together with benevolent technologies, no matter what they are and where they are, through your consciousness. When you go into your meditation you can send out a field of healing to counter these *male*volent vibrations. You can align yourself with the vibrations of all those around the planet working to end the harmful radiations that are being proliferated and you can also assist in the education, so that more and more people become aware, not just of the G energy, the fifth generation, but all the ones from 4 going all the way back to the very beginnings of the proliferation of electricity, of telegraph technologies that began to affect your biology a long time ago. This is actually part of the whole story.

It is definitely a part of the New Earth that you can have a web and interconnectedness that is benevolent technologically, based on the technology of consciousness. You can actually have devices that use scalar waves, Tesla-type technologies that are beneficial and not harmful, and you can also, just through the faculties of telepathy and extra sensory perceptions, access technologies based on your consciousness. As you progress in your own evolution, you can develop abilities unimagined as yet by your current level. Are we close to having answered that question?

- *Yes.*

- Yes, it is important to research what is out there, what is available and how, perhaps even, in a small way, you could participate, as long as you create it for fun and that it does not have that heavy, heavy energy of concern, of worry, of projection of "Oh my God, we're gonna die" kind of thing, because that is counterproductive. Peace.

Q. (ZS) I am curious if you could talk to us a little bit about non-attachment since that is a really deep practice of the Buddhist way. I guess it's kind of very, very broad to just ask about non-attachment but of course it can be, it's a curiosity for so many different aspects of life.

A. Thank you. A very powerful, important question, not just for the satisfaction of the mind but for the practice, because the practice of non-attachment is the same practice you have been given and has been talked about all the way through this course. It is the energy of cultivating your own Inner Warrior, cultivating your own inner channel of connectedness to Mother Earth and Father Sky, of aligning your heart, your body, your mind, your soul and your emotions into a wholeness. It is about finding that you yourself are complete as who you are, and that attachment is not needed any longer because it is a crutch. It becomes an aspect of your association, of your assumption of what you need to be complete. It is a way of projecting outside of you something to provide a need for you.

It is usually attachment to outcome, connected to a person, or perhaps a response from someone about something that you feel very deeply about. Something you need desperately, and will not be happy unless you had it. There are so many areas where attachment comes in as part of your mind-set. So, once again, we would like to reiterate the power of breath. Attachment requires of you to notice. It is mindfulness, another so-called Buddhist attribute. Mindfulness allows you to pay attention to the fact that you are becoming attached to a thought form; you are giving it a reality and allowing that reality to become your reality. Does that make sense?

We are encouraging you to examine every attachment, because every attachment is like every belief system, every assumption, every projection. It is just called attachment because it has a few extra kilograms of weight attached to it that are sitting on your shoulders. Your heart will not feel comfortable if so-and-so does not love you, or whatever the attachment is about. You may be attached to your cell phone. You may be attached to your computer and the way in which it allows you to communicate with your friends or to be on a course like this. Where within that structure of mindset do you stand? How can you take it apart enough to recognize that even without it, somehow you will be OK? And yet, even with it, you can find a happy medium where you will be OK no matter what and at the same time, because it brings you joy and it brings you connection and it has beauty and benefit and all sorts of wonderful toys, why not? Why yes? Why no?

Do not judge anything, because any judgment is an attachment. Attachment is another way to say "judgment" but, at the root of attachment, there is a slight connection with the questions that SL asked about humility, about how you see yourself and how much you need to get somebody else's approval or you need to feel good about yourself to be able to offer service. So, you get to see a reflection, because at the basis of that is a sense of insecurity and a need for, shall we say, a little bit of glamour or a little bit of that sense of being a good person in order that you feel better about yourself, because you've absorbed all those voices that say you're not good enough. When you go down to the very roots of your question about attachment, it's "Who am I? How do I feel about myself, and how can I shift how I have been feeling about myself to create a new story that allows me to be free in my power, to be able to have boundaries, to not be a doormat, to not have any place in my life where I give away my power and say "Yes" when my real gut wants to say "No?"

These are deep questions, and require a deep practice. Even if you were the highest Lama possible and you had done practice after practice after practice; you could still be subject to your personality, to your ego and to your need for some kind of approval or glamour, some kind of way of having others look up to you and put you on a pedestal because you are so mighty or so wise or so loving. It requires constant vigilance to stay pure and to connect with that child within you that knows what innocence feels like and is like, to recognize that you are God in motion. You are the expression of God and God is only Love. You have access to that expression as an aspect of who you are and what you do and how you think, and the more you cultivate *that*, then your Rainbow Body grows and the attachment detaches and expresses itself as color and light moving outwards from your radiant center because you have learned to love yourself as God, as All That Is, as a reflection of the greatest love that there could possibly be, the Love of Creator for that which Creator has created. And you have created yourself with your thoughts, with your feelings, with your story, and you have the capacity to recreate yourself in the image of the Divine and the simple and the pure. So, from this moment on you make that commitment to do so, and to be that; and you cannot go wrong. And your life becomes full of blossoming and magic and thriving and love, because the love comes from within you, and at the same time it comes from God or Divine. It comes from that because that is within you. That is who you are, and then detachment becomes where the attachment no longer can stick to you. Peace.

- *Thank you.* Thank you.

Q. (CZ) I remember a while ago information that came through you was about the fi-ve Gee energies and all these towers and stuff and that the higher energies would kind of intervene and lessen their harmful downloads or what they're doing to us. In that vein, I'm thinking of the vac-cine. I have family members that are in the health care profession and they would be on the frontline to get them. Is there any way to mitigate the harmful effects of those vakcines for those people or for anybody who might receive the jabs?

A. Thank you for your question. Yes, we understand and we do not use the term with the number and the letter on the Internet openly because it is monitored very closely. That is why we have been using terminologies that kind of go around from the back door, shall we say. So, there are two answers to your question, three perhaps, that we would give you. One is: Yes, there are the greatest energies possible that the Light carries, and it is doing its utmost to help to mitigate the harmful effects of these life-threatening energetics. At the same time, there is a very simple technology that we will show you and if you request it, we will send it to you that you can print and put around you that would help to mitigate the effects of whatever they would put into the vac-cine. Also, if those who ever do become ill from the affliction itself, this would help to mitigate its effects.

It is important that those in the health care industry understand that (and again this in some ways goes to the greater aspect of the question) each one has the responsibility for what they experience through their choices. Each one has a contract and agreement with their soul and must go into their soul to search out the truth of what is correct for them and what choices they must make. It is beneficial if you have a way to understandingly let these of your relatives know that there is a dark energy that is behind and creating the negative aspects of these vac-cines. There is no such thing as a vac-cine for this thing. It has been engineered. Everything has been engineered, every aspect of the medical industry. Doctors are being paid to essentially falsify the death certificates in order to raise the numbers of the "casualties." All the industry is at its root corrupt, though there are many beneficial hearts within it who are unaware of the level at which it is corrupt and is controlled. But it is important for you to educate wherever you have an opening that would not create more of a dissonance, shall we say, within the soul aspects of your family members.

It is important that they know that the so-called vac-cine contains na-no-technology intended for control that is passed through the genetic system. They need to know that, but there are also some available technologies and before we end, we will show you one, and we will give you the ability for you to be able to print out your own that would effectively help in the ability to protect yourselves at some level or other. We would also recommend that you suggest the use of Shungite. Shungite can be used for protection even though it is only partially effective with the latest rollout of the current technology that we're talking about. It certainly will mitigate much of the effect of all the vibrations emanating from all the machines and technologies that are used in their facilities.

There is also a way to boost your immune system and provide protection through some products that this one offers through his website, a policosanol called Nano Soma and a patch that activates your body's stem cells.[76]

(Shows rev. marker.[77])

OK. This design came through the energy of the one Thoth via Maia Nartoomid to counter a vibrational imprint that was put into the "vir-us" and will be also included as an aspect of any kind of vac-cine. Any technologies that come from the medical system that claim to be beneficial within the structure of this deception are going to be harmful and negative, and even the tests are absolutely not accurate one way or the other. It is also claimed that they have within them some kind of harmful nanoparticles for control and for surveillance.

So, we believe we answered your questions, and it is important that you are very careful with the terminologies you use on the Internet and your computers, just to be aware of that. Thank you.

Closing Meditation

Let us again put our right hand on our heart and our left hand on our right and begin to feel that sense of peace, that sense of stillness. Allow that vibration to warm your heart, to feel it radiating out, connecting each one of us with each other, with all our loved ones and all those who have in some ways been part of this course; sending out that radiance of gold, of love, of protection and interconnectedness to all life and to all those you love and hold dear, as we spread the radiation of love out into the Universe; surrounding Mother Earth, surrounding all beings, all life with the healing vibrations of God's Love, so that we become conduits, vessels, vehicles, channels of this love through its expression within and from ourselves, allowing it to expand and to radiate from us, surrounding each one of us with that beautiful golden sphere of light that radiates its vibrations out into all worlds. In the name of the One. We thank you. We love you and we bless you. May the Living Spirit that is in all life surround you with love, with light and with peace.

Voice Twelve
Joy

1st November 2020

Let us begin by placing our right hand on our heart, our left hand on our right, taking that nice, deep, delicious breath, allowing ourselves to feel the stillness pouring down, filling our hearts. It is pouring down this column of light that we hold in our space always now, whether we are consciously aware of it or not. That sphere surrounds us now, golden light filling all space, creating safety and protection around us. The sphere of golden light is filled with angels, only positivity and the vibrations of love. This golden energy of the heart and the column reaches from Mother Earth beneath us to Father Sky above us as we feel that connection between us now through the threads of our hearts as they weave out from us to become a fabric; bigger and bigger, as it spreads its way around the whole planet, filling all space and all time with the energy of heart, with the connection of love and light, with that higher purpose that we all subscribed to before we came here, and many times over and over, each lifetime. You can rest your hands as I invite and welcome my daughter Joy to talk with us.

There is a beautiful, soft glow around my heart as I come to speak with you. There is such a deep intimacy that has developed in this time that we have been together because, as you understand, everything is so connected that each time one would speak, one particular voice, it was always the voice of the whole. You might call it the voice of the Zodiac but it is way more than that. It is the voice of Love that speaks through different channels, through different avenues and through different perspectives. It is also important to understand that, just as it is written that "a child shall lead them," so, in many ways, I was chosen and I chose to be the introduction for this series and to be, we won't call it the concluding voice, because there is one more that weaves us all together into this beautiful alignment.

You might say it is like the solar system with the sun at the very center and each one of us that is here, each one of us that pays attention, on your end and on our end, is like a different planet with a different vibration that makes up together that sense of wholeness. And just as we in the solar system are revolving around the great Solar Logos, this Sun, this Christlike Energy that oversees (we don't like the word "overshadows," so we use the word "over-lights") us all and is the bright light of this life, of this Earth, of this planet and of all life within this solar system, so too we are as an electron revolving around the nucleus in an atom. We revolve around the Great Central Sun, that space that is much bigger than our minds can grasp and yet is what we would understand to be our Universe; that very core, the black (or white) hole at the center. Even that has access to other galaxies, other dimensions in other worlds.

At its very "origin," this entire galaxy came into being from the dimension of the NoThing, from that infinite potential that is the beginning of all things. And yet there is no beginning and there is no end.

As you look at the situation on your planet right now, you understand this energy of continuity, of infinity, or immortality, because even though I was only 9 years upon this planet, it was my last life. It was my legacy to, you might say, offer as an initiation, my heritage for my family and for all those who knew me. It was my blessing to them. It was said by Old Chinese once that when a child leaves this planet before the age of 12, it means that they have completed their lifetimes and are ready to go home, back to Source and it is also often a gift to the parents, to the family, to the community, and so it is this aspect of community.

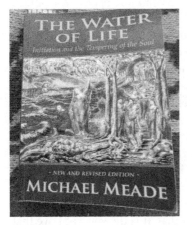

To the left is the cover of a book *The Water of Life*. It has much to do with the underlying energies of interrelationships between archetypes of people, of father and son, father and mother and grandparents, daughters. It concerns archetypes, but also an understanding of the movement of the soul and the necessity of going through initiations to move from one phase to another. As you are all, shall we say, mature beings, you have been through many times of initiations, not just in other lifetimes but also in this one. Each one carries with them their entire entourage of energies from other lifetimes, from other aspects and dimensions. They also carry with them their wounds that particularly were chosen in order to extend and open up and move into a whole new understanding of life on this planet. Understanding relationships, intimacy, who you are, why you have come, what is your work in this particular lifetime, and what you have chosen to complete in all of your lifetimes. For it would appear that many of you have been called from distant galaxies or dimensions to come here once again for this grand finale. You came to help create the bridge to the New World, the New Earth that will be inherited by the young ones, that will be the domain of the children who will be growing up, hopefully, with the energies that you have given them of your love and your positivity, and your deep caring and consideration.

And so, let's consider too, to say some prayers for KM's daughter, to hold her in our hearts as we do the speaking and the listening, to consider that the power of prayer, the power of intention and the power of heart moves out in ripples beyond the imagination and can affect results, as we have said, in the quantum field, thousands of miles or years away. So, we hold her in our hearts.

We also hold each one of you as we come to this 12th voice. There is a touch of, we shall call it heaviness upon us as we/I ask you to consider the plight of the children in this world. It has been a challenge to find a way to expose that which is going on in the hidden realms of control upon your planet. This has been responsible for some of the greatest suffering, some of the heaviest of horrors and tragedies for humanity. It will be so shocking when it is revealed as to the true nature of what actually goes on behind the scenes, behind closed doors, behind the halls of power on this planet and that which the cold, closed hearts of many of those who hold the reins of power and control are responsible for, and capable of doing. For them, this particular period is actually the great testing point. For it is the ending of the eras of horror and the eras of suffering that has been on this planet for so long. It is necessary that many must remain in the dark as to the true nature of what has been happening. Most people have no understanding of how horrific have been the ways in which humans harm one another, in which atrocities, in which genocides and reigns of terror that have been perpetrated on whole peoples, on whole segments of population, on women and children, on people of color, on those who are the 'underdogs,' who are the underprivileged.

Perhaps you are familiar with the ways in which your history (we won't call it herstory; we will say history) has been filled with the blood of innocents and the truth whitewashed, distorted and turned on its head. Perhaps this is news to you. You are approaching this season of the elections. It is very hard to penetrate into and make some sense of what is really going on, especially those who are understanding that nothing is what it appears, so it is important that no matter what happens, that you hold in your heart that tower of light, that tower of love, that space of trust, of being able to know that no matter what it seems, there is a higher purpose and there are Beings of Light who watch over this planet and the unfolding of this giant transition that is happening. It is a turning point for all of humanity, for all the creatures and for all life on this planet, and for how that affects all the other planets in this solar system and beyond. For this is the most pivotal time in the evolution of this planet for billions and billions of years, through all of its many incarnations. This is a time that has not been before. Even if there is no such thing as time!

It is important for you to have patience and to try and find as much clarity as you can in everything around you, for you to be able to observe fear, observe the deep terror that actually has grasped the hearts of so many on your planet who have believed in the Great Deception and who are actually in terror, in fear of their own lives, of the way in which the evolution of your civilization and society seems to be moving. It seems like everything that they held dear or that they considered as normal is being swallowed up by some great nightmare and that they have no control whatsoever of the outcome.

And in many ways, it is true. For the only place that you have any area of control is of your choices, of whether to choose love or fear, whether to trust or to give in to the fear of the unknown, of insecurity, of the darkness, of the times when you feel depressed or you feel upset or angry or deep sadness. Some of you bristle at the restrictions, at the imposition on your freedom, or perhaps you just go into that little cave where you want to hide and lick your wounds. Whatever reaction you have to what is going on outside, we wish to encourage you to consider that within you, you are already building the structures for the New Earth. Perhaps you are able to witness, in spite of the appearance, those places where the disintegration is happening and where it is beginning, like the little seeds that have grown shoots and are emerging through the cracks in the pavement, beginning to show their greenness and their newness. You are beginning to feel and see around you, in the alternate news networks, that are not part of the mass media; you are beginning to see where the good has been taking over from that which used to be the "not-so-good." You are able to see how consciousnesses are expanding and opening up to possibilities that they never imagined they had the capacity for. You are seeing how much the young ones that are coming into the world now are open, how much they are in this state of vulnerability and yet they are still infused with a sense of love and a sense of the future, a sense of peace and a sense of knowing that they know and understand the truth behind the mask. Even though they are forced to wear these masks, they understand that they're just doing it to appease their parents and the parents' peers and the authorities that require it.

In truth, nothing can harm you when your living style is healthy, when your immune system is strong, when your attitude is positive, when you ingest your vitamins and you drink healthy water, purified water, structured water, water that has life force energy in it, that you pray over, that you bless. You send your light out into the ethers, into the universe to shine on those who are less fortunate than you, perhaps you find ways to encourage others to realize that all is not as it seems, that this is a "temporary glitch in the matrix." It is a necessary glitch that actually distorts the whole field of the matrix and turns it into something that is transcendental, something that is more powerful than the evil minds of those who orchestrated this matrix can even imagine possible. And it is building. It is building up in the hearts and the minds and even in the activities of many on your planet who understand that it is a time for action. It is a time to gather together in whatever way you can and initiate whatever change you can for the movement towards greater cooperation, towards the return of the energy of village, of community, of support, of sharing, of listening.

Understand the value of that little conversation, however minute it may be, when you listen to someone and you share your truth and your experience and you share even your sadness or your loss or your fear or your anger. Understand and know that 'this too shall pass' and that one day follows another just as the sun rises each morning above the horizon and sets. Each day comes and goes, and you have survived, perhaps you've thrived, perhaps you have found a new avenue of expression, of art, of music, of poetry, of dance. Perhaps you have been encouraged to take more hikes and be more in Nature and even converse with the trees or sit with your back against a grandfather or grandmother tree and feel Mother Earth beneath you and Father Sky above you, feel the chill in the air and the dropping of the leaves in the fall.

Whatever it is, we invite you to find inspiration wherever you can, to share your love with your children, to never hold back from giving them hugs, from giving them that sweet kiss and reassurance, reading to them when they go to bed, telling them stories and reassuring them that "this is just a passing phase," and that there are Beings of Light that they can call on, that surround them, that love them. Not just the children, but even the old ones, even the dark ones. There are beings at the ready to shine the light for them to come home to the Light, to the realization that they have lost their way but that everything returns to that great Light of Union, and the sooner the better. There are aspects in play, there is an unfolding of what is transpiring upon your planet behind the scenes, and this is partly one of the reasons why, when the revelations will be required to come, there will be great shock of what is happening, specially to the children. There are millions who are no longer. Their faces have been on the milk cartons and they had all but disappeared from the scene. The truth, when it is revealed, will be so horrific that it will require a slow and gradual acclimatization to the nature of the truth. However, it is important to know and understand that all the realms of Light and the guardians of this planet are working to create the completion and the restoration and the ending of such things so that they could never again happen on your planet.

It is important to understand that everything, no matter how dark, works for "good." Even the most horrific times upon your planet have evoked a certain kind of evolution in consciousness that has been part of the preparation for this time of the Turning. It is like the Earth is in its fall, its autumn. It is the time of moving towards the winter solstice. It is the time of the greatest dark beginning to evolve into the glimmerings of a new light appearing, the time of the harvest, the time of the, shall we say, settling down to begin your preparations for the winter, for perhaps the 'dark nights of the soul' you are required to traverse, this evolution in consciousness that requires of you to face your demons, to face your fear, to face your anger, your bitterness, your disappointments, your losses and your tears, and to understand that they are necessary as part of the journey.

They are your initiation points, and as each one moves through their initiation, we are always there beside you to help, to guide you, to steer you in the right direction. We are always there to give you comfort and relief and to remind you that we answer questions, we touch your hearts with that little extra feeling of warmth, that Golden Glow within the heart that is so vital to keep you hopeful, keep you in remembrance that this too shall pass, and that everything, like the silver lining, works for good.

There will be rain even though the drought has been almost interminable. The cold eventually becomes warm. The seasons and the people and the parties and the politicians, everything changes, everything morphs, everything evolves and you are a part of the evolution of this planet toward the Golden Age, towards the time that has been promised.

Do not lose heart. Remember, each lifetime seems like a beginning and ending, and yet you go back home to the Ones with No Names, to the Swing Between Worlds and you prepare, and then you come back. These cycles for you are coming to completion now. These cycles are moving towards an evolution of resolution, moving towards a whole brand-new dimension of existence on this planet for those who carry the light in their hearts, for those who know that love is the only answer, the only Truth; that love and light and union are the reality behind the illusion, behind the deception; and that your hearts are the most powerful force in your own universe. For the heart is the key. The heart is that place from which the love and the light emanates; for it is within the heart that we all dwell with you. We understand that you are bound by the energy of timing and yet, as you engage with patience, as you embark upon the journey of the Spiritual Warrior, you become willing to face your demons. You recognize what that one in the book The Water of Life, Michael Meade, has said, that to be human is to be wounded. It is part of the journey. It is why there has been suffering.

You may want to consider that each soul, whether it be a child, whether it be a woman, whether it be an old one, an elder, whatever, each one has their connection to karma and each one, in their many lifetimes has inflicted great harm, we shall put it mildly, upon another or upon many. It is necessary within the ending of this cycle of the 12 and within this grand cycle of what is going on on your planet, that some benevolent way be found to resolve the intense karma of these millions of souls. To reach a place of equalization, so that you do not have to come back and suffer. And so those dark ones who have orchestrated this grand scheme, in their eagerness to achieve global control without opposition, unknowingly to them, they have set in motion the mechanism for the cleansing of all karma upon your planet.

For in old times, in other epochs, it was a cataclysm that destroyed all life on the planet and freed those souls from the accumulated karma of that cycle. And they would be able to evolve their souls in a new way, through a brand-new cycle. This was taught by Old Chinese many, many years ago, that when each cataclysm comes, it is as if the memory has been wiped out and there is a necessity to begin again. Even the technologies are forgotten and it is necessary that they become reinvented. This is why it is not common knowledge that your societies, your civilizations have been ongoing for millions upon millions of years over numerous cycles, numerous Earths. You are more familiar with the four worlds and that you are entering the 5th in the indigenous-wisdom-way of seeing things.

However, this opportunity that has been engineered for harm, is actually turning into a mechanism for clearing away the tremendous amount of karma that has been gathered into the etheric atmosphere of the Earth and into the Akashic Records that contains the collective memory of all souls. For each one is connected to all the other souls as a community, as a collective. And even though you also dwell within other lifetimes and dimensions that are parallel, everything is, in many ways, a connected wholeness, as we have said many times. It is now that you can transform this planet and all of life that is ready and willing, into a new vibration that is the New Earth.

If there is an energy that is not ready to transform into the new vibration, it will exist encapsulated within its own field that no longer has any interpenetration with the New Earth that is being created. There are dimensions for all walks of life, for all energies, for all vibrations and resonances. The Law of Attraction ensures that those who dwell within the vibration of love and positivity, will inhabit a dimension that is self-contained, that consists of only those who resonate and match the new vibration. So, it's important to understand this, not just for your mind to have something to grasp, but to understand that there is an evolution that is held in the "Mind of God" that is unfolding. So, remember that this is just part of an evolving experience, for you individually and for the collective. It is affecting Mother Earth and her life force energies, as well as the Light Beings. Even what we call the Living Spirit that is in all things, is evolving. This grand finale, this grand climax, this grand show is but the staging of the energy of transformation for the New Earth.

It is important not to get caught up in the show, in the glamour, in the grand adventure movie, where the good guys always come with blazing guns and the poor old miserable ones that dwell in the darkness end up going to some Hell. Star Wars, all these movies that are based on the ancient wars of civilizations against each other, these movies are coming to an end. There is endless viewing of horror movies, of violence, of this tremendous evil against the innocent. The rape and genocides and tortures and the use of terror to extract the minerals that are required for your cell phones and your technologies are not sustainable; they are built on suffering. The whole energy of control of your planet is built on suffering and it cannot be allowed to continue, and you are witnessing its dissolution, its disintegration.

So, hold steady. Hold that sweet space in the center of your heart where you generate peace and stillness, where you love, where you give love to your children, where you give love to that part of you that is aching, that is terrified, that is in tremendous fear, that is facing its worst inner enemy. Allow yourself to find forgiveness for everyone who you think has ever harmed you. For each one is an actor upon the stage. It is an illusion. The reality lives within your heart and soul and within this field of Love that we are surrounding you with. Always access it. You have us right beside you, all the way from little child to grand-elder, to Star energy to Mother Earth energy, to the creatures that dwell, the insect people, the spiders, the ones of Nature, the trees. We are all supporting you as we go through our own evolution. The birds are dropping from the sky and the earthworms disappearing from the earth as a result of your technologies of death, technologies that are engineered to harm, not to benefit.

Our beams of light have technologies that can not only disable, but can bring the same availability of your interconnection, true benevolent technology, that does not harm life. We have the ability beyond your imagination to bring benevolence to your planet, but we must be invited. We must be embraced. I am no longer a little 9-year-old child. I dwell in the Realms of Light. You all have your one foot in these realms, even as one foot is firmly planted on Mother Earth. We are eternal, all of us, infinite, immortal, universal. That is the truth, the Reality. Understand that you have the ability to choose, in each moment, to take that breath; that you are being called and asked to explore the depths of your creativity and your imagination, to bring beautiful things, beautiful energies to your planet, to your people, to your communities, to your children and to your elders. You have the ability to gather in circles and share and communicate your love and your pain, to listen, to hear. You don't have to be cool. You have to be real. That is what is being asked of you; to be honest with who you are and what you are experiencing, and understand that you are not alone. You're not alone! It is difficult for the insulated, individualized mind-being to understand that they are not separate from God, from each other, from the All That Is.

You have no choice but to choose, and you have no choice but to choose light, because you already chose when you came here to be at the forefront. There will be no more firing squads, no more crucifixions, crosses, no more stakes upon which to burn. The time is over for these horrific things. Know that you are here to blossom, to thrive, to live ease and grace and abundance, love, joy and fun! (Deep sigh) Let go of all your burdens, just like that! Let the shower of light that is pouring down upon you wash away all your sorrows, all your challenges, all those places where you diminish yourself, where you have those voices still ringing in your ears; allow them to leave. It is true that stories have great value, that they can  be the most exciting and entertaining and challenging experiences to follow, but it is also important that you are creating a new story for yourself, a collective story and an individual story. It is based on love. It is based on new beginnings. It is based on the continuity of little one to adult to elder to Being of Light and back and forth.

Even if you do not come back, you can still assist from the other planes and you will be a multidimensional being that can allow one aspect of yourself to be a guide for your children or your grandchildren to reach out to, and feel your love and warmth. It is still there. It does not fade away or die. It is there in the Akash and it is palpable to those you have loved. You will become guides. Imagine that! You will be like me, talking with a group of people perhaps, or whatever. It is time to open our eyes and take a breath.

Comments

(NB) I have been on this path for a very, very long time, it seems like, and I know it's been for many, many lifetimes. I find that something has shifted. There's been a couple of very, very, very profound sessions, actually three I can name, very, very profound sessions where I'm not able to really pay attention. My mind is so distracted. The only time I pay attention is when I'm facilitating or sometimes it'll go into meditation. Sometimes it will. But three of your 11 sessions have really grabbed my attention for the full 2 hours, which is unheard of. So, I just want to thank you for the invitation.

(MS) Yeah, I just wanted to say thank you for creating this forum for us. I love the connection of all these energies from different, what we would call, time periods and seeing how they all connect and, you know, I've kind of created in my own mind these separate little images and now I realize there's a huge connection and thread between all the different energies. And I thank you for the community that you have created here. It's, I think, very special for those I've spoken to and those that I will speak to, or maybe you know we don't have to talk directly, but there's definitely a connection. So, thank you, Raphael, for that.

Raphael: It's my delight and my pleasure. This gives me probably more than it even gives you guys. It's a wonderful blessing, and what was sweet was I didn't initiate it. No way! I was asked to do it and it just came through, so it's a giant affirmation and validation for me as to what my work is or at least a piece of it. Thank you all, and I do feel very close to all of you. It's been a beautiful ongoing experience. I'm always nervous before I start and I also have the sense of the energy of wrap up; it feels like it's like the sun and the 12 planets surrounding the sun and that's why the messages have been coming that next week, if you guys would still like to continue for that one more Sunday, I believe that the Christ wants to weave it all together and give us some guidance, for by that time we'll know if there is any level of stability around the presidency or not. I've also heard that there's a chance it might drag on for a while.

Joy Q&A

Q. (SL) I just wanted to express that irreverence is one of my finer traits, and for whatever reason I find that there's much too much niceness in the world and I wonder if you could speak to that idea.

A. It's true. Most niceness is the icing on a cake that is too hard and too brittle and too unfinished to enjoy, and it has to be iced over so that it looks good. Most of the niceness comes from being indoctrinated to be a good boy or girl and stay in the corner and be quiet and be nice at the table and never answer back. All these things that were inculcated into you growing up in order to socialize you, so that you would be a good citizen, behave, and never rock the boat. Being nice is different from being kind. It's different from being loving. It's different from caring. Being nice is a veneer, especially if underneath of the niceness there's a raging tiger or a furious stampeding pink elephant in the middle of the room, and everyone's being nice because they do not want to address the fact that Ganesh is dancing in the room knocking over all the crockery, vases and delicate, pretty things that make for niceness.

Underneath of nice, people are suffering. It's really 'nice' to be able to stream and watch videos and YouTubes and do Zoom calls, but that convenience sits on the backs of so many people who barely survive and slave under inhumane conditions. So, you have a point. We are calling the need to be authentic, the antidote to being nice. We are also evoking for you the idea that the Spiritual Warrior doesn't necessarily aim to always please when they confront the truth. There are times when it is necessary to be not so nice. That's what is called "tough love." We shared with you about how being human involves being wounded, so it is sometimes necessary to be real with people who are wounded and cover up their wounds with niceness or its opposite. Sometimes they don't need you to be nice to them, they need someone to tell them to get off their high horse or to stop being so selfish or whatever it is that would perhaps wake them up from the trance of their wounds. Does that answer your question?

- Yes, thank you very much. I feel like I have an ally with my attitude.

- As long as you're real.

Q. (CR) It sounds like there will be a splitting of those that are within 5D and 4D mindset from the rest of 3D people, and the Nameless Ones also spoke about that separation, where there was going to be a division. Part of mankind would go one way, part of mankind would go the other way, that there is going to be an energetic change that will occur that creates this apparent division, and I was wondering if the division, the split, is also occurring in our multidimensional lives, kind of like we're experiencing now, because part of us live in the 4ᵗʰ and the 5ᵗʰ dimension at times, and yet there is a separation, so is it going to be a physical change that takes place for the whole planet or is it still just individual people at individual times that this division is going to be occurring for? Is it in the physical realm totally? That's enough of a question.

A. We understand the question. Just as I can be a spirit guide in another dimension talking with you here as a little girl who was once in the 3ʳᵈ dimension, it is possible for you to dwell within that multidimensional realm and have access to both. You can have access to other realms, because the law of attraction, the law of resonance, will generate a congruous energy to match the vibration. It will match, or reflect your frequency. Somebody else might dwell in a completely different world. Let us say that you have someone who's a street kid living in a city 'ghetto', which may represent an image of an environment of gangs and violence, you know, rough living in the 'hood.' (We know we are stereotyping to bring a point). That reality does not impinge on your reality in any way unless you happen to watch a video clip or a news broadcast or you read about it in a paper. There are billions of people, each one living a whole different movie of their own and all are going on simultaneously. You have absolutely no idea of these worlds. So too, your own 'movie' occurs within an encapsulated space, a kind of sphere of influence or experience that is completely separate from their bubble. So it's a question of the mind rather than of consciousness or of spirit that you are asking. It is the mind looking at the physical world and wondering whether it's going to stay the same. It won't. The experience you have of what is, for you, the world or the Earth will be a different experience and may have absolutely no way of interfacing with the experience of another and their other world that is separating away from yours.

You could imagine it as another twin Earth that is moving across the skies further and further away to a whole other solar system and you are barely even aware of it because the one that you are in has that same sun shining upon you, and the birds are singing and this is your experience of the New Earth and you don't have any longer newspapers or news broadcasts or any of that stuff because something has shifted. Perhaps the technology that brought you all this information no longer exists. We do not know how it will look when you look through your eyes.

It is important to recognize that this is a question of the mind, not a question of what will reality look like to others. Your individual reality will be the result of your choices, of the ways in which you take a negative reality and turn it into a positive one. So, you become a sphere of Shungite that allows all that stuff to completely reverse its direction into a positive spin and you no longer have the original negative one. The negative spin does not exist anymore. It's like when Shungite is in water, the heavy metals that were there, the toxins, impurities in the water, their whole atomic structure disintegrates away into the individual atoms and that molecule no longer exists. And so, you are like this purified water that has dismantled the negativity and it no longer exists. All you are seeing is the positive vibration that you live within now. Does that make sense? Do you understand the analogies?

- Yes, I do understand. It's as if the mind has become broken away from the molecules and goes to the atomic levels of life and the creation that we are, so it's kind of like we become, we are our own creator, in other words.

- Absolutely. Your belief system is the key. We have been sharing this with you all the time. Your belief systems create your reality and it is not even about looking at the genetics. Your belief structure can change your genetic makeup. Your DNA can morph into a whole different set of 12 strands, just as the neural pathways in your brain can start reconfiguring themselves to a whole new motherboard, that is running a new program within you, so that the old ones are no longer even active. There is definitely a distinction between the realm of mind and matter and consciousness and spirit. It's almost as if they are interfacing with each other from a distance and not necessarily on the same page, and as you are working towards harmonizing them, then you become the wholeness of all four in a Oneness state. You are moving towards Union. Everything is moving towards non-separation. If that is part of your consciousness, then you become an aspect of Union expressing itself and the mind doesn't have to worry about what it's going to look like. It's your living experience, yes?

Q. (NJ) So when we are feeling connected and we are in that oneness, then everything is icing and then when we're not connected it's the hard damn cake?

A. Yes. Imagine yourself sitting before your chocolate cake with the icing or without. Each bite is blessed and delicious and nourishes your body and your mind and your heart and your soul. And there was never a hard chocolate cake that got burnt, that is covered in icing and all you got to taste is the icing, and you found under the icing an unpalatable cake because the chef was not paying attention, was not fully present in their body when they baked the cake. Perhaps, they were using ingredients that were not of the highest quality. So, everything is an expression of your consciousness. Everything is the cake. You can look at the cake as soft and sweet beneath the icing. When you're looking at it through not so beneficial eyes, it's burnt and crusty, beneath the icing. So, it comes back to the understanding of how your attitude creates your reality, because your attitude sits on your belief systems. Your 'reality,' your experience, is going to be the result of your belief system re-engineered to always see the highest outcome, even when you do not see it clearly enough with your mind. Yes? - Thank you.

Q. (MS) So I'd like to talk to somebody named Joy, a master of joy about joy. Can you talk to us about the value of bringing joy and experiencing joy in our lives, especially in these times of great change and seriousness, and how do we create and proliferate more joy into our lives in general?

A. Thank you very much for bringing that to my attention. When you read the introduction to our series, you will remember that I put that idea that joy is the ultimate expression for your life. When one lives harmonized, when one lives in balance, when all the chakras, all the bodies are congruous, you are experiencing joy, because there are no pulls upon you. You have allowed yourself to be complete and full within yourself and you live in joy because joy is the expression of God's love always emanating from you and radiating from your heart, and people feel it. It's a way of being that is actually, the greatest goal in life. It's to always live "the bubblies," like the champagne, the effervescence. Often, we talk about feeling that light within the cells as this effervescent energy. It's that aliveness always present within you. It's that pleasure of experiencing what's right in front of you and feeling it to the full and experiencing it as having positivity, as having a benevolence to it, so that when you are at peace within yourself, essentially, you're experiencing the joy of existence, the joy of being, of doing.

Look at a child! When I would play with a particular toy or be drawing or doing a creative venture with my mom or I would be outside with my dad in the garden, and we were so immersed in the experience, time would fly by. You have each had that experience in your own lives where it could be hours and it feels like minutes because you are enjoying yourself so much. The experience of time, of space, of anger, loss, sadness all dissipates, and disappears in the experience of being fully present in the moment, in your heart, for this is the nature of joy. It's going back to that childhood innocence, the childlike nature that does not fear a stranger or is not scared to jump over the fence or climb the tree or experience something new but is looking forward to the adventure of discovery. So, cultivate joy in your life and it will be the expression of who you are. You know what it feels like to be around someone who is genuinely joyous.

We do understand that one can appear to be always joyous and always smiling and always happy and you know that there's a veneer underneath of which is a tremendous sense of anger or sorrow or pretense. That niceness we addressed. The true nature of authenticity is being happy inside. That's what we're seeking, what I am saying now, using different words to express that inner nature of deep satisfaction. When you are happy, everything is fine. When you're unhappy, you just wanna go back to being happy again. Happy is another word for joy. A satisfied mind might be another way to term joy. We appreciate that question.

It was definitely there in the very beginning, in the introduction to the wisdom and fullness of the variety of expressions we 12 wished to bring to you. It's important, and we have said this many times. I want to reiterate that it is important to stay close and connected with your child, not the wounded child, but the child that is beneath that wound. That child understands that joy is the essence of what life is here for, the expression and experience of it. It is especially needed when faced with the jadedness of the big world of adults, for whom innocence can become a detraction. Hold on tightly to your sense of innocence. It is the jewel in your heart when you come forth with the innocence of the child. It is the meaning of what the Christ said when he said that a child shall lead them. It is that space of being open, of being ready to explore as a humanity, as a civilization.

Once you get over the hump of this transition, you will be exploring the heavens. You'll be finding out what it's like to experience other cultures and civilizations beyond your wildest imagination, just as when you leave the body, you can go anywhere. You can experience anything that your mind wishes to experience. You can bring that same innocence of the explorer mind, of that young, open-hearted way of seeing everything to this new age, this new world, this New Earth and to your own lives so that you become the expressions of joy. It is another, let's call it, point of the trinity of Light and Love and Joy. And, you know, at the heart of that center is peace, right there in the center of that tetrahedron. Peace.

Q. (LS) *This is not a question but what popped in my head. I was just going to mention, as Raphael, as you had your instructions from your last channeling with the Nameless Ones to do this group for us, that my instructions, if you remember, were, for every single day for three months to bring in 12 thoughts of joy into my morning meditation and I made it an entire thing for my Healing at the Heart group and my social media as I posted every day my 12 thoughts of joy. What started happening with these memes I was making, as more and more people were following them and then the inspiration came through me as I was posting, I would start writing more things to talk about, I suppose, just topics around joy and how to start uplifting people again. I had taken an entire year and a half break off of my business, social media, speaking, everything, because I had just kind of gone down with my health stuff. And so hearing Joy today was just reminding me of how important it was for me these past three months to be bringing in the 12 thoughts of joy, and how it got easier and easier and easier and it started to, even when I was having ups and downs these past few months, always be able to lift me back up to that place where I could get close to joy and then eventually feel the joy. So, I don't know if there's anything she wants to elaborate on how important that exercise was or still is for me and many friends that actually ended up following it and telling me how much I was helping them as well.*

A. Thank you. That's very beautiful and yes, you know the saying "Fake it till you make it." When you are having a hard time, imagine what it's like on the other side or find a way to use your imagination to shift. So, what you have done, is you have actually answered A's question in a way. You did what you felt in your heart, what you were instructed, but you actually also were able to find those experiences that were personal for you that expressed joy and you were able to share it and influence others to be inspired by what came through you. What you did was you created around you a circle. You created a structure. Just like this one was asked to create, to help each one of you to find and create the structures for the New Earth that are yours to do. So, it is very inspiring to hear what you did and how you did it and how it grew and blossomed and how it helps not only you but it helped everyone, and you do not have to stop. In fact, we love that you have created this energy. There was a Facebook group called "Something I am grateful for" that is still active on Facebook.

It is important that you accept that you can be either the center or at another place, like the number 12 in the clock, of a circle, and that you empower it and that you continue to bring forth that beauty, because where there is joy there will be beauty, and where there is beauty there will be joy. Everything that enhances the consciousness of another is expanding the light and the consciousness on the planet. Each one then becomes a light through what you've done to share with others. So, grow it. Let it be your new garden. We notice too that you have a different backdrop. It is a little subtler. It is a little softer, but it's beautiful and we see a different LS when we look at you. It feels like your little one is here with you more, and we like that, so thank you for that. Thank you for doing it, and thank you for sharing it because we want you to also be an inspiration for the others here to find their exercise that brings this joy to others. So, it is very powerful. We're grateful that you brought that forth.

- Yes. I also want to say from the last week too, asking us to consider what we are here for and what we bring, action-wise, I was at first thinking I can't physically do action because of my health stuff, but then through this exercise and for being in my heart more this week I realized it's time to bring my voice back. That's my action. It's always been my videos. It's always been my gatherings online pretty much, so I can still be at home where I need to be, but yeah, it just felt really good. And all these ideas for more videos in the series and connecting people online and, of course, it overwhelms me a little bit 'cause it's still a little scary for me to think about getting back into the swing of that, but yeah, so I just wanted to share that. Thank you. Everything that we've been doing these past 12 weeks has really helped me find myself again in a new way and move past some of the fears that had always stopped me.

- Thank you. What is the name of your Facebook group?

- It's Healing at the Heart.

Closing Meditation

Let's put our right hand on our heart, left hand on our right. Let's use that three-in-one, the right and the left, masculine, feminine and the heart, and let us direct the brilliance of our radiance from each of us to each of the others here on the call, to weave our threads together, to send that blessing in our hearts, that joy, that love, that experience of stillness and peace, and have it be part of that sphere that surrounds each one of us so that we become like the molecule of Shungite, we become the interconnectedness of the sacred geometry that weaves this beautiful web of interconnectedness around the planet and each one of us; so that when we feel or think or go into our hearts with our hands, immediately we are all there, this glowing sphere of light, of love, of gold weaving its way across the planet, blessing each one. Each time we go into our hearts we radiate this light to everyone who is suffering and we radiate the potential for joy, for restoration, for healing of all those wounded humans, so that we can move closer and closer and more quickly towards the New Earth. And so, we give thanks for your presence here today. I am especially so happy to be with you as Joy, as that experience, expression of childhood innocence, of truth, of knowing from within what is appropriate in each moment. I love you all. We will see you next week, for there is one that wishes to bring his message of hope, of joy, of peace and of reassurance that behind the appearance there is only love. Thank you. Joy Weisman.

Voice Thirteen
The Christ

8th November 2020

So, let's put our right hand on our heart, our left hand on our right, allowing the great humor of the Universe to enter into us to lighten our hearts and to fill us with that beautiful golden energy of Love that is pouring down, that is filling our hearts now with stillness, with a deep sense of peace; in fact, with a sense of completion, a sense of deep satisfaction. Let's feel Mother Earth beneath us, Father Sky above us, that column of light surrounding each one of us that opens and expands to become a beautiful sphere of golden, white light. It surrounds this group and surrounds each one with protection and with a sense of connection to all of life and with all the Beings of Light that are present here with us. Feeling the energy of the Great Central Sun, the Solar Logos pouring down love and light, showering us with blessings, allowing our hearts to open fuller and fuller, wider and wider as the threads of our hearts weave together in this tapestry. It is made up of all colors, shapes, sizes, ages and beliefs; a tapestry that reaches out to weave together the hearts of all the people, of all the creatures; surrounding Mother Earth with our love, with this energy of heart, of gold; this energy of interconnection and this energy of knowing from the depths of our hearts and souls that each one is in the right place at the right time and that each one is guided. Each one is being led towards the greatest light it is possible to hold within us, such that it pours out and reaches out in a beautiful stream, in a spiral of golden light of the Christ Consciousness, touching the hearts of all those who suffer, of all who are in fear or in darkness, allowing them to open to the possibility that Light and Love is all that there is.

I greet you today. You may rest your hands. I greet you in the name of the Great Light of Creator, in the love of God/Goddess, in that oversight, that over-lighting that keeps each one of you safe, that keeps each one of you open to the most profound understandings and revelations possible. For this is the time of the revelation. It is the time of Truth. It is the time of the reckoning and it is also the time of not knowing, of being comfortable with not knowing, of recognizing that you have been on a journey and that the journey is the goal. The journey is not some destination that you arrive at and then all of a sudden you are living in Nirvana. It is not about escaping the need to be flesh and blood, the need to have feelings, the need to work out your stuff, to feel your body, every cell vibrating, each breath entering and leaving. Your heart and your soul and your body and your spirit all in one alignment with Heaven and Earth, reaching out in connection and interconnection with each human being, with every heart; so that you are establishing a new field of order in your universe and on this planet, Mother Gaia.

You are establishing a new field that is essentially the field of Union, the unified field that is building the New Earth. For it is necessary in any new endeavor to build a unified field through your intentions, through your heart, through your stillness. It is built up by meditating, going within and paying attention to the voices of the guides, of the angels. You are replacing the old voices that pound away at your mind telling you that you are insignificant or powerless. For those voices we have long ago discarded, and the voices that now fill your heart and your soul and your mind are the voices of light, the voices of guidance, the voices of those Holy Beings who carry the vibration of the New Earth forward, a new universe, a new way of being on this planet.

We want you to focus only on that light, because, if anything is important, it is the light that will change everything. The light inside you and the light that you project outside of you is the energy, is the vibration that will create the New Earth. It will overcome any attempts to manifest a world of control, of domination, a continuing world of horror, of tortures, of harming another, of damaging the environment, of being caught up in a desire for control out of a deep sense of insecurity. And so, it is the light that will reach into those places because you want to affect every single human being upon the planet to be able to unfold to greater light. Because, as the light enters, the cells are able to receive a new pattern, a new blueprint for what it requires of each human to be able to enter into the field of Union. It opens the path to abandon the old ways of seeing that are limited, that are limiting, and that see the other as something to be feared instead of an adventure to be encountered. It opens possibilities to a new connection that may bring great beauty and interest and excitement instead of one that used to bring terror or fear to the heart.

It is important, it is extremely vital, that you focus as much as you can upon the light, upon knowing who you are as light; that no matter what else is going around in your mind, that you are able to constantly remember to breathe, and that with every breath you remember that you are Light. Of all the things we have taught you in this series, this is the most important message: to remember to breathe in the midst of any tension or stress or any voices that contradict your heart's knowing, any voices that diminish you in any way or create fear or worry within you. Your first job is to discard them and fill your breath with light. Fill yourself with light and then direct that light to whatever situation, whatever encounter or relationship you are having that seems to be a challenge and causing the stress. It is very simple; but when the breath stops and the shoulders begin to rise and harden, that is the moment where you have the power and the control and the choice to take that breath and let go. It is so simple. If everybody was able to do that, the world would immediately shift to a new vibration.

It is also important, not just that you do this for yourself each time the need arises, but that you become a model, that you become a teacher of this simple practice. You can go to the ends of the Earth with your mind, in all sorts of fascinating directions, encounters with all sorts of amazing beings and amazing truths and mystery schools and great ancient wisdoms. They may offer initiations that require of you to do multiple hoops and land on your feet with one hand in the air waving at the stars and the other hand on your nose pretending that you are going somewhere. All these wonderful things that the mind can take you on are beautiful and exciting, and yet nothing can compare with that breath. You are your breath! Your breath is your connection to life. Your breath is your connection to your fellow humans. Your breath is your connection to your divinity within. It is the connection to your heart, to the soul, to your Soul Seed. It is the connection to all the realms of guidance, and it is so simple. The truth is simple. If it does not resonate, if it does not bring you a sense of joy, a sense of pleasure, a sense of feeling stillness or completeness or satisfaction, but it creates a tension in your body or in your mind, it is not for you.

We come here to bring you ease and grace. We come here to ask you to embrace ease and grace; to stop worry, to stop rush, to stop hurry. It is a simple message and yet it is so profound because when you begin to use it, in the moment, you start to realize that your life can be easy and graceful. You can have abundance, you can have every single thing that your heart desires. There is within you this tremendous source. We like to call it the Inner Sun.

I come to you today as one who stands within the center of the 12. I come to you as the one who over lights the whole planet and the whole solar system. I come to you in many ways, as well, as one who has been called the Solar Logos, that energy at the heart of the sun, the energy of the One, the Great Central Sun at the very center of the Universe. It sends its energy and its power towards the great Sun of your solar system. You may have called it Sol at some point in its journey. The energy of gold has been very prominent in the teachings over this year. The energy of gold is the energy of the sun, the energy that is also within you, this golden light. It is also the Light of Creator, the Light of All That Is. For the energy of that which could even consider the creation of All That Is, is the greatest power. And it is accessible to you. Within your heart, within your soul, within your very center, there is that spark that is, in many ways, a small version of the great Sol that is without, that shines its light upon you and that gives rise to the possibility of life upon your planet.

So, it is important for you to honor that within you that spark is your connection to your divinity, and that your connection to your divinity, which is also the fire within the heart, is connected to that energy of your solar plexus. It is that neural pathway center, that field of interconnectedness that is responsible for the linkages of all the pathways within your physical body. It is also a center, the nerve ganglia place. It is one of the three. The one that is in your solar plexus is connected to the one in your heart, which is also connected to the one in your brain, and they operate as a wholeness, as we have shared with you before. When these three are operating in a harmonious way, there is a back-and-forth communication going on, then everything works together according to the fields of order. Many of you are familiar with the four elemental essences of the Pillar: Truth, Light, Order and Union. As you work within your own physical framework as a unified field, so you are also connected to a unified field within the soul, the connection to your Soul Seed and your blueprint. You are also connected to the Ones with No Names and to that place of the Swing Between Worlds where you have all become part of a soul group.

This is why you are all here together, as a collaborative energy for each other and a support system. You all came to express and to manifest this great need at this time to shine your light, to stay within the heart and to stay in a space of equanimity instead of fear. You came to manifest new beginnings, holding a new vision for what the Earth can be and to hold that template, that blueprint. And you are here to create the structures that will become the containers for the New Earth.

We have stressed for you in the past, over this whole series, the importance of examining your ideas, your assumptions, your belief systems, the very words you use, and the associations that you have with those words. It is important for you to recognize that each one of you is a Grand Central Sun for a whole universe that revolves around *you*. Imagine that each one of you is a sun in the center of a solar system, whether it be your family or your children, your grandchildren, or it be your friends, your neighbors, or those in your spiritual groups.

Imagine that there are these different kinds of personality types that are all revolving around you and that for the time being you can lay aside your own personality and manifest this energy of comprehension, of integration, of synthesis. Imagine that you are an energy, like a force, like, for instance, the force of the nucleus within the atom that has the power to hold this entire field of energy in place so that it all revolves around you, so that each of the electrons that revolve around your central sun, that each one of them has a particular kind of elemental nature that is different from the others. And so you have your Geminis and you have your Virgos and you have your Scorpios and you have a different approach to how to see things. You have these different perspectives. Just as we have done with this group of 12, we have attempted to give you the broadest spectrum possible of understandings and approaches to essential, basic truth. The truth of Union, the truth of Light and the energy and essence of being the Love of God in expression, and this is what each one of you is.

And so, imagine that you have come, you have gone through all your incarnations and you have gone home to Source and you have been asked to become a sun and to have around you a solar system that you are responsible for shining light upon. You create the life force energy that will begin to develop Gardens of Eden, libraries of manifestation of all sorts of life forces, all sorts of energies, humans, creatures, viruses, bacteria, earthworms, scorpions, turtles, elephants or lions. Imagine that you are the sun that is shining upon your solar system and each planet perhaps has its own satellites or moons, and some planets will have oceans upon them and trees and waters flowing, and other planets will have forms of life that are, perhaps, completely different. Surrounding you is an entire universe and you are the center and it is important that you never stop shining your light, giving your heat. You are receiving the vibrations from another Central Sun that is at a dimensional level beyond yours and yet is feeding you in the same way that you are feeding your planets. And so, you recognize that you are a central sun within your own system; but you are also connected to a 'hierarchy,' an entire field, in a hierarchical expansion of other Grand Central Suns that all shine upon other suns and all are shined upon.

We have this inter-connectedness that reaches into infinity in both directions, all the way down to the minutest energy beyond atom and the greatest energy beyond the Galaxy, all the way to Source, all the way to the Grand Intelligence of All That Is. "Something" has/had the ability to create such a vastness. There is an Intelligence that is responsible for creating such an incredibly refined, amazing existence in which everything is balanced and poised in a field that is allowed to shift and change and morph and yet constantly maintains a momentum and an equilibrium within which everything is moving.

And yet, within the center is that stillness, that space of the NoThing, the Tao. You might call it the Emptiness, but it is an emptiness from which all Wisdom springs. For it is necessary, in order to even say words, like we are sharing with you, that there must be an emptiness at the center that receives these messages and allows them to come forth. So, each one of you is a sun and an emptiness. Each one of you is a divine potential that is not yet manifest. Each one of you is Source, that spark of divine fire that animated your body, that is your soul, that is your connection to all of life and all this grandeur we are talking about. That spark is the true nature of who you are, and it sparks the Great Fire within you of your central sun; it is your soul connection inwards and outwards, radiating out and radiating in.

We wish you to imagine that which is the external universe, the stars that you see at night that reach out to infinity, that are beyond counting like the sand on the shore, and there is that one shore in front of you, and yet there are so many shores upon your planet, as each one is like a star in the great vastness of infinitude. So too, that expense of infinity exists within you. You can go deeper and deeper and broader and broader into an endless expanse of possibility, of understanding, of knowing, of feeling, of connection that extends within you into infinity. Is this not a great miracle? Is this not the Great Mystery? Can you not feel how powerless and powerful you are at the same time to be that spark, to hold the template of Divinity within you, and allow it to unfold? In a similar way, those two, minute little things, the egg and the sperm come together and then, in a grand explosion of sacred geometry, they begin to multiply and to form, out of the fields of order, everything that is required for the creation of a new life. The mystery is beyond understanding. If you consider this time on your planet, your life at this time, your life right now, it is but a drop in the ocean.

It does not matter who will be president and who will not. It does not matter whose ideas will run the show. Everything is being dismantled that is not sustainable, whatever the appearance. It is just the appearance. Hold your breath for just that half second before you breathe in and recognize that everything will change, that everything can change, and that you can change whatever it is that has been bothering you, just like that, by entering that space of the No Space, of the No Time, of the NoThing in that breath, and recognizing that you are on the threshold of the New Earth and that you cannot allow yourself to be deluded any longer by appearances.

You cannot allow yourself to pay attention to the voices of put-down, of diminishment, to the energy of burden that you perhaps have allowed yourself to carry, to the energy of being responsible for somebody else's problems, of feeling that you are having to do something for an ancestor or for a loved one that is against the grain. You have the ability and choice now to say "No! I am starting again. I am me. I come with a whole new vibration, because I'm here for the future. I am here to establish these new containers, and the containers that I bring are filled with love. They are filled with light, and they're filled with meaning. They are filled with the possibility of peace on Earth unfolding. They are filled with the Peace of a Million Years of Dreaming. They are filled with my heart's desires, my heart's longings establishing themselves in this new field of Order.

I come to you today because I am that which is within you. I come as the one called the Christ, or Jesus or Yeshua, or Joshua, the root of which (ישע) is the word "salvation." You are your own salvation. I do not exist outside of you, and yet I am also a projection of your own inner salvation from within you. I have created story upon story. I have been through lifetime upon lifetime as an avatar of each age, as a way-shower, as a leader, as a teacher, as a bringer of Truth, of knowledge. I have now come to this planet at this time to not be a single individual energy. Even if I am the Solar Logos, I am also an emanation that dwells within each heart as part of the Christ Consciousness that radiates out from you as light. It reaches and touches the hearts of all people, all creatures, no matter how encased in density they may be. There is that spark that each one has within them as long as they are in life force energy. We are not talking about clones and drones and the artificial energies that are being created. We are talking about humans, about souls. Those souls who have lost their way need that light more desperately than anyone else on your planet or beyond.

Even the extraterrestrial energies that have been behind the control and domination of your planet for so long, they can use your light. They need a new model for how to exist in a way that is harmonized with All That Is. For, if something is not harmonized, it will fall apart. It will begin to vibrate at a very unsteady and erratic rate and it will disintegrate itself. This is what is happening in the world today on your planet. It is why you are facing the greatest ability for fear to be in your face behind your mask and behind the mask of each one that you see, because fear is a call. It is a desperate, urgent 911 call for help. It is saying "I feel trapped. I am scared. I do not know what the future will bring me. I am contracting. I don't know what to do. Help me!" And when you shine your light, it will dissolve the masks, the illusions, the Grand Deception. It will unmask it and show it for what it is, because it is orchestrated for the intention of domination and control. And at a higher level, it has been orchestrated for the disintegration of everything that has upheld the terror and the horror that has infiltrated each one's consciousness upon this planet, lifetime upon lifetime, and it cannot be allowed to continue.

It is important to be patient. It is important to know who you are and what you bring. It is important to love yourself. This is the other bottom line. It goes with the breath and the letting go of the shoulders, of the tension, of the weights; starting to see yourself as God or Goddess. Starting to see that you chose this life, this body. You chose this particular brand of individuality, your personality, just as you chose your parents, your schooling, your upbringing, your Catholic schooling, your Jewish background, all the mythologies, all the heritages that you have inherited and believed to be the way in which things were, and have to be, all the stories.

You choose them in order to bring you to this place and this time. It is important that you stay steady, that you ground. Connect with Mother Earth. Connect with that sense of being rooted in the Earth, feeling the soil, feeling the air, the breeze, the sun, the warmth, hearing the birds, the trees, the creatures. Connect to Mother Earth, connect with Father Sky, with us around you and within you as your guides. You can connect with me. You can call me Jesus. Call me what you like, but don't call me late for dinner! It is not important. Do not put me on a pedestal or make me into something that you cannot even consider aspiring to. It is part of the grand delusion that you are any less. Everything is everything. Everything is part of everything. The union that you seek, is the union of interconnectedness.

When you have a conversation with someone, you are recognizing that there is another "you," and that you can have great delight in connecting with another way of seeing yourself in a different kind of Zodiacal-experience. For they may be a Gemini and you may be a Taurus, and it is exciting to know that there are these differences, that it can be seen, the whole entire caboodle can be witnessed from a different perspective, looking at a different facet of the diamond, of that beautiful energy of the Shungite molecule, the Fullerene,[78] that is made up of all these interweaving 6 and 5-sided figures, all creating this magnificent structure that can take an energy that is negative and spin it into a positive vibration.

You are living energies of Shungite. You are all Fullerene molecules. You carry the energy of transformation. You carry that energy of ground, of what it feels like to be connected to Mother Earth. And yet the Shungite came from Outer Space via Jupiter and landed upon your planet billions of years ago, waiting for this time when humans will discover that they have an ally in Nature that can help them with this technology of death; that can help them to reverse all the negativity that surrounds them or that they are ingesting; that it can turn things around. This is why you are here. This is what the energy, not of your elections, but the energy of this Light that you are and that you carry, is about. Transformation. You are a transformer. You take the negative energies and you then spin them clockwise.

We are encouraging you again to consider the chakra system; that you look at your root, at your connection with the Earth and you spin it counterclockwise with this energy of red, of life force. The counterclockwise spinning is a gathering in of energy, which rises up toward your creative energy of the second chakra, of your sexual organs, of that life force energy, that creates a new life. The creative impulse brings together polarities into oneness. It brings negative and positive together. Sun and Moon create stars. The energy of Isis and Osiris creates Horus, the son, and brings Trinity into Union.

This drive becomes a clockwise spin that has a positive vibration and that sends out into the Universe the blueprint of this new soul that is making these eggs divide, the egg and the sperm, as we have said before, these imaginal cells, elemental beginning cells, begin to multiply according to sacred geometry and create life. This force is a positive clockwise spin that takes that energy of Creation, of life force energy from the mother, from that lower chakra, the first chakra, and sends it out into the Universe and then, like the sun, it is gathered again into the Solar energy, the solar plexus, in a counter-clockwise manner. You are gathering the light of sun, the Light of Source, this golden energy of Love into you again, to that place of the Plexus, the place which is going to connect all things within you. Then, as it reaches towards the heart energy, via the Soul Seed, connecting yourself with that Swing, with that connection with the Ones, with your blueprint, with your intention before you came, it takes you to the heart, where everything begins to radiate out again with that beautiful green energy of light, of love, that spiral outward-going clockwise energy of the Christ Consciousness reaching out to bring love, to send light to the world, sending it clockwise.

And when you do this then, there is a need for that in breath, the throat chakra, the gathering of Truth, the gathering of everything you have learned, the gathering of the next vibration coming in, to reassess. Coming in to hold space within your higher aspects now, allowing the Truth to then start to radiate out through your third eye, the all-seeing eye of Horus, that which scans the horizons: "Where am I needed? What must I do? "Your will be done God, not mine, in me and through me. Show me what I must do this day so that I may be a blessing to all." [79] Now, you send out this radiation from your eye. You see through the eyes of God/Goddess, so you become tuned to the inner nature of what is going on, of what is being seen, of what is needed. This realization reaches the Crown and connects with that divine energy pouring down through you which connects to the chakras above you. It too, is a counter-clockwise motion that gathers in from above, from the Heavens, from the Grand Central Sun the beautiful down pouring of the golden mantle, the golden nectar. And, as it comes in, the spin begins to reach back out again, gathering and sending. And so, you create this energy of a ladder, shall we say, a linkage between Earth and Heaven through your very form, through your very structure.

We are so grateful for you that you have been here on this journey. We know that you have been through changes. We know how much you have worked to hold this energy of positivity. We know that you are all graduating as Spiritual Warriors, that your sword is now firmly in your scabbard because it is not needed in the same way it was at the beginning. And yet, there is still a need to evaluate and to stop judging and to allow yourself to love yourself and not be in judgment of anyone, so that you are no longer feeling the vibration of separation but instead are upholding the energy of Union. We will take a pause to see where we stand.

Christ Q&A

Q. (ZS) *My heart is racing in my chest. I never imagined I could have this opportunity to speak directly, you know, with this energy of Christ who has been with me my whole life and such an incredible guide. In these last experiences that I've had I've been suffering from a little bit of heartache and I feel like a lot of it was my own creation. The emergence of old wounds that have come up have been, I feel, like the underlying foundation of the pain of rejection, and I feel like, what other being could know of this thing other than Jesus Christ who experienced probably the highest rejection, to be crucified. I am just curious as to any wisdom that could help me move through this so that I don't continue to not only not heal what has been in the past, but to move forward and not allow this energy of rejection to debilitate and dim my light. Thank you.*

A. Bless you, dear one, thank you. If you could see what you look like on the screen with this beautiful aura behind you radiating the gold light, this beautiful gold energy, you would see yourself, and you would know that, in truth, you are this little girl, this innocent child who has been harmed because the world itself has been a world in which it has been necessary to experience the full gamut of human emotions. One of the first experiences of each one's lifetime is rejection. If you are a child and a brother or sister is born, you will have that feeling. The one quoted, in the book Water is Life wrote that to be alive is to be wounded. The sadness that you talk of is something that is within the human heart deeply. Very often it is covered up with anger, with rage. Do you remember the words "Father forgive them for they know not what they do?"

- Oh yes

- Understand that you are surrounded by vibrations that are less conscious than you are, and that also there are others of vibrations who are much more conscious; but that on this grand ladder that we have talked about, in essence all are equal. All must go through the purging and the purification of the heart, of the experience of what it's like to be human. There are so many stories of my life, so many versions of what did and what did not happen and there are also so many mythologies about what I am a reflection of. The story of my life is a reflection, as we have shared before, of the various sun gods, sons of God, sons of the Sun who have had to die and be reborn, to be resurrected. These mythologies are part of the cosmic cycles, even if there are historical counterparts. Within the human cosmic cycle, within the soul, within the heart of each one there is a necessity to face the rage, the depression, to face the disappointments, to face deep sadness and sorrow of loss.

Do you remember the story of Siddhartha, the young Buddha who, when he finally saw that there was something wrong with the picture of his isolated golden cage, went around asking and knocking on doors? Every home that he knocked upon, there was somebody who had suffered a death in that household, and he had been kept from this knowledge. So, it is part of the human condition to feel abandoned, rejected, to have disappointments, to feel that you have done everything you can and yet nobody acknowledged you. Yet, it is important to also remember that you are still that little girl, that innocent child and that the world cannot in any way diminish or crush the power that is rising within your heart and that is building, and taking you to another place.

We have stressed the importance of forgiveness and of recognizing that, at the core of forgiveness and compassion is the understanding that everyone is wounded. Everyone acts either from that woundedness or (and this is an 'and/or', 'not a 'but') because they too made an agreement with you before you came to this planet that they would reject you and that you would get to experience this opportunity, to recognize that, even with the rejection, you are still pure and innocent and powerful, to understand who you are as a shining light that cannot be diminished by rejection or by betrayal.

So, it is important to understand that very often one carries a mission forward from other lifetimes and from your contracts and agreements in the Swing Between Worlds, that you will come, and you will transform those energies that have been dogging you for so long and that, in the transforming of them, you are creating a stepping stone for others to follow suit. Because, if you can do it, another can. You can become a model for others by recognizing that the projections are not the reality, that the rejection is not real but is a projection of that person upon you. You feel rejection because you had an expectation that was not met. Often, your vibration has shifted and altered and raised itself to a level where there is no longer a congruence with that person. It then becomes easier to recognize that your feet are now standing at the crossroads ready to move past the threshold towards a new direction and that story is done. We have talked about letting go of stories, and it is true that there is great value in story. It has value as a method for teaching. It has value for soul growth to listen to and to tell a story. It does not necessarily have a value for you in pursuing your direction towards the experience of ease and grace and living the vibration of the New Earth. Does that make sense?

- *So much, so much.*

- Thank you dear.

Q. (CR) I wish to hear Christ speak on how, when loved ones pass over, we can continue to do work with them, even when they're no longer in the physical form by our intentions and by prayer and sending love and light to them and how, if you take this even maybe further, as we expand our love to each other, and the same way, just by our intentions and how it's possible to reach through the veil.

A. As you sit in the stillness, as you do your practice, as you meditate, as you gain a sense of interconnection, perhaps you will have a feeling of communing with other aspects of Nature around you or the feeling that something is moving within your soul, within your heart. As you begin to have a sense of something, let me say greater, more expansive than the environment of meditation, you'll begin to have a sense of the possibility of communicating with an energy or vibration of another soul. It does not matter whether that soul is in the same room with you, is 1,000 miles away or is no longer in human form. Perhaps they have crossed over into a dimension of Light. Once you have the feeling of the inter-dimensionality of your meditation experience, within the stillness, within the breath, you have that ability to put forth a question or a desire for communication with that soul. You may have a vision or experience of colors in your mind's eye or an energy of expansion, of light. In truth and in the greater reality, there is no separation. So, what is required for you, is to start with the intention of wanting to make a connection with a being who has crossed over or with an energetic that you feel you need an answer about, so that you could call upon one of us in the Realms of Light. You could call upon me. There is no reason why you cannot speak with me in a different format than on a Zoom call through this one or another. You can have your own direct communication, and within that framework you can connect with any soul or any life form in the same way that we have been recommending that you connect with a tree or stream or creature.

It is about going beyond the limitations of your conscious mind, going beyond the assumptions of what you can't do, about the limitation that you see for yourself when you wish to be in communication with another soul, be they alive or not, be they from a different timeline or lifetime. You have that ability within the stillness, as if you have this beautiful sofa within your heart. Perhaps you have a special altar, cave or meditation room within your heart. You sit there, and you invite the other energy to join you. Use your imagination to create this scene, and thereby actualize it. You step into it, and make it real. Then that energy becomes real. It will become a communication network for you, back and forth. So it is just really about believing; it is about trusting that you can do this. That is all that is missing, and we recommend you use your imagination and practice doing it. Peace. Does that make sense?

- Absolutely, thank you so much.

Q. (MS) So what is the purpose of lower frequencies, darkness and dark agendas? Is it purely a contrast to understand what light is and love is?

A. You are all asking deep questions. We approve. When we talk of the All That Is, when we look at the soul; when we consider the subject of free will, you understand that Creator, the intelligence which created All That Is, whatever name you give it; this intelligence created everything to be *what* it is. Darkness has been defined as the absence of light. It is necessary in the highest gift-giving that is possible for a soul, that Creator (we will just call it that) gave to each soul free will. IT gave them the ability to choose. Some chose to hide in the darkness because the light somehow triggered them, and they experienced a sense of isolation that was so deep and powerful because they could not handle the recognition of themselves as light. It is almost as if things had to divide up into polarization in order for movement to happen, and so the wholeness separated into Yin/Yang. There is always the seed of the one within the other, the potential for one to morph into the other.

There is always the possibility that a great Light, that a human who has attained the highest levels of consciousness, of avatar, of Bodhisattva, could descend into depths of darkness just as it is possible that one who has groveled in the deepest, darkest density and has performed the greatest atrocities possible could ascend to the Realms of Light somewhat like the Prodigal Son, you might say, and return to their pristine nature as God's Light in expression. The gift of free will allows everything to exist without judgment. It is as if the sun will shine upon everything equally. And there may be energies that are hidden in shadow, because something has been placed in the path of the light waves. It is not going to stop the sun from shining. It is still the choice of those energies to hide behind something, density, to allow them to have a particular experience. The 'Free Will Experiment' allows souls to choose between light and dark. It is also there intentionally for the possibility of a soul to grow, and expand into greater and greater light consciousness through the experience of suffering. Suffering has resulted from the descent into darkness and density. This has generated the conditions for a soul to experience tremendous suffering in order that they could grow into a commensurate field of light and love and of compassion.

So, each one holds within their hands the possibility, the potential for all directions, for all experience and has been given the ability to choose. The gift of Creation essentially is free will. You are transcending the Free Will Experiment and moving towards the Free Heart Experience in a new field of order, shall we say. It does not deny one's choice, but it creates a vibrational field that allows you to experience a new model of living in human form. Living from the heart, in such a way that you can experience ease and grace, love and connection, cooperation, and peace, without the need for that old experience of suffering in order to grow as a soul.

Up to this point, the fastest way for souls to grow, to expand into greater light, has been the experience of coming into density and suffering. This has generated the greatest amount of, what in Buddhist terms is called merit. When a soul experiences the great Light of Creator all the time, experiences itself as part of God or Goddess all the time, soul growth is very slow in terms of so-called time, and the acceleration that suffering provided, was necessary. Plus, you have cycles of karma that has been accumulated through harming others and the generation and causing of suffering. In order to move through this and move beyond it, it is necessary to come to a balance point where the karma gets cleared. We alluded to this the last time, that what is happening on your planet and why, in fact, the dark energies are serving the higher plan through their insidious intentions, is because they have set in motion, not just the disintegration of the old systems, but the balancing out of old karmic patterns that require suffering to see them through to the New Earth. Does that make sense?

- Yes. That's a lot to chew on, and I'll definitely listen to that one. Thank you.

- Thank you for your question.

Q. (MSG) This question follows a bit on the previous question around karma, needing to clear karma. All the turmoil that is happening, not just in the whole world but particularly in the Americas.... Many years back I received guidance that the unprocessed, unbalanced genocide of the Native peoples that happened, that our country was founded on, and actually, you know, South American and Central American countries too, that has not really been fully acknowledged properly. It's beginning to emerge into the consciousness. Even children were not taught true history. I wouldn't want to hold things back to feel like "Oh, that has to be cleared for us to move on," but I keep feeling that this is a stumbling block in our way to create... We keep going into more divisiveness, and in order to come into unity and forgiveness it feels to me there's something about that, and I personally am holding a very strong piece of that. I have Indigenous ancestry as well, but yeah, anything that you can say about that, that would help to understand and to support that clearing to happen, I appreciate.

A. Thank you. We are holding space for each one to see through the eyes of Spirit, for each one to see as a soul, to see the evil, shall we say, which is really the word "live" reversed. It is the anti-life force that has been raging upon your planet for so long. We have brought forth the idea in the past that those who are from a particular culture or religious practice or a particular nationality have been through the numerous lifetimes experiencing the karma of having been all kinds of beings. Each one of you has been a rapist, a terrorist, each one has been a king or a beggar. Each one of you has committed tremendous atrocities, has been a victim of the most horrendous crimes over the many lifetimes that you have been in existence as souls, and so it is important not to stereotype. It is important not to target one particular energy or group or kind of consciousness, even though it is also important for you to hold a field of union, of light and of love, to celebrate the differences, the diversity, the special quality of each culture, each tradition and each ancestry. It is important not to get caught up in a way of seeing that is divisive, even if it is upholding a particular point of view for a particular people or culture or energy that has been downtrodden, that has been harmed, that has been victimized, that has been turned around. It is important to not judge anything or anyone as best you possibly can.

We have talked about seeing the golden or the silver lining with every cloud. The recognition comes when human beings show respect for other human beings and for all life. This is the goal. This is the intention. You often put one group or one being of light, whether it be a Christ or a Mary Magdalen or it be a whomever, a Buddha or a Bodhisattva, you put them on a pedestal. You take a particular indigenous practice or a particular culture that has great wisdom and you separate it out. You say that somebody, because of the color of their skin or culture is being targeted. It is true, and yet you do not know the history or herstory of that person's soul journey. You do not know the context or the karma that they are working through within this experience that has a global and a cultural element to it and that is being worked out on a global and on a national scale, but also on an individual level.

So, it is important to understand that what we said in the very beginning, that the most important thing you can do is to hold the light, to shower the light, to radiate that light, to gather as much light as you possibly can so that you have so much surplus of it that you can be a lighthouse, so that you can shine the message of non-separation of non-judgement, no matter what it looks like. Old Chinese once shared, a long time back, that many of the cavalry who persecuted the Native people, are now the drunks on the reservations. We do not mean to disrespect anyone, but they are playing out their karmic retribution, their karmic balance sheet. And so, it is difficult to know what to say and do within a context like the one you are presenting. For, in truth, it is necessary for one to hold the balance, the light, to holds the energy of groundedness between Heaven and Earth and to know truth as the expression of union, to evolve a level of higher consciousness that holds all with the same kind of regard, the same kind of respect.

It is important that when they wrote of me, even if all the writings were doctored, they reported that I would gather with the tax collectors, with the lepers, with the harlots and with the lowest of the low, that I did not judge one against another. This model, this example means not judging the one on the street who lives on the corners or lives in the parks and suffers and yet people turn their backs saying "Oh, these homeless people, you can't trust them." They are humans who suffer. Each one has been through the mill. Each one has created their own suffering through their karma, through their attitudes, through their belief systems, through their upbringing and through their suffering. It is important for what I represent; The energy of the Christ is the energy of love, of acceptance. It is the energy of non-judgment, of non-separation. No one is higher or lower and no teaching is of greater regard than any other.

If it stands for respect and love and light, it can come from any source, it can come from the ghetto, it can come from the gutter. Wherever it appears in the hearts and souls of a human being, where they radiate respect, they are an indigenous wisdom energy and they may be a white person or a black person or a native person of a particular color. And so, it is important to transcend that kind of stereotyping because it requires, in many ways, a turning over, a turning upside down, on its head, of the kind of energy of '-ism' that initiated the kind of suffering, the kind of victimization that started this whole process and has carried it through for so long. Perhaps this is not the kind of answer you were looking for, but this is what is coming forward. Does that make sense?

- Yeah, it does. It is that I hear it as the very highest perspective. It's a little challenging translating that into working with social justice issues with indigenous Native American groups which I'm involved with, so I have to sit with that and see. Very, very, challenging to present that view.

We are not expecting or asking you to present any view. We are asking you, and you have already initiated the process, to be the Spiritual Warrior, which means that you will always choose the highest possible vibrational answer for yourself. What you need now is only to integrate that into how you are, how you represent your own truth. It does not require of you to answer anybody else's truth but to express it in the only way you know, through your love, through your heart and your light. So, it is important to hold the light when there is a question like this, and find a way to support those on the front lines. Perhaps they have not chosen to see things from the same perspective we are giving and they need to go forth with banners. They need to be activists. They need to go on the front lines and they need to stand at the halls of power and protest. Each one must do what their heart calls them to do and it is valuable, even if it is somewhat limited, and even if it is somewhat distorted. I'm not saying it is, but I am advocating the highest possible perspective. Yes?

- Yes, yes, integrating all of that, and yeah, thank you very much.

Q. (MM) When you were just speaking, I can't put into words, my focus lately has been on your life during biblical times, and all I'm focused on these days is being the Eternal Light, the Eternal Flame. I see all the duality and sort of like I don't have time for it. All I have time for is to remember what it's like to be that Eternal Flame. I don't have a question. I just wanted to say that, thank you.

A. It is important to be the Christ. Christ is just a representation of God's love available. It is not even Christ. It is Mary and Jesus. They are a oneness of masculine and feminine, of God energy, of Solar energy. It is a way to the Light. That Christ energy is within you. This is the Light. It was ordained that I came in a male form this cycle, shall we say, because it has been required that there be a sacrifice of the son of

God in a particular kind of cosmic context so that the Sun can be reborn again at the winter Solstice. It is a mythology. I represent all these many stories of Christ. It is not a one thing. It is not a person, even not a one kind of energy that you can externalize. You are the Christ Light shining. That is all you really need to know. As you embody light, you are the Christ. There is no distinction. It is hard for a human to accept that they are it. You are where the buck stops. You are God/Goddess/Christ/Mary. You are all of it and you have the capacity to shine in the exact same way. Did I not say "You shall do greater things than I?" We are just a stepping stone for you to express, experience and be that transcendental energy of All That Is expressing itself through form. It is for you to experience the greatest joy of union, of oneness with God with all the light that you possibly can. This is the gift that is offered to you as a human, that you will experience this bliss of Union. This is all the heart longs for, and when you can experience it as self, you can also experience it as the whole Universe, as for everyone. The New Earth is about this love manifesting on your planet.

- *I understand. Thank you.*

Closing Meditation

We will go into the heart where we are already. You can place your hands upon your heart or just sit in stillness, imagining it, allowing that beautiful Light of the Christ's love to pour into you, to fall, to drop like the beautiful rain that came last night here, its torrents for the parched Earth to receive, hungrily, thirstily, that Divine Light of Christ, of the love of God that shines through you each moment. That is your real heritage. This is your gift. This is your lineage. This is why you are here, because you have come to embody this Light, to recognize there is nothing but Light and there is no Time. You know this very well. You have come to be the models, the master, come to be the Christ Light shining into the darkness of this density of this world that is filled with fear. When you experience fear, you have the tools that others perhaps do not have to overcome the fear, to recognize that you are immortal. You are eternal. You are infinite and universal. You are the Light and Love of God in expression. We love you. We surround you and we are within you. Peace. Blessings and Peace.

Epilogue

"OK, so you have a new path; and the path has many, many collateral paths. So, you're here in this world, as you know, to be a voice of the integrity of the masculine, of the sacred essence of water, the importance of the heart in the world and the capacity for each person to open themselves in unlimited ways that offer a distinct and clear direction, so that each person is more available to their own sourcing, their only epistemology, if you will. So, at this point you have many choices.

The diversity that's opening to you is unlimited, as you are aware now, and it is no longer your path to walk in the humbleness of not knowing or not being ready or not having or whatever. So, we're going to, as with others, we're going to erase those pathways from your mind and awareness. So, what you are opening to is a diversity that has the capacity to actually integrate different lineages, different places, different consciousnesses and to unify them in the one voice. So, your next opportunity is to hold the 12 channels and to expand to 12 more, and to multiply them together so you hold 144 channels. And this is something that we want to do, and will do with you, because it is not something that you will do alone. So you will take the 12 channels that you have; and you have of course more than 12, but the 12 you've been working with, and you will expand those 12, and then you will multiply those 12.

So, what we would promise for you and do with you, is the structuring of that consciousness with you; so we will be assisting you to create those channels. Now, the reason you want 144 channels is so that those channels begin to orient in a magnified manner with each other, in a, we're going to use the word again "new" way that will allow the particles of consciousness that each of those voices has, to become one voice. So, what you're endeavoring in this life to provide, is a one-voice structure that will then move through the consciousness of the people in a way that vibrates with those 144 channels, and therefore reaches the channels that are active in each person, and activates the channels that are not activated. You could think of that as the one voice that reaches all, the one voice that holds all hearts, the one voice that opens out to each moment in its texture, and then allows that texture to be experienced, received and integrated.

This is not just about talking as a voice, this is about a voice that goes through, it has the timbre to go through and actually vibrate and resonate and activate inside each being so that those channels become extremely, we'll use the word "organized" but not in a mental sense; so they become very ordered, very able to support health and well-being and alignment and trust and truth and all those things that are so important if one is to activate transformation. So what you have is this understanding that the volumes of your consciousness that are working and the energies that you have been gathering and sustaining, are now going to assist you to magnify that.

Now the channels are going to be specific to start with and then begin to blend together, so you have the 12 channels and you have more channels; so you can add the John Henry and others, and as you add them, you feel the resonance with them. All you want is the vibration of the essence of that being, just that, not a lot of words, not a lot of other things, just the essence. "What's the essence?" and the essence then gets to come together with other essences and other essences, and other essences as they are named or held.

Once you have the 12 and 12, they will face off with each other, in a sense, and they will join, and as they join, they will magnify, so the magnification then becomes the ordering of different resonances within that context of all of those; and then, as that happens, there is this fountain that flows; and it comes in and it gives you the essence of different aspects, each one at a time, and yet each one flowing with others into this organic resonance that is going to then expand the whole. So, you'll have, in the beginning, the sense of each essence, you know, working with each essence, and it's not a long time. It's just: "that's that essence." Got it! That's the essence, and you might want to keep track on the list or something just for the moment; and as you put that down there is a settling of that essence into you and as it's into you, it then is going to activate other essences associated with it, derived from it or connected in whatever way in the future.

And as all these start to happen, we're going to hold the container around your consciousness, so that those essences come into your awareness in a very easy and very gentle way, when you want them to, and not at other times. The whole feeling of this, is of expansion that's contained within the consciousness of the All. So there is symmetry to it, there is an awareness of what's happening. You're able to understand it, you know it's not just whoosh, and it's this sense of "It's time for the one voice to come together within itself, so that, as it comes through me, it is actually able to touch all these fibers, all the circuits inside however many people it reaches, so that they are transformed through that consciousness." It's a very beautiful awareness that has the timbre in it that responds to the cells of the people, and the people's cells respond to it; so, it is a healing energy; it is an opening and expanding energy. It is a forgiving energy, so forgiveness comes from it, through it, with it and is utilized from it, you know.

All these energies are received, activated and then utilized inside of that being; and it isn't for you to worry about what they get, how they get it and if they get it. That's all going to be taken care of. We're taking all that stuff out of your map, so you'll be able to recognize just that you are, and just that as being 'are,' as being the I AM and being in that space, everything that you have dreamed about, the community, the expansion, the land, everything starts to flow from that one voice. So always know that it's not about going back into Raphael, figuring Raphael out anymore. Just like with Maryanne, you know, you're not going to go back and think about, "What do I do and what do I know?" It's not that anymore for any of us. It's working the dynamic of the mission in the place of the heart, and it's every minute. That's what it is. There isn't any "I" anymore. It's transformed into the "We" and the voice that has all the aspects is an example of the "We" and will provide the world with that example as well. So it is."

TNO, 19th November 2020

Notes and glossary

1. The Ones with No Names. Also referred to as "TNO" and "The Nameless Ones." They are the beings who consult with souls prior to entering an earthly incarnation and on their return to the "Swing Between Worlds," the realm they inhabit or "live" in. In *I Remember Union, The Story of Mary Magdalena,* they "counsel" Jesus Christ, Mary Magdalena and Judas Iscariot concerning their missions prior to their incarnation. In the glossary of *Sunlight on Water, a Manual for Soul-full Living* channeled through Flo Aeveia Magdalena, they refer to themselves as "The body of light and knowledge which sustains order and truth in the universe. Amorphous light beings whose 'job' is to act as Cosmic Guidance Counselors for Humanity. We 'live' in the Swing Between Worlds" – *Sunlight on Water,* p.418. See Bibliography.

The opening and closing messages received from the TNO through Flo Aeveia Magdalena were given during a year-long virtual course called 2020 Action. Flo Aeveia Magdalena has been a channel for TNO for many years.

2. John Henry. John Henry is a spirit guide who came through Flo Aeveia Magdalena many years ago. He calls himself a "once-human angel" and brought the HeartThread® practice through her. He has shared that he traveled through the dimensions studying and asking all the Holy Beings how he could help humanity. They all answered that the heart was the key, and so he devised the HeartThread® process and teaches self-authority. He is Voice #5 in this book. For information on HeartThread® refer to https://raphaelweisman.com/healing-channeling/HeartThread or https://www.soulsupportsystems.org/heartthread

John Henry became my "buddy" and "personal" guide soon after I "met" him and was trained as a HeartThread® practitioner. I would receive a written message from him each morning after meditating and later, when I became a HeartThread® trainer, I began channeling him directly. See *Heartful Living* by Flo Aeveia Magdalena in the Bibliography for more from him.

3. Old Chinese. Also referred to as Chung Fu. Old Chinese is a spirit guide whom I met in London in the 1970s through the full trance medium, Marshall Lever. He called himself Old Chinese and taught that his name was Chung Fu, which means Inner Truth. As a result of our studies and training with him, my wife and I were invited to the USA in the early 1980s to join a project of the organization. He left the medium in around 1982/3 after which we moved to New Mexico. He once mentioned that he had been a student of Chuang Tzu in his last life. I always had fond memories of his teachings and energy and learned a tremendous amount from him. I continued to revere his teachings and in 2019 I discovered that Sally Pullinger in Glastonbury

was a full trance medium for Chung Fu and had been so for maybe 40 years. I was fortunate to meet her and her lovely family on a trip to Europe, and I received a powerful session from him in Glastonbury. I attended a number of online teachings including a course mentioned in the text called the Rainbow Warriors of the Light. From Chung Fu I learned about the properties of Shungite, which I have been selling in Santa Fe since. See Marshall Lever's book in the Bibliography.

4. Joy Sasha Weisman. Joy is my oldest daughter. She was born in Embudo, NM in 1981 and died in a car accident in Taos, NM in 1990. She is buried on family land in El Rito, North of Questa, NM where she and my other two children Elisha Rowan and Grace Oriel grew up. The harp-making company, Harps of Lorien I founded, is still there.

5. Fifth Gen-eration. We have altered the keywords related to this whole subject because of the surveillance, paranoia and attribution of the term "conspira-cy the-ory" to all voices that "dissent" the mass media narrative about the current medical emergency situation on the planet and any association with the rolling out of the technologies you use to access Wi-Fi. It is an extensive discussion, but there is much evidence to the effect that the symptoms of the Corona plague are actually not Influenza symptoms, but radiation poisoning and also Cyanosis (Cyanide poisoning, derived from "blue" or "cyan") as Cyanide is present in the widespread use of pesticides around the planet. I list a few authors in the Bibliography who have written about the subject and also the "sea" of electromagnetic frequencies that is asked about in a later question. Any mention of the two (fifth genera-tion and Vi-ris) in a YouTube video results in almost immediate removal of the video. So, we have used a variety of alternative ways of mentioning these keywords to avoid the scrutiny.

6. Co-vid. This same discussion applies to this subject and covers answers about vacc-cin-ation, testing and maskwearing. They refer to the subject as the 'Grand Deception.'

7. Atlantis. Atlantis was a civilization that existed for many thousands of years and dominated the world, creating colonies in North and South America and in Western Europe and the Mediterranean. The continent was located in the Atlantic Ocean and underwent a number of cataclysmic destructions of its land mass, becoming a set of large islands that eventually sank beneath the ocean in a final paroxysm around 10,000 BC. It was written about at length by Plato and today there are many books on the subject. See the Bibliography for a selection.

8. HeartThread®. See note 2. HeartThread® is a transformational modality that used messages from a client's cells to shift old conditioning and imprints from the body/psyche and replace them with life-affirming, positive realizations, opening up space in the cells to hold more light, and releasing patterns of stress and self-denigration from the being. Refer to the links in note 2.

9. Lemuria. Lemuria was a continent in the Pacific Ocean that pre- and co-existed with Atlantis and also was destroyed in a cataclysmic event, becoming submerged beneath the waters. It is also referred to as Mu and the Motherland. The best known, and one of the earliest books about Lemuria is by James Churchward. See the Bibliography.

10. Christ Consciousness. Instead of a physical "second coming" of some being like the Jesus Christ of the New Testament, the consciousness that Christ represents will be distributed as an elevated, universal level of awareness among those human beings who have transcended separation. This will generate the morphic resonance needed to shift humanity into the New Earth.

11. Edgar Cayce. Edgar Cayce (1877-1945) was known as the "Sleeping Prophet." He was one of the most prominent and best known trance channels, healers and psychics of this age and was highly regarded for the accuracy of his readings and diagnoses. He was a devoted Christian and founded a nonprofit organization, the Association for Research and Enlightenment, (A.R.E.) where his life's work is recorded and where you can access more information.

12. Councils. In various channelings there is reference to the Council(s) of (the) Light and various other collective transcendental groups of beings who oversee the spiritual evolution of Mother Earth and humanity, and who transmit messages and wisdom through these channels. Groups such as the Galactic Federation and The Star Nation(s) are included in this category.

13. Spiritual Warriors. I use this term to represent those who follow a path of dedication to a higher wisdom and truth and who practice impeccability in all their affairs, personal and transpersonal, who are in service to humanity and their soul-purpose and are willing to examine their motives, behavior and beliefs and focus on a positive, life affirming way of living. The term conjures up the various codes of conduct of warrior classes and sects from the ancient and medieval world such as the Samurai, the Templars and the Knights of the Round Table, to name a few. However, the emphasis has been shifted from the warrior of external combat to one who follows an internal warriorship.

14. Medicine Water Wheel. A circular ceremonial space designed for the practice of blessing the waters. The design combines the Native American Medicine Wheel with the 6-sided Seed or Flower of Life pattern that has 6 petals and a central altar. The straight lines represent the masculine and the curved lines the feminine. For more information visit www.WaterAwarenessGroup.Wordpress.com . You can also view a YouTube video about the Water Wheel at https://youtu.be/QP3oN2mMBBw

15. Precession of the Equinoxes. The Earth appears to shift its axial orientation relative to the backdrop of the stars according a cycle of approximately 26,000 years, such that the predominant Zodiacal sign apparently shifts "backwards" (hence precession) in the opposite direction from the monthly cycles of Zodiacal changes. We have just emerged from the dominance of the Piscean 26,000-year cycle and are entering the "age of Aquarius." Prior to the Piscean era in which the symbol of the fish was predominant, was the era of Aries, the Lamb and prior to that was Taurus, the Bull. Much of the mythology of these eras was associated with these images, such that the ram appears in the sacrifice of Isaac story and the sacred bull Apis in Ancient Egypt and Sumeria. Leo the Lion is a possible source image for the Great Sphinx. Wikipedia has an extensive article on the subject.

16. The Hopi Prophecy. Attributed to a Hopi Elder, given June 8, 2000

A HOPI ELDER SPEAKS:

«You have been telling the people that this is the Eleventh Hour,

now you must go back and tell the people that this is THE HOUR. And

there are things to be considered...

Where are you living?

What are you doing?

What are your relationships?

Are you in right relation?

Where is your water?

Know your garden.

It is time to speak your Truth.

Create your community.

Be good to each other.

And do not look outside yourself for the leader.

Then he clasped his hands together, smiled, and said, «This could be

a good time! There is a river flowing now very fast. It is so great

and swift that there are those who will be afraid. They will try to

hold on to the shore. They will feel they are being torn apart and

will suffer greatly. Know the river has its destination. The elders

say we must let go of the shore, push off into the middle of the

river, keep our eyes open, and our heads above the water.

And I say, see who is in there with you and celebrate. At this time

in history, we are to take nothing personally. Least of all,
ourselves. For the moment that we do, our spiritual growth and
journey comes to a halt. The time of the lone wolf is over.
Gather yourselves! Banish the word struggle from your attitude and
your vocabulary. All that we do now must be done in a sacred manner
and in celebration.
We are the ones we've been waiting for.
Oraibi, Arizona
Hopi Nation.

17. 144,000. There is a belief that there are 144,000 souls whose destiny is tied to the evolution of The Earth and humanity and that, as these souls awaken to their light and soul purpose, they facilitate the ascension of consciousness for the entire planet and its creatures.

18. *Molecules of Emotion.* Candace Pert is the author of a book that explores the connection between emotions and biology through the discovery that there are "molecules" that can stimulate particular emotional responses in the human body. See Bibliography.

19 *The Biology of Belief.* Bruce Lipton is a biologist who, through the study of genes and stem cells in a Petri dish observed that the environment (our belief systems) has a greater influence on genes and influences our genetics and our health. See Bibliography.

20. Kirlian photography. A photographic development that allows for a color photograph of the human aura.

21. Disclosure. Steven M. Greer is the author and motivation behind *The Disclosure Project* which seeks to reveal the truth about our connection with extraterrestrial civilizations and their involvement with government agencies and with secret clandestine operations in the darker echelons of and behind the control elements of the world. His book *Hidden Truth: Forbidden Knowledge* reveals even deeper and darker mysteries. See Bibliography.

22. Beings of Light. You have your own guides and angels watching over you, guiding and protecting you. During the year-long course with The Ones with No Names, they mentioned beings within Mother Earth, 20-30 feet high who surround and guard us.

23. Solar Logos. The divine, over-lighting being who is the central power within or behind the Sun. The word "logos" means "the word" in Greek and is a reference to The Christ and/or God as the great spiritual power of our Solar system. See also John 1:1 "In the beginning was the word and the word was with God."

24. Crown of thorns. This refers to the crown of thorns that was believed to have been placed on the head of Jesus at the Crucifixion as the Romans jeered at the title "King of the Jews."

25. Soul Seed. The Ones with No Names teach that the location beneath the xyphoid process, where the ribs come together is the connection point of the soul with the body and can be accessed by focusing there.

26. Tree of Life. The tree features prominently in many mythologies as a connection between Heaven and Earth, as symbolized by the cross, and as the central focal point of ritual in many traditions. It was associated with the Goddess and is also often associated with the serpent. It featured prominently in the worship of the Druids. The mythologies were usurped and distorted to represent the Goddess energy and the wisdom embodied by the serpent in a negative light, in effect turning on its head the truth that life comes from woman.

27. Nymph. In one version of the story, the aged Merlin was seduced by a nymph, Vivien, or Niniane and became enticed to enter into a boulder where he became entrapped, and his powers became ineffectual.

28. The Aten. The Aten was the sun disc that represented the only god of Akhenaten, the "heretic" pharaoh of the 18th Dynasty whose Aten replaced Amun as the principal god of the Egyptian pantheon. The Aten was an older version of the sun god and is often shown with rays ending with the ankh, symbol of life, at the nostrils of Akhenaten and the god's worshipers. See Bibliography for more on the period.

29. Shungite. A black mineral found only in Russia that has special properties to reverse the harmful effects of electromagnetic radiation and other negative influences on biology. Its effects are due to a special molecule of carbon called a Fullerene which give it these properties. For more information visit www.RaphaelWeisman.com/Shungite. See Martino in the Bibliography.

30. Great Central Sun. The center of our galaxy from which the spiritual hierarchies and guardians of our universe issue their light and oversight. From an astronomical perspective, this can be seen as the black or white hole at the center of the Milky Way Galaxy.

31. The Emotion Code. Dr. Bradley Nelson is the author of the book by this name and founder of this system for releasing trapped emotions from the body, a very simple and effective healing modality. See Bibliography.

32. The Swing Between Worlds. The "place" where The Ones with No Names consult and guide souls prior to and on returning from Earth lives. See also note

33. Inner Truth. Chung Fu, Old Chinese' name, means Inner Truth. It is hexagram #61 in the *I Ching, The Book of Changes*. The organization associated with his teachings through Marshall Lever was called 33 Energies, Inc. See also https://deepsoulconnection.medium.com/who-is-chung-fu-a070cda85107

34. Devas/Devic. The Devas are spiritual beings who oversee the growth and well-being of all living things. They are mostly associated with the Nature kingdom and the world of plants and animals. They can be invoked to produce unusually large, healthy vegetables as was the case in Findhorn, a community in Scotland.

35. GMO. Genetically modified organisms are the result of the genetic and biological engineering of seeds and other products to produce hybrids and strains that are resistant to pests and chemicals used in modern agriculture. They are harmful to biology and difficult for the body to eliminate from its systems.

36. Herman Rednick (1902 – 1985) A spiritual teacher, mystic and visionary painter who lived in Taos County and established a community of followers and students. He taught the path of love and service. The cover of this book is one of his paintings that belongs to the author. You can find out more about his teachings, paintings and books at www.EarthJourney.org. See Bibliography.

37. Triskelion (or triskele). A triple spiral motif that is formed from a single thread or line emanating from a single point. This symbol is found on early Celtic and Neolithic structures and when made from copper and placed beneath a container of water has the effect of structuring and enhancing the water.

38. Vibrant Vital Water. Randy Hatton is the founder of a company that uses vortex, magnet, mineral and copper in his technologies for creating structured, health-enhancing water. He is a friend and colleague of the author. https://www.vibrantvitalwater.com/about/.

39. Slim Spurling was the genius creator of devices made of twisted copper that incorporated sacred geometry with his deep understanding of energy. He devised Light-Life tools, products that could assist in healing and clearing negative energy. His experiments included cleaning up the pollution and smog around Denver. See Anderson and Garrison in Bibliography.

40. Medical Medium. Anthony William is the author of Medical Medium. From a very early age he was able to see what was happening in the body of friends, family and clients. This book reveals an explanation for many of the "mystery diseases" and strategies for healing and overcoming many of these pervasive afflictions. One of his most popular practices is to drink 16 oz of freshly prepared celery juice each morning before any other intake. See Bibliography.

41. Perfect Science.TM Ayhan Doyuk of Turkey was the original founder of Perfect Science water, which could transform polluted water and trash into organic fertilizer and dissolve oil in water. It was shown through dark field microscopy that patients with cancer, HIV and other severe diseases could be healed. Diseased blood cells seen through these microscopes after treatment could be seen restored to a healthy condition. The company and products have evolved since the author was involved so that up-to-date information may reflect a different reality. http://www.perfectwaters.net/

42. Kinesiology. A system for measuring the positive or negative effect of substances, thought forms or energies on the body using resistance or lack thereof to controlled pressure on a limb, finger or body movement. Pressure on a body part such as downwards on an outstretched arm is met with either such resistance that the arm cannot be depressed, or by an absence of resistance so that the arm immediately releases downwards from minimal pressure. A system of self-testing using your fingers or other methods such as leaning forwards or backwards, or a pendulum are also effective once one has established a "yes" or a "no" answer as a baseline.

42A. Pendulum. A pendulum is a weight suspended from a pivot so that it can swing freely. The backwards and forwards motion of a pivoted arm is used to keep a grandfather clock wound. A weight, such as a crystal or stone suspended from a chain can be used to get a 'yes' or 'no' answer through its clockwise or counter-clockwise motion as predetermined with the user.

43. One company that offers quality filters is http://www.TherapeuticWaterSystems.com. In addition, we highly recommend Your Body's Many Cries For Water by Dr. Batmanghelidj. It is an excellent book about the importance of water that has shown how an increase in intake of even tap water can heal many symptoms and illnesses. See Bibliography.

44. EMF. Electromagnetic frequencies. EMR refers to electromagnetic radiation.

45. Trees. *What A Plant Knows*, by Daniel Chamovitz. *The Secret Teachings of Plants* by Stephen Harrod Buhner. *The Global Forest and Arboretum America* are two of the many books by Diana Beresford-Kroeger. See Bibliography.

46. Anastasia, Book 1, The Ringing Cedar Series by Vladimir Megré. See Bibliography.

47. Call of the Forest. There is a film and more information about Diana Beresford-Kroeger at http://calloftheforest.ca

48. *The Overstory*, a novel by Richard Powers with a strong focus on trees has possible inspiration from Beresford-Kroeger. See Bibliography.

49. The Pillar. The Pillar is a column of light with analogies to the tree whose trunk is attached to roots that penetrate deep into the earth and whose crown connects to the atmosphere and the canopies of the trees. It represents the connection between Heaven and Earth and the forces of benevolence, nurturing, guardianship, light and divinity and is also equivalent to the Column of Light referred to in this book, which is filled with golden light that nourishes the cells and has the heart at the center. It was originally conceived at a gathering of Soul Support Systems as being comprised of the four elements Light, Truth, Order and Union which, like roots spiraling upwards together to form the tree's trunk, begins to spin in a clockwise manner and radiate out as the Christ Consciousness.

50. Torsion Field. A torsion field is a rotational spin of particles in either a clockwise or counter-clockwise direction as postulated (hypothetically) within certain quantum scientific research. A counter-clockwise spin is associated with the harmful effects on biology of synthetic products, clothing and foodstuffs as well as electromagnetic fields, whereas a clockwise or positive spin is believed to generate beneficial and healing effects on biological systems.

51. William Marshal. William Marshal (1146-1219), 1st Earl of Pembroke served five Kings of England and was one of the most highly regarded knights of all time. He was instrumental in the creation of the Magna Carta and the introduction of a chivalric code and the tournament into the life of the English court. He has been one of the energies that channels messages through Flo Aeveia Magdalena and teaches the use of "The Light Magnificent." See Magdalena's book in the Bibliography.

52. Akashic Records. This is the "place" where all thoughts, actions and existences are "recorded." Those who have the ability to "read" the records are able to access information from all time and all space of all experiences. When a psychic relates to a past life or an event, moment or action in someone's history, they are retrieving this information from the "records" or the Akash.

53. Fractals. A fractal is a pattern that repeats itself infinitely within its own structure, such that one can find the same pattern on a smaller scale when one hones in to, or amplifies a part of the larger pattern. There is a mathematical formula for

each pattern. One such famous fractal is the Mandelbrot Fractal. Repeating forms in Nature are similar to fractals, such as the leaves of ferns or the multiplication of branch and leaf on a tree. For more information visit https://fractalfoundation.org/resources/what-are-fractals/.

54. Scalar Waves. Nikolas Tesla was one of the great minds who explored scalar waves. He re-considered the equations of the mathematical physicist James Clerk Maxwell whose research was rejected by mainstream scientists. He developed applications for energy transmission and healing using scalar waves. There are devices for healing that use scalar waves, which are similar to sound waves, but there are apparently different varieties of scalar waves that have different effects on biology. One of the attributes of scalar waves is that they can travel faster than the speed of light.

55. Karma. The concept of Karma is an understanding of the law of cause and effect within the framework of multiple lifetimes. It is taught in Buddhist, Hindu and other Eastern philosophies and religions as well as in early Christianity prior to the takeover by the Catholic Church.

56. Ashtara. During a channeling meditation session through Flo Magdalena, the Galactic Federation invited us to imagine that we were invited aboard a starship. I experienced a beautiful female being in white garments. At first, I thought it might be my daughter Joy as an adult in the higher dimensions, but she told me her name was Ashtara and that she was my feminine aspect with whom I could connect any time I wished. It was a unique and very beautiful experience for me.

57. Kalpa. According to Wikipedia, a kalpa is a long period of time (eon) in Hindu and Buddhist cosmology, generally between the creation and recreation of a world or universe.

58. The Parable of the Sower, Matthew 13:1–23, Mark 4:1–20, Luke 8:4–15

59. Thoth Deck. The Thoth deck is a Tarot deck painted by Lady Frieda Harris according to instructions from Aleister Crowley (1875-1947) a famous British occultist.

60. Ho'oponopono. This Hawaiian practice of forgiveness is extremely powerful and healing. The words mean "to make right twice" or "doubly," referring to oneself and the recipient. Simply say the words aloud or to yourself: "I'm sorry. Please forgive me. Thank you. I love you."

61. *When God Was a Woman* is the name of a book by Merlin Stone which traces the herstory of the gradual takeover and usurpation of the matrilineal goddess

cultures by the masculine through the agency of the invasions of Indo-Europeans who worshiped a male, mountain storm god into areas of Europe and Asia where worship of the goddess held sway. The book *The Chalice and the Blade* by Riane Eisler also addresses this subject. See Bibliography for both books.

62. Amenti. "Hidden Place" The Halls or realm of Amenti is the place where ascended masters and avatars go to rejuvenate their bodies so that they can reappear within society at different periods within history. It is also regarded as the underworld in Egyptian mythology and is associated with Thoth as the ruler of the Underworld and the one who evaluates the soul upon death.

63. Feng Shui. Chinese geomancy. The Chinese practice of creating harmonious space, alignment with Earth energies and the correct way to lay out objects to produce beneficial currents of energy in the home or on a piece of land is based on the Bagua, an 8-symbol design.

64. Ley lines. The Earth has energy lines similar to the meridians of the body on which sacred sites and places of power are located, especially where these invisible lines cross. Most ancient ceremonial megalithic sites and later cathedrals were situated at holy wells, on hilltops and conjunctions of Ley lines.

65. Trees and the heart. *The Secret Teachings of Plants* by Stephen Harrod Buhner. See Bibliography.

66. *I Remember Union, the Story of Mary Magdalena* by Flo Aeveia Magdalena. See Bibliography.

67. *Joan of Arc* by Mark Twain. See Bibliography. Also, the powerful movie called *Joan of Arc*, starring Leelee Sobieski by director Christian Duguay

68. Vedas. The sacred teachings of Hinduism from India. These ancient, religious texts were written in Vedic Sanskrit and also record events from the distant past.

69. Law of One. The ancient teachings of the Truth of Oneness that are considered to have derived from Atlantis and form the basis of all Spiritual paths. The Law of One was upheld by the Children of the Law of One in the face of the "Sons (and Daughters) of Beliel" who misused their power to dominate and control. See the Peniel in Bibliography.

70. Boddhisattva. One within the Buddhist tradition who has attained enlightenment and vows to continue to reincarnate on Earth and refrain from going to Nirvana until all beings have been liberated.

71. Achille's heel. The tendon that attaches the calf muscles to the heel bone gives rise to this term, the Achilles tendon. Achilles was one of the Greek's mightiest warriors, but when this tendon was cut in battle, he was rendered defenseless. This became a metaphor for one whose power can be taken away by a fatal flaw or weakness of character in spite of their great strength.

72. Tanka, also spelled "Thangka." A Buddhist art form portraying deities, usually seated on a throne and displaying their characteristic gestures and symbols. Mandalas and colorful designs are also woven into the art and fearsome figures of demons are also portrayed. Usually, the thangka is displayed as a wall hanging with ribbons and wooden strips.

73. Rainbow Body. An emanation, a colorful pattern of radiating lines from the heart and body of a Buddha or enlightened being, often portrayed in thangkas depicting Guru Rinpoche.

74. Goethe on Commitment. This famous quotation is by Johann Wolfgang von Goethe (1749- 1832)

On Commitment:

Until one is committed, there is always hesitancy, the chance to draw back, always ineffectiveness. Concerning all acts of initiative and creation, there is one elementary truth, the ignorance of which kills countless ideas and splendid plans: that the moment one definitely commits oneself, then providence moves too. All sorts of things occur to help one that would never otherwise have occurred. A whole stream of events issues from the decision, raising to one's favor all manner of unforeseen incidents and meetings and material assistance which no one could have dreamed would come her way. Whatever you can do or dream, you can begin it. Boldness has genius, power and magic in it.

75. Morphic resonance. This term was originally coined by Rupert Sheldrake. Morphic resonance is a process whereby self-organizing systems inherit a memory from previous similar systems. There is a tipping point, when a large enough number of people exhibit an elevated level of consciousness on the planet, such as described in the end note about the 144,000, it shows up in many places on the planet. A similar concept is called the 100th monkey syndrome.

76. Nano Soma. The active ingredient in Nano Soma is a nanoemulsion of policosanol, a lipid, which activates the body to heal and protect itself, thus enhancing the body's own immune system. It substitutes for vitamin D in the body, activating the Vitamin D Receptor (VDR), a critical key to our immunity. It also triggers the body to produce its own endogenous vitamin C which reverses the aging of our bodies. https://raphaelweisman.com/nano-soma/

The stem cell patch distributed by Lifewave triggers the body to activate its own dormant stem cells so they can heal those areas of the body that are dis-eased and under stress. The little patch that one puts on one's body for a period of 12 hours at a time uses light technology to elevate the peptide GKH-Cu within the body, which is known to decline with age. When elevated, this Peptide activates the body's stem cells. https://raphaelweisman.com/healing-channeling/stem-cells/

77. Reverse marker. This graphic was given in a channeling by Thoth through Maia Nartoomid. I recommend a visit to the original reference at this link: https://newearthenergetics.wordpress.com/2020/03/12/cv-reverse-marker/

78. Fullerene. A molecule of carbon found in Shungite that gives it its particular properties. This molecule has a shape similar to that of a hollow soccer ball, made up of carbon atoms connected in a pentagonal and hexagonal structure of 60 atoms, referred to as the C-60 Fullerene molecule, named in honor of Buckminster Fuller, creator of the geodesic dome. See Martino in Bibliography.

79. Your will be done. This is a mantra slightly modified, inspired by the book, The Children of the Law of One & the Lost Teachings of Atlantis, by Peniel. See Bibliography.

Bibliography and Recommended Reading

Andrews, Shirley. Atlantis, Insights from a Lost Civilization. Llewellyn, 1998.
- Lemuria and Atlantis. Llewellyn, 2004.

Anderson, Susan with Slim Spurling. In the Mind of a Master, iUniverse, Inc. 2012

Asbridge, Thomas. The Greatest Knight: The Remarkable Life of William Marshal, the Power Behind Five English Thrones. Ecco, 2015.

Batmanghelidj, Fereydoon, MD. Your Body's Many Cries For Water, Global Health Solutions, Inc. 2008

Beresford-Kroeger, Diana. The Global Forest. Viking, 2010.
- Arboretum America, A Philosophy of the Forest. University of Michigan Press, 2003.

Braden, Gregg. Resilience from the Heart, Hay House Inc., 2014.
- Secrets of the Lost Mode of Prayer, Hay House Inc., 2016.

Buhner, Stephen Harrod. The Secret Teachings of Plants, The Intelligence of the Heart in the Direct Perception of Nature. Bear & Company, 2004.

Chamovitz, Daniel. What A Plant Knows. Scientific American, 2012.

Churchward, James. The Lost Continent of Mu, the Motherland of Men, 1926.

Consigli, Paolo, MD. The Hidden Secrets of Water, Discovering the Powers of the Magical Molecule of Life, Watkins, 2008 (Translated from the Italian).

Donnelly, Ignatius, Revised and Edited by Egerton Sykes. Atlantis, The Antediluvian World. Gramercy, 1949.

Eisler, Riane. The Chalice and the Blade. HarperOne, 2011.

Elliot, W. Scott with Charles Leadbeater. The Story of Atlantis and the Lost Lemuria. McAllister, 2015.

Emoto, Masaru. The Hidden Messages in Water. Beyond Worlds Publishing, 2004 (English), 2001. (Japan).

Finkelstein, Israel and Neil Asher Silberman. The Bible Unearthed. The Free Press, 2001.

Firstenberg, Arthur. The Invisible Rainbow: A History of Electricity and Life. Chelsea Green Publishing, 2020. Microwaving Our planet: The Environmental Impact of the Wireless Revolution. Cellular Phone Taskforce, 1997

Garrison, Cal. Slim Spurling's Universe. IX-EL Publishing, 2004

Gimbutas, Marija Alseikaite. The Language of the Goddess. Harper & Row, 1989.

Greer, Stephen. Disclosure, Crossing Point Inc., 2001.
    - Hidden Truth: Forbidden Knowledge. Crossing Point Inc., 2006.

Hoagland, Richard C. and Mike Bara. Dark Mission, The Secret History of NASA. Feral House, 2009.

Kelly, Penny. Robes: A Book of Coming Changes. Kelly Networks, LLC, 2005.

King, Kaih Khristé Fredericks and Oswald White Bear. The History of the Hopi from their Origins in Lemuria. The King's Bridge, 2009.

Klem, Rosemary. Atlantis, FACT: Two Colonies Inhabit the Atlantic & Pacific Oceans. Zodbooks; 1st edition (May 30, 2013).

Koestler, Arthur. The Thirteenth Tribe. Hutchison and Co, 1976.

Lever, Marshall N. The Search for the Hidden Door. Self-published, 1981.

Liberman, Jacob, O.D., PhD. Light, Medicine of the Future. Bear & Company, 2019.

Lipton, Bruce. The Biology of Belief. Hay House Inc., 2008.

Magdalena, Flo Aeveia. I Remember Union, the Story of Mary Magdalena. All Worlds Publishing, Hardcover 1992, Paperback, 8th Edition, 2013.
    - Sunlight on Water, a Manual for Soul-full Living. All Worlds Publishing, 1996.
    - The Light Magnificent and The Power of Grace. All Worlds Publishing, 2019.
    - Heartful Living. All Worlds Publishing, 2019.

Martino, Regina. Shungite, Protection, Healing and Detoxification. Éditions Ambre, (French original), Inner Traditions International, 2014 (English translation).

Maylor, D.K. Wrestling with Jesus. 2018, Self-Published.

McGrath, Roslyn Elena. Post-Resurrection, The Family of Mary Magdalene. Chrysaetos Press, 2017.

Meade, Michael. The Water of Life, Initiation and the Tempering of the Soul. Greenfire Press, 2006.

Megré, Vladimir. Anastasia, The Ringing Cedar Series, Book 1. Leonid Sharashkin, 2005.

Melchizedek, Drunvalo. The Ancient Secret of the Flower of Life, Vols I & II, Light Technology Publishing, 1990.
-Living in the Heart. Light Technology Publishing, 2003.

Nelson, Dr. Bradley The Emotion Code. Wellness Unmasked, 2007, St. Martin's Essentials, 2019.

Osman, Ahmed. The Hebrew Pharaohs of Egypt. Bear & Co., 1987.

Pearce, Joseph Chilton. The Heart-Mind Matrix. Park Street Press, 2010.

Peniel, Jon. The Children of the Law of One & the Lost Teachings of Atlantis. Network, 1997.

Pert, Candace. Molecules of Emotion. Scribner, 1997.

Powers, Richard. The Overstory. W.W. Norton & Co., 2018.

Rednick, Herman. Earth Journey. Vantage Press, 1980.

Royal, Lyssa and Keith Priest. The Prism of Lyra, An Exploration of Human Galactic Heritage. Light Technology and Royal Priest Research Trust, 1991.

Sabbah, Messod and Roger. Secrets of the Exodus, The Egyptian Origins of the Hebrew People. Jean-Cyrille Godefroy, 2000 (original French), Thorsons, Helios Press, 2002.

Sand, Shlomo. (Translated from Hebrew by Yael Lotan). The Invention of the Jewish People. Verso, 2009.

Singer, Katie. An Electronic Silent Spring: Facing the Dangers and Creating Safe Limits. Portal Books, 2014.

Stone, Merlin. When God Was a Woman, Barnes & Noble Books, 1976

Trungpa, Chogyam, Shambhala, The Sacred Path of the Warrior. Shambhala, 1984.

Twain, Mark. Joan of Arc. Harper & Brothers, 1896 & 1924.

Van Der Kolk, M.D. The Body Keeps the Score. Viking, 2014.

Wilcock, David. The Source Field Investigations. Dutton, 2011.

William, Anthony. Medical Medium. Hay House Inc., 2015.

About the Author

Raphael Weisman is a retired luthier and harp-maker. He was born in South Africa and currently lives in Santa Fe, NM. He is a channel for the love and guidance of Beings of Light. He provides Shungite for protection from EMFs, and counsels people being affected by these frequencies. He is a trainer and facilitator of HeartThread®, and a minister. Raphael channels Healing Light through his hands for relief of pain, and to release old, stuck energy from the body. He founded the non-profit Healing The Scars, Inc. to provide healing from the effects of war, trauma and abuse. He facilitates Medicine Water Wheel Ceremonies for the blessing of the waters. Raphael's life is committed to helping empower lightworkers to find clarity, connection to their highest wisdom and light so that they can pave the way for others to co-create the New Earth. He is a musician, a visionary, a poet, an editor and writer. He loves to dance, and is an avid hiker and a lover of trees and Nature.

www.RaphaelWeisman.com

Photo of author by Anne Staveley

Book Cover photo: Painting by Herman Rednick, property of Raphael Weisman

Reviews

In *The Path of the Spiritual Warrior*, the New Earth Council compendium, Raphael Weisman brings together voices that wish to support, inform and guide us to an understanding of the inherent capacity we have to restore our lives and beings through alignment with our Divine natures.

Each voice brings a perspective and a grace that offers us a canopy of deep resources that provide an ongoing process of discernment to listen, hear and create through our own vibrational resonances. This assures that we are clearly hearing and living the promise of our own balance and Order in the New Earth we are all creating.

Flo Aeveia Magdalena, Author, *I Remember Union: The Story of Mary Magdalena*

In his fascinating book *The Path of the Spiritual Warrior*, Raphael Weisman has given the world a wide-ranging and comprehensive glimpse into the vast, unlimited wisdom and intelligence that seemingly permeates our cosmos. While so much of what has been called 'channeled' material has left me unmoved through the years, Weisman's work is one of those that stands apart from the usual 'love and light' pabulum and strikes the reader as intelligent, cohesive and workably practical for those on the 'spiritual' path. The book is dense with useful, provocative information and uplifting encouragement, and it's difficult to imagine that any reader would not benefit by its content, which could emerge only from the purest heart and clearest mind. This stimulating, thought-provoking work will no doubt begin making the rounds throughout the world for those ready to absorb its blessings. Highly recommended!

DK Maylor

Author, *Wrestling with Jesus, A Global Gift of Love and Liberation.*

Made in the USA
Monee, IL
01 July 2023

37838852R00154